TWO CONCEPTS OF
ALLEGORY

TWO CONCEPTS OF ALLEGORY

A Study of Shakespeare's *The Tempest*
and the Logic of Allegorical Expression

A. D. NUTTALL

Yale University Press
New Haven and London

First published in 1967 by Barnes & Noble Inc., New York, N.Y.
First Yale University Press edition 2007.
Preface to the Yale edition copyright ©2007 by A. D. Nuttall.
Copyright ©1967 by A. D. Nuttall

Printed in the United States of America.

Library of Congress Control Number: 2006938857
ISBN 978-0-300-11874-2 (pbk. : alk. paper)

A catalogue record for this book is available from the British Library.

The paper in this book meets the guidelines for permanence and
durability of the Committee on Production Guidelines for
Book Longevity of the Council on Libary Resources.

10   9   8   7   6   5   4   3   2   1

To
MARY

CONTENTS

PREFACE TO THE YALE EDITION

I wrote this book nearly fifty years ago (it was the second of my books to be published but the first to be written). After so long a time I know that I am no longer quite the same person as the author of *Two Concepts*. I read my own pages with a strange mixture of identification and distant objective assessment. The book, it now seems to me, is in some ways an artless performance, but I believe it contains the most important idea, or critical insight, I have ever had.

I – or he, the young graduate student – noticed a curious coincidence. In one of the earliest allegorical poems, the Latin *Psychomachia* of Prudentius, there is an apparently trivial technical problem: in the *psychomachia*, or 'battle within the soul', virtues must defeat vices. It is a fundamental requirement of allegorical form that particular virtues be represented by figures who are themselves characterized by the virtue in question: courage will be represented by a brave person, mercy by a forgiving figure and so on. In like manner, on the other side, the vice of cruelty, say, will be a figure that delights in the infliction of pain. But how on earth is Mercy going to smash Cruelty on the field of battle if she can do nothing but forgive any injury offered to her? Meanwhile, 'in another part of the wood', Plato in his *Parmenides* becomes entangled in a serious philosophical problem. Beauty, the universal, that beauty in respect of which all the beautiful *things* are beautiful, is itself – supremely – beautiful. His universals, like the figures in an allegorical poem, are 'self-predicating'. This causes Plato to say that there must now be a *further* universal, standing behind and beyond Beauty, in respect of which Beauty and all the particular things are beautiful. And then, if that remoter universal is itself beautiful, there must be yet another universal, even further off. And so on, *ad infinitum* (an 'infinite regress'). The modern reader wants to say that we are confronted by a simple failure to think abstractly. The great stroke of originality in Prudentius's allegory is his perception that there are other conflicts besides those on a physical battlefield; virtues and vices exist in tensely antagonistic relation to one another. In this secondary engagement mercy will be pitiless to something like cruelty; merciful people, of course, will forgive and turn the other cheek, but mercy itself, abstracted so that its relation to vices (as distinct from vicious persons) can now be seen, will be the reverse of merciful. 'Self-predication' begins to look like an awkward hang-up, an overspill from concrete thinking into the abstract field, disturbing the exciting purity of the initial allegorical move from body to spirit. This awkwardness will impede later allegories: Spenser's St. George in the *Faerie Queene* is, allegorically, Holiness, but because the poet must imagine him a holy *man,* a good Christian, he must be purged of his sins in the house of Caelia. This is absurd: holi*ness* does not require purgation. Caelia's house, meanwhile, is called 'the House of Holiness', but it is not St. George's house! One senses that a Platonic regress of absolutes is beginning to form within the Elizabethan poem.

So far, Prudentius's problem still looks trivial – something that a foolish poet could get himself into but a philosopher will 'analyse away' without difficulty. But Plato is a philosopher, and he seems to have the same problem. It struck me that universals were themselves differently conceived before the modern era. Plato's Ideas are not abstractions, though they discharge functions discharged for us by abstractions (hence the difficulty discussed in the *Parmenides*). Beauty for Plato is not a logical construction, designed to assist our talk about such things as sunsets and Helen of Troy; it is a spiritual individual; it is itself supremely beautiful – not 'beautiful and a horse' but *just* beautiful – beautiful all the way through. Suddenly the whole business of self-predication had to be considered more carefully. I felt that I had happened upon the explanation of a general feature of poetry written before the eighteenth century: its ability to move from particular to universal without any sense of 'bloodless abstraction' supervening. Shakespeare writes about lovers and also about love; but when he moves to love there is no draining away of imaginative colour from the texture of the verse. In his late plays a conception of love and reconciliation disengages itself as quasi-Platonic, conscious not of its own abstraction but rather of its own spiritual quasi-transcendence. In the late 1950s and 1960s F. R. Leavis was immensely influential. He demanded of poetry a 'quality of felt life': concrete particulars could be sensuously vivid, but abstract universals could never be so. This metaphysical presumption on his part was, I now felt, a huge error, critically, historically and perhaps philosophically. The vast field of literature before 1700, this great dance of particular and universal, has an imaginative warmth that is, so to speak, freely circulating.

I was sure that Plato had to be brought in or my work would lose any claim it might have had to originality. But Plato was 'Philosophy', and I was a student within the subject 'English Literature'. I was passed from supervisor to supervisor like a hot potato. They refused to say what was wrong with my thesis, instead murmuring, over and over, 'But that would be philosophy'. I said, 'Send me to the toughest philosopher you can find'. At last an interview was arranged with the Waynflete Professor of Metaphysical Philosophy, Gilbert Ryle. Ryle read my stuff and told me that some of it was rather corny but that there was real interest in my contention about the different character of universals in early European thought. The relief on my side was enormous. I had begun to think that my work was completely unintelligible to anyone but myself. Ryle understood everything without difficulty. After that everything changed. I was assigned first to Anthony Quinton and then to Iris Murdoch (who was a wonderful supervisor). I moved from Oxford to the then-new University of Sussex and found to my delight that, now, I no longer had to fight to pursue an inquiry that was 'interdisciplinary', but instead my studies were eagerly welcomed.

I can see now, looking back, that the whole book is against premature brusqueness in reasoning: C. S. Lewis's clear opposition of Platonism to confessedly fictive allegory, like Erich Auerbach's similar opposition of medieval *figura* to *allegoria,* comes unstuck when one enters the intricately engaged field of older literature. Indeed, as I think about this all over again in the year 2006, I find myself warming (perhaps predictably) to the views of my younger self.

A.D.N.
June 2006

PREFACE

This book began as a rather eccentric B.Litt. thesis for the University of Oxford. It was at that stage in its composition that I received really crucial assistance from several of my teachers, particularly Mr. Anthony Quinton and Miss Iris Murdoch, who not only directed me to much useful material but also laboured tirelessly to straighten the many crooked notions I brought to its organization. For all of which I am deeply grateful. A more recently incurred debt is to those who read and commented on my manuscript, in its various stages of completeness: that is, to my friends, Christopher Taylor, Gabriel Josipovici, Laurence Lerner and Stephen Medcalf. In fairness to these readers I must explain that what follows in no sense carries their *imprimatur*. The absurdities from which they saved me are numerous; those which remain are no fault of theirs. Needless to say, in this short paragraph I have not presented a full and honourable record of my obligations. Those I have acknowledged are certainly real enough, but I am very conscious of an additional (and enormous) debt, to the participants in innumerable half-forgotten conversations and discussions – a debt which is none the less real because I am quite unable to pay it.

A.D.N.

The University of Sussex
May 1966

INTRODUCTION

The fundamental subject of this book is a particular habit of thought – the practice of thinking about universals as though they were concrete things. The place in my scheme of Shakespeare's *The Tempest* is essentially subordinate to this first concern. The play has, for the purposes of this inquiry, the status of a complex, extended example. The same book could, conceivably, have been written round a different work of art; conceivably, but not (to me) imaginably; for I cannot think of any work of comparable suitability. Nevertheless, the investigation is intended incidentally to increase our understanding of the play, much as crystals can be used to reflect light back upon its source. The book takes the form of an inquiry into certain conceptual questions raised, in the first place, by the allegoristic critics of *The Tempest*, and, in the second place, by allegorical and quasi-allegorical poetry in general. My argument has the further consequence of suggesting that allegory and metaphysics are in practice more closely allied than is commonly supposed.

The reader may find a short programme useful. I begin with a brief account of the allegoristic *Tempest* criticism of the last century. In the second chapter I isolate a logical oddity – my 'particular habit of thought'– which is fundamental in the conceptual structure of such criticism and show that something very like it is to be found, not only in the writings of allegorists, but also in works of metaphysics. On the strength of this observed affinity between allegory and metaphysics, i attempt to weaken the practical force of C. S. Lewis's strong opposition of the two. In the third and fourth chapters an account of the psychological foundations of the problematic concept is offered as a partial, though not exhaustive, explanation of it. In the fifth chapter I make some tentative suggestions as to how some of the deficiencies of the psychological account may be supplied by an examination of the language of 'intuitionistic' ethics, and of Shakespeare's treatment of love and value in his *Sonnets, Troilus and Cressida* and last Romances. The final chapter is a study of *The Tempest* itself.

In general, I have been occupied with logical rather than historical relations. Where I have touched on the subject of Platonism, I have been concerned not with the historical transmission of that philosophy but rather with such conceptual overlapping as can be found between the philosophical practice of Plato and the poetic practice of others. This essay is not, however, a radically philosophical treatise on either logic or ethics. Throughout, whether from intellectual modesty or cowardice, I have restricted myself to the task of answering the question 'What (in matters relating to ethics or universals) *can be thought* by a sane man?' and leave to others the larger question, 'What (in such matters) *ought* to be thought?' Psychological possibilities have been my quarry, not philosophical proprieties. But because the psychological activity in question is *thinking*, and not the motions of the unconscious, for large areas of the essay the distinction between logical and psychological analysis is not explicit. Some readers will find the mass of material handled uncomfortably heterogeneous. Yet I would plead that the book is not a rag-bag. It is constructed on the principle of a chase. I have allowed a single governing idea to draw me wherever it wished to go and have tried to resist all temptations held out by a false conception of relevance.

NOTE

All Shakespeare references are to the three-volume Oxford Shakespeare, ed. W. J. Craig, (i) the *Comedies*, the 1952 reprint of the 1st edition of 1911, (ii) the *Histories and Poems*, the 1958 reprint of the 1st edition of 1912, (iii) the *Tragedies*, the 1956 reprint of the 1st edition of 1912.

The following symbols and abbreviations have been used:

E & S	= *Essays and Studies*
NS	= New Series
PA	= *Palatine Anthology*
PAS	= *Proceedings of the Aristotelian Society*
Proc. Brit. Acad.	= *Proceedings of the British Academy*
RES	= *Review of English Studies*

I

THE TEMPEST
AND ITS ROMANTIC CRITICS

In 1875, Edward Dowden observed of *The Tempest* that 'it has had the quality, as a work of art, of setting its critics to work as though it were an allegory; and forthwith it baffles them, and seems to mock them for supposing that they had power to pluck out the heart of its mystery'.[1] The practice of allegorical criticism, at any rate in its more naïve forms, is alien to many of us today; our sensibilities recoil from it, and our intellects tend to dismiss it as not being criticism at all. But Dowden has put the case in a peculiarly challenging way. Whatever you may think of it (he seems to say), here it is. Whatever the propriety of allegorical criticism, it is an incontestable fact that it gets written, and that some works of art come in for more of it than others. Thus, a body of allegorical criticism relating to a particular work of art is set before us in a new guise. It is no longer a conflicting set of candidatures for our belief. Instead, it appears as a subject for investigation. Saying no to rival exegetes can be a tedious business, but the concrete situation, comprising the work and its exegesis, may be of surpassing interest as a phenomenon both historical and logical. All that follows is, in a manner, an attempt to meet Dowden's implicit challenge. I shall therefore be asking not 'What does *The Tempest* signify allegorically?' but rather 'What sort of thing are people doing when they talk of allegorical significations; what sort of reasons prompt them to do so in connexion with *The Tempest*?'

[1] *Shakespere – his Mind and Art*, London 1875, p. 423.

I propose to investigate these questions in a descriptive rather than a legislative spirit. I shall therefore begin, ὕστερον πρότερον Ὁμηρικῶς, not with the play, but with the critics; and in order to generate the maximum degree of bewilderment and mystification, I shall restrict myself in this first chapter to a tradition which is peculiarly obnoxious to us, perhaps because we have so recently cast it off. I mean the romantic tradition of allegorical criticism. The sooner my reader is induced to acknowledge the conceptual oddity of much *Tempest* criticism, the sooner will he be persuaded to follow out the rest of my argument. That oddity attains its grossest and most obtrusive aspect in the nineteenth century. I keep back the play itself till the last, not because I think it is the least important thing, but because I am certain that it is the most important.

The nineteenth century, then, saw the real efflorescence of allegorical criticism of the most unabashed kind, and altogether it makes an excellent Deep End into which the reader may be pitched. Dowden, of course, was writing in the very thick of it. For the beginning of this kind of criticism – though 'beginning' sounds much too definite – we must go back to Schlegel's lecture[1] on the comedies of Shakespeare.

Schlegel appears strongly in this work as the great innovator. In it one can find various ideas which were to reverberate in England many years later. For example, he gives a cue to Hazlitt[2] when he distinguishes the primitive and 'essentially poetic' rudeness of Caliban from the 'prosaic' vulgarity of the drunkards, Stephano and Trinculo. More importantly for our purpose, he relates Ariel to the airy elements and Caliban to the earthy, thus opening the doors to an allegory of the soul in terms of early seventeenth-century psychology. But he does not walk through them. A vein of eighteenth-century sobriety is still in him, so that he writes, 'Yet they are neither of them simple, allegorical personifications but beings individually determined.'[3] In a way, there is more of the nascent romantic criticism in his description of the love of Ferdinand and Miranda –'an affecting union of chivalrous magnanimity on the one part, and on the other of the virgin open-

---

[1] *A Course of Lectures on Dramatic Art and Literature*, trans. J. Black, revised A. J. W. Morrison, London 1846. The German text was printed in 1811.

[2] See *The Complete Works of William Hazlitt*, ed. P. P. Howe, London 1934, vol. IV, pp. 238 ff., and vol. IV, p. 346.

[3] *Dramatic Art and Literature*, pp. 395–6.

ness of a heart which, brought up far from the world on an uninhabited island, has never learned to disguise its innocent move-
ments'.[1] It would of course be idle to argue that the abstract nouns
in this sentence make it a piece of allegorical criticism, that they
are anything more than a *façon de parler*. Yet it is just *this* sort of
observation which, when warmed by the ontologically assertive
imagination of subsequent romantics, turns into full-blown allegorical criticism. Such cool, historically minded observations as
that concerning the elements are, in comparison, innocent. As the
fervour of the imagination is heightened, so the attribute of reality
is more largely invested in abstractions, and the supposed allegory
glows more brightly.

Some twenty years later a Mrs. A. B. Jameson wrote a book
called *Characteristics of Women, Moral, Poetical and Historical,* and
was excited to even stronger language by the character of Miranda.
'Had he never created a Miranda,' she writes, 'we should never
have been made to feel how completely the purely natural and the
purely ideal can blend into each other.'[2] The snowball is beginning
to roll. The stylistic audacities of Schlegel have undergone a
vaguely Platonic hypostasis. 'The character of Miranda', she
continues, 'resolves itself into the very elements of womanhood.
She is beautiful, modest, and tender, and she is these only; they
comprise her whole being, external and internal.' The Platonic
notion is hovering in her mind: Miranda is Womanliness, that is
(to borrow Cornford's[3] phrase) she is womanly-and-nothing-else.
We can no longer be confident that nothing beyond common sense
is involved, that she intends no more than that Miranda is typical
of the best kind of young woman. Our quarry here is not what a
reductionist philosopher would make of Mrs. Jameson's words,
but what Mrs. Jameson herself intended by them. And that intention is clearly infected with certain vaguely ontological presuppositions about ideality. There is a particularly curious and
interesting passage where she stresses the tension between
Miranda's 'palpable reality' and her unearthliness. It is difficult to
know how much we should make of her later use of imagery
drawn from Scripture – she speaks of Miranda as the 'Eve of an
enchanted Paradise'. Perhaps we may class it tentatively as an
additional indication that she is thinking in transcendental terms,

[1] *ibid.,* p. 395.
[2] *op. cit.,* London 1832, vol. I, p. 210.
[3] F. M. Cornford, *Plato and Parmenides,* London 1939, p. 87.

that the antithesis Spiritual/Unspiritual is just as prominent in her consciousness as is General/Particular.

The impression grows stronger as we turn to Heinrich Heine. In 1838, inspired by some engravings depicting Shakespeare's heroines, he printed some observations under the title *Shakespeares Mädchen und Frauen*.[1] To the last he thought the pictures superior to the reflections they provoked. The visual felicity of early romantic drawings from Shakespeare runs through the whole book, and makes of it a wonderful garden of 'knights and ladies, shepherds and shepherdesses, fools and wisemen',[2] antlered deer and so on. The novels of Scott may be said to be instinct with the atmosphere of his own day and at the same time landmarks in the evolution of the historical sense. Similarly, Heine's romantic garden, redolent as it is of the early nineteenth century, holds, in the first joyous franchise of the historical imagination, more of the 'golden' quality of, say, *As You Like It* than many a modern production can be said to do. But it is when he comes to describe the characters of Juliet and Miranda that his language begins to burst at the seams, and accordingly it is here that our vigilance should quicken:

> . . . to what can I compare you, O Juliet and Miranda? Again I search the heavens for your prototype. Possibly it is hidden behind the stars too far off to reach my sight. Perhaps if the scorching sun possessed the moon's tenderness I might compare thee to the sun, O Juliet! Perhaps if the tender moon possessed the sun's heat I might compare thee to the moon, O Miranda![3]

The Platonic language is quite explicit here, though the spatial conception of the ideal seems to be given rather too warm a welcome. At least, we feel, Plato was worried about the status of his term χωρισμός ('separation'), but here is Heine, obviously extracting a keen poetic enjoyment from it. We cannot, it is true, believe that Heine really thought Miranda was beyond the stars, so that an exceptionally powerful space-ship could investigate her and present a report. If we suspect this, can we be sure of our initial imputation of Platonism? Might not that also be 'poetically entertained'? Perhaps if we asked Heine how much of this he 'really'

[1] Trans. Ida Benecke under the title *Heine on Shakespeare*, Westminster, 1895.
[2] *ibid.*, p. 176.
[3] *ibid.*, p. 189.

meant, he would be at a loss for a reply. But I do not think he would have said 'None of it.'

The same year, 1838, saw the publication of the seventh edition of the *Encyclopaedia Britannica,* containing De Quincey's article on Shakespeare. In a slightly cooler style than Heine's we can find the same strain, the ideal world and our world, differing from one another ('as it were') in their degrees of density. Religion, however, is set carefully on one side:

> In the *Tempest* again, what new modes of life, preternatural, yet far as the poles from the spiritualities of religion. Ariel in antithesis to Caliban! What is most ethereal to what is most animal! A phantom of air, an abstraction of the dawn and of vesper sunlights, a bodiless sylph on the one hand; on the other a gross carnal monster . . .

A third production of the year 1838 was Thomas Campbell's *Remarks on the Life and Writings of William Shakespeare.* Campbell was, as far as I know, the first to make an allegorical connexion between Prospero and Shakespeare himself. Prospero drowns his book and Shakespeare takes his leave of the London theatre. Campbell thus stands at the head of a tradition which is to run through Montégut, Dowden and Raleigh and crop up unexpectedly in many more places. Montégut, indeed, produces some rather startling extrapolations from the notion of Shakespeare's Farewell to his Art. He begins in a sufficiently familiar strain: '. . . la Tempête est très évidemment la dernière pièce de Shakespeare, et n'est autre chose, sous une forme allégorique, que le testament dramatique du grand poète'.[1] He soon grows bolder, however, and affirms that *The Tempest* as a whole is a poetic synthesis of Shakespeare's entire dramatic career. In a few pages he grows confident enough to ask rhetorical questions like this:

> Et l'histoire de l'île enchantée telle que Prospero l'expose dans ses conversations du premier acte avec Miranda, Ariel et Caliban, est-ce qu'elle ne raconte pas trait pour trait l'histoire de théâtre anglais et de la transformation que Shakespeare lui fit subir?[2]

He goes on to identify the foul witch Sycorax with the foul

---

[1] 'Une Hypothèse sur *la Tempête* de Shakspeare', *Revue des Deux Mondes,* LVIII (1865), p. 733.
[2] *ibid.*, p. 746.

English theatre of earlier times. A similar impulse for elaboration carries Dowden as far as suggesting that Ferdinand is 'the young Fletcher in conjunction with whom Shakspere worked upon *The Two Noble Kinsmen* and *Henry VIII*'.[1]

The twentieth century has, of course, seen hypotheses equally bizarre, if not more so. In 1925 the curious genius of Robert Graves was willing to identify the drunken sailors of the play with 'Chapman and Jonson with a suggestion of Marston'.[2] A Miss Winstanley who corresponded with Graves found[3] in Sycorax the reputed witch Catherine de Medici and in Caliban Jesuitism and Ravaillac, who was entrusted with the task of murdering Henry IV, and is described in pamphlets as a spotted monster and a degenerate. He was, it seems, first racked and then pinched to death with red-hot pincers for the murder.

Such historical allegorizings seem, apart from a mysterious inner principle of self-multiplication and extension, to be conceptually fairly innocent. The discovery of parallels between fictional and historical personages is a blameless occupation. As criticism or interpretation its constant danger is that it will make too large a claim upon the intention of the author, and clog the pleasures of the historically uninitiated reader. But to say this is to describe the abuse rather than the use of the approach. It is entirely free from the ontological smell of more transcendental allegorizings. For some tastes, indeed, it will always appear much too sublunary and mechanical. Few would dispute that it is much more important to remember that Spenser's Una represents Truth than that his Artegall represents Lord Gray.

But, if the supernatural was banished by De Quincey and ignored by the historical allegorists, it is brought home in triumph by François-Victor Hugo, in a cloud of Gallic rodomontade. In 1859 a massive French version of the works of Shakespeare began to emerge, of which the second volume was devoted to '*féeries*'. Hugo wrote in the introduction to this volume:

Cet homme, ce fut Shakespeare.
Shakespeare ne fit pas comme Reginald Scot.
Il ne rejeta pas les traditions de la Bible et de la légende; il les arbora.

[1] *Shakspere – his Mind and Art*, p. 425.
[2] R. Graves, *Poetic Unreason*, London 1925, p. 214.
[3] *ibid*., pp. 221 ff.

Il ne contesta pas le monde invisible; il le réhabilita.
Il ne nia pas la puissance surnaturelle de l'homme; il la sanctifia.[1]

A few pages later his language is equally forceful, if a little less Chadbandian. The categories of comparison seem to multiply until they shimmer before our eyes, abstract/concrete, general/particular, spiritual/unspiritual. Also we find once more the suggestion of Paradise. The connexion of the Enchanted Island with the Garden of Eden is older than Mrs. Jameson or Schlegel. It goes back to the seventeenth century and is linked with the Paradisal dreams of the great Elizabethan voyagers.[2] Hugo writes:

> La Tempête symbolise l'action de l'homme sur le monde invisible . . . Dans cette île enchantée 'pleine de chansons et de douce musique,' on croirait par instant entrevoir le monde de l'utopie, la terre promise des générations futures, l'Éden reconquis. Qu'est-ce en effet que Prospero, le roi de cette île? Prospero, c'est le naufragé qui atteint le port, c'est le banni qui retrouve la patrie, c'est le désespéré qui devient tout puissant, c'est le travailleur qui devient tout puissant, c'est le travailleur qui, par la science, a dompté la matière Caliban, et, par la génie, l'esprit Ariel. Prospero, c'est l'homme devenu le maître de la matière et le despote de la destinée, c'est l'homme-Providence![3]

Hugo had mentioned not only the Promised Land but also Utopia, which suggests the interesting possibility of adding political allegories to the theological. In 1860, Alfred Mézières produced a book called *Shakspere, ses oeuvres et ses critiques* and published it in Paris. Kreyssig had, it seems, made certain political observations on the play between 1858 and 1860.[4] Mézières devotes some space[5] to Kreyssig's treatment of Caliban as the Mob, and then, after observing sarcastically that he himself is not capable of such insight, suddenly jumps in head first with 'il représente simplement l'homme primitif livré à lui-même . . .' and more of the same sort.

The sociological approach links itself with the transcendentalist

---

[1] François-Victor Hugo, *Œuvres complètes de W. Shakespeare*, Paris 1859, vol. II, Introduction, p. 84.

[2] See below, ch. VI, pp. 137 ff.

[3] *Œuvres complètes de W. Shakespeare*, vol. II, Introduction, p. 87.

[4] T. A. Th. Kreyssig, *Vorlesungen über Shakspeare, seine Zeit und seine Werke*, Bd. I–III, Berlin 1858–60.

[5] *op. cit.*, p. 448.

approach, as one might have expected, in Ruskin. In *Munera Pulveris*, which was first published in New York in 1872, he compares Caliban to the slave in Plato's *Republic* and says:

> . . . there is an undercurrent of meaning throughout, in the Tempest as well as in the Merchant of Venice; referring in this case to government, as in that to commerce. Miranda ('the wonderful', so addressed first by Ferdinand, 'Oh, you wonder!') corresponds to Homer's Arete. Ariel and Caliban are respectively the spirits of faithful and imaginative labour, opposed to rebellious, hurtful and slavish labour. Prospero ('for hope'), a true governor, is opposed to Sycorax, the mother of slavery, her name, 'swine-raven', indicating at once brutality and deathfulness . . . . For all these dreams of Shakespeare, as those of true and strong men must be, are 'φαντάσματα θεῖα, καὶ σκίαι τῶν ὄντων' divine phantasms, and shadows of things that are. We hardly tell our children, willingly, a fable with no purport in it; yet we think God sends his best messengers only to sing fairy-tales to us, fond and empty.[1]

The tone may seem excessively exalted for this world of politics and labour relations, yet the name of the chapter is 'Government', and the Greek quotation is taken from the seventh book of Plato's *Republic*.

We have seen an historical *Tempest*, a political *Tempest*, a sociological *Tempest*. All we need now is someone to put all these together and give us an Evolutionary *Tempest*. As a matter of fact, we have a prize specimen. The Darwinian Daniel Wilson published in 1873 a book called *Caliban: the Missing Link*. Wilson's precise intention in this book is extraordinarily elusive, even for his century. Sometimes he seems entirely content with the sheer interest of pointing out affinities between the Missing Link and Salvage Men from Mandeville onwards; sometimes he seems to be saying, 'If you want to know what the Missing Link was like, his feelings, his glimmerings of reason and imagination and so on, then read *The Tempest*'– and this is rational enough. But at other times he speaks of Caliban as an *anticipation*, in allegorical form, of Darwin's theory. The gap in the great chain of being corresponds to the gap in the evolutionary story. Caliban fills both.

We are soon led back, however, to the religious import of the

[1] *The Works of John Ruskin*, ed. E. T. Cook and A. Wedderburn, London 1905, vol. XVII, pp. 257–8.

play. The year 1876 saw the publication of the most audacious theological allegory yet. At last it is out; Prospero is God.

We must be permitted to suggest a deeper purpose. In the epilogue the poet says his project was to please, but be sure it was to please himself as well as his audience. Let anyone to whom the idea has not previously occurred re-open his Shakspeare with the special intention of appreciating what we may call the Manichaean element in this delightful poem. Postpone the pleasure of letting the mind glide gently down the current of the poet's dream. Cast a gaze of scrutiny into its depths. Fear not lest you should be too polemical. The supreme poetic charm of the Tempest will not be easily dissipated. But if for the time you manage to analyze this gossamer thing of beauty, what will you see? A man perfectly wise and gracious, scarcely distinguishable in purity and benevolence from what we believe of God, and endowed by magical studies – or rather (for our present purpose) by the dramatist's will – with superhuman power. Prospero, by this happy fiction of magic lore, is put, without profanity, almost in the place of Deity. In one passage [V.i] in which he puts forward his humanity, asking whether he shall not be as kindly moved as Ariel towards his prisoners in the lime-grove, seeing that Ariel is but air, while he is 'one of their kind, and relishes all as sharply passion as they', it is just possible that there may be an allusion to the experiences on earth of the great High-priest. . . . May we not consider the rest of the play an answer, as this passage is an echo, to the weary doubts of ages in the presence of calamities caused by Omnipotence, which seems malevolent in not having prevented them?[1]

Edward R. Russell's proposal is too bold to be plausible. Even the the reader who was prepared to find a sort of sanctity in the play as a whole has some difficulty in bowing down and worshipping the irascible old Duke of Milan as the God of his fathers. Yet by trespassing where angels fear to tread Russell proved to be a seminal writer.[2] Nearly eighty years later we find critics still

[1] Edward R. Russell, 'The Religion of Shakespeare', *The Theological Review*, no. LV (Oct. 1876), pp. 482–3.

[2] In that he finds in *The Tempest* an emergence into the Kingdom of Heaven, and in the Incarnation and Passion of Christ our best comfort against the fact of evil, Russell might be held to have linked two features which later appear in the work of Charles Williams. For Williams in his 'Essay on the Cross' (in *Charles Williams,*

searching the play for a solution to the Problem of Evil. K. J. Spalding supposed that he had found it – and here his theology falls well short of Russell's – in the lines

> Whom best I love I cross; to make my gift,
> The more delayed, delighted.[1]

Few of his successors, however, were willing to follow him to the full limit of his doctrinal assertions. As the years passed, it became more and more unlikely that an intelligent man would state the case in so crass a form. Critics began to search, dimly and tentatively, for some sort of prior field of the consciousness, in which the poetic and religious insights are not dissociated, and critical pronouncements can be made without obligation to notice the truth or falsity of the factors involved. Statements of the form 'Prospero figures our Lord Jesus Christ, and the play is a shadowing of our salvation through His Incarnation' tend to give place to statements of the form 'Ideas of redemption seem to have had an especial importance and validity for Shakespeare at this period'. Yet it is hard to write always in the language of Limbo. Dover Wilson, with all his circumspection, suddenly slips right back into the nineteenth century with the rhetoric of '. . . what is the enchanted island but Life itself . . .?'[2] Even the use of capitals dates him.

But the religious approach never completely subsumed the 'Platonic'. In the same year as Russell's article, J. Surtees Phillpotts wrote: 'There is a real resemblance . . . between the characters of Nausicaa and Miranda. Each stands before us as an ideal of maidenhood . . .'[3] Between 1907 and 1911 J. W. Mackail de-

---

[1] See his book, *The Philosophy of Shakespeare*, Oxford 1953.

[2] *The Essential Shakespeare*, 1937, p. 142.

[3] *The Tempest of Shakespeare*, London 1876 (the 'Rugby Edition'), p. xxi.

Selected Writings, chosen by Anne Ridler, London 1961; the essay first appeared in 1943 in a Symposium, *What the Cross Means to Me*) proposes just such a comfort for Christians, and in *The English Poetic Mind* (Oxford 1932) worked out a theory of the poet's intelligence (especially Wordsworth's and Shakespeare's) as passing from the innocence of youth through a time of 'subversion', in which the discrepancy between the ideal and the real first shows itself vividly and produces a kind of despair, to a just and pure vision at the last. An account which similarly links Shakespeare and Wordsworth, though in more exclusively aesthetic terms, can be found in J. Dover Wilson's *The Essential Shakespeare* (Cambridge 1932), pp. 134–45. The historical thesis, about the development of Shakespeare's genius over the years, cannot be extracted from Russell's article. But any subscriber to William's account would be tempted to say that Russell had observed in *The Tempest* the effects of that development.

livered at Oxford various lectures on poetry. In one of these, 'The Note of Shakespeare's Romances',[1] he spoke of a special tension between the idealities of fairyland and actuality, and affirmed, with a slight shift of terminology, that Shakespearean romance attained to a higher degree of actuality than Shakespearean tragedy. As late as 1920 we can find a sentence – dealing this time with a different romantic drama of Shakespeare – having the authentic nineteenth-century Platonical ring: 'Chastity, faith, fidelity, strike the ideal chord in *Cymbeline*; and Imogen is their exemplar.'[2]

Of all the romantic allegorist-critics, however, perhaps the most interesting is James Russell Lowell. He is no shyer than his contemporaries of religious parallels, and he does not shrink in style or in thought from the sort of Platonic bravura we have seen in others of his time. His proposed allegory is elaborate and detailed. Yet to all this he brings a not inconsiderable critical awareness. He is interesting because what he does he does reflectively and deliberately. We have had some experience in tracing the development of this sort of 'interpretation' through a twilit world of 'merely poetical' and enthusiastic assertion. In Lowell we see it in the full light of consciousness. He merits an extended quotation:

> Outside the tragedies also, the *Tempest* makes an exception worthy of notice. If I read it rightly, it is an example of how a great poet should write allegory – not embodying metaphysical abstractions, but giving us ideals abstracted from life itself, suggesting an under-meaning everywhere, forcing it upon us nowhere, tantalizing the mind with hints that imply so much and tell so little, and yet keep the attention all eye and ear with eager, if fruitless, expectation. Here the leading characters are not merely typical, but symbolical – that is, they do not illustrate a class of persons, they belong to universal Nature. But in the *Tempest* the scene is laid nowhere, or certainly in no country laid down on any map. Nowhere then? At once nowhere and anywhere – for it is in the soul of man, that still vexed island between the upper and the nether world, and liable to incursions from both. . . . But consider for a moment

---

[1] Published in *Lectures on Poetry*, London 1911.
[2] H. Granville-Barker, *Prefaces to Shakespeare*, New York 1958, p. 530. The work was written *c*. 1920.

if ever the Imagination has been so embodied as in Prospero, the Fancy as in Ariel, the brute Understanding as in Caliban, who, the moment his poor wits are warmed with the glorious liquor of Stephano, plots rebellion against his natural lord, the higher Reason. Miranda is mere abstract Womanhood, as truly so before she sees Ferdinand as Eve before she was wakened to consciousness by the echo of her own nature coming back to her, the same, and yet not the same, from that of Adam. Ferdinand, again, is nothing more than Youth, compelled to drudge at something he despises, till the sacrifice of will and abnegation of self win him his ideal in Miranda. The subordinate personages are simply types: Sebastian and Antonio, of weak character and evil ambition; Gonzalo, of average sense and honesty; Adrian and Francisco, of the walking gentlemen who serve to fill up a world. They are not characters in the same sense with Iago, Falstaff, Shallow, or Leontius; and it is curious how every one of them loses his way in this enchanted island of life, all the victims of one illusion after another, except Prospero, whose ministers are purely ideal. The whole play, indeed, is a succession of illusions, winding up with those solemn words of the great enchanter who had summoned to his service every shape of merriment or passion, every figure in the great tragi-comedy of life, and who was now bidding farewell to the scene of his triumphs. For in Prospero shall we not recognize the Artist himself, –

That did not better for his life provide
Than public means which public manners breeds,
Whence comes it that his name receives a brand –

who has forfeited a shining place in the world's eye by devotion to his art, and who, turned adrift on the ocean of life in the leaky carcass of a boat, has shipwrecked on that Fortunate Island (as men always do who find their true vocation), where he is absolute lord, making all the powers of nature serve him, but with Ariel and Caliban as special ministers.[1]

Lowell's essay is an excellent specimen for examination. His whole language is, of course, suffused with value, and perhaps does not wholly meet the descriptive ideal of twentieth-century objectivity. Yet here, very clearly, is a man who means what he

---

[1] 'Shakespeare Once More' in *Among My Books*, first published in 1870. The text of this quotation is taken from the Everyman Edition.

says. The full religious affirmation of E. R. Russell is absent from his essay; but almost everything else is there. Even the historical allegory connecting Prospero and Shakespeare is to be found, neatly dove-tailed into an entire transcendentalist world-view. And here we come to the point. Concepts which we are nervous of assessing in the works of Mrs. Jameson or Heine attain full visibility in Lowell. We can no longer be confident that this sort of criticism is conducted without metaphysical presuppositions. The allegoristic criticism of the nineteenth century differs from the common run of criticism today in that it was metaphysical. With varying degrees of seriousness and vividness, the romantic men of letters felt that when they were talking about *The Tempest* they were talking about the structure of the universe also. They felt, by and large, that *The Tempest* itself impelled them to this course, but they did not feel that they were expounding the curious opinions of a man long dead. The metaphysics they proposed was, they felt, quite as much their own as it was Shakespeare's. Ontological assertions are woven into the very fabric of their criticism. Lowell's relegation of what he calls the 'metaphysical' to the realm of tenuous artificiality and unreality does not alter this fact. The very relegation is a piece of metaphysics. The phrase 'ideals abstracted from life itself' is still more ontologically assertive. It is significant that he spells 'imagination' with a capital I, and the significance is metaphysical.

Further, it looks very much as if his metaphysics bears a more than accidental relation to his allegorizing. For the primary peculiarity of his conceptual scheme (and it is a peculiarity which runs through nearly all the critics we have mentioned) is that he thinks of (certain) universals as if they were very important instances of themselves. He thinks of the concept 'womanhood' not as a logical construction designed to assist talk about a set of concrete individuals, but as an ideal entity, existing not here, so therefore somewhere else, to which concrete particulars stand in a curious para-physical relation, of 'embodiment'. The Platonism is rather more than skin-deep. He is thinking of womanhood as something supremely womanly. What more natural, then, than to compare her, end even to identify her, with Miranda? For if we think of womanhood as something womanly, we are already thinking the way allegorical poets write. We are not likely to say 'Prospero is a perfectly reasonable man', when, since Reason itself is also perfectly reasonable, it seems equally proper and much more forceful to say 'Prospero is *like* Reason itself'; or even 'Prospero *is* Reason itself'.

I do not suppose that Lowell thought the word 'embodiment' was anything but figurative. Yet I do think that he would find it exceedingly difficult to 'demythologize'. It may even be that if he had read a slightly brutal analysis of his views such as the one I have just given, he would abandon his metaphysic. But there is no doubt that he is still wedded to it here. The antitheses he makes will scarcely stand up without it. What, for example, are we to make of the contrast between illustrating 'a class of persons' and touching on 'universal Nature'? What is the difference between the way in which Ferdinand is pure Youth and the way in which the subordinate personages are 'simply types'? In each of his antitheses there is one term which might be felt to burst the bonds of common sense. We understand well enough what is meant by being typical of something; we are less sure of what (beyond this) can be meant by saying that someone is 'mere abstract woman-hood' or what not. When we use the expression 'She is stupidity itself' we are employing in little a form which is fundamental to allegory. It is also by no means superficial in the structure of Lowell's *thought*.

The business of the next chapter will be to inquire how far the critical practices we have outlined, together with the poetical practices of other ages, necessitate a revision of our stock conceptions of allegory.

II

TWO CONCEPTS OF ALLEGORY

The general purpose of the last chapter was to bring out the fundamental, if imprecise, connexions between the allegorical criticism of the romantic movement and a body of metaphysical beliefs. All the examples given could, without straining language, be called allegorical; all, save only the historical allegories, can be felt to retain some metaphysical force; both functions are simultaneously discharged by the same sentences. But at this point some doubts may arise as to whether these 'fundamental' though 'imprecise' connexions amount to anything more interesting than confusions. Perhaps, it might be said, the whole attempt to relate allegorical composition and metaphysical thinking is barren, tending to the elucidation neither of metaphysics nor of allegorical poetry, but calculated to turn its followers, as Sir John Davies put it, from sun-gazing eagles into bats, fitted only for the darkness.

The objections come in their strongest form from C. S. Lewis:

> This fundamental equivalence between the immaterial and the material may be used by the mind in two ways, and we need here be concerned with only one of them. On the one hand you can start with an immaterial fact, such as the passions which you actually experience, and can then invent *visibilia* to express them. If you are hesitating between an angry retort and a soft answer, you can express your state of mind by inventing a person called *Ira* with a torch and letting her contend with another invented person called *Patientia*. This is allegory, and it is with this alone that we have to deal. But there is another way of expressing the equivalence, which is almost the opposite of allegory, and which I would call sacramentalism or

symbolism. If our passions, being immaterial, can be copied by material inventions, then it is possible that our material world in its turn is the copy of an invisible world. As the god *Amor* and his figurative garden are to the actual passions of men, so perhaps we ourselves and our 'real' world are to something else. The attempt to read that something else through the sensible imitations, to see the archetype in the copy, is what I mean by symbolism or sacramentalism. It is, in fine, 'the philosophy of Hermes that this visible world is but a picture of the invisible, wherein, as in a portrait, things are not truly but in equivocal shapes, as they counterfeit some real substance in that invisible fabrick'. The difference between the two can hardly be exaggerated. The allegorist leaves the given – his own passions – to talk of that which is confessedly less real, which is a fiction. The symbolist leaves the given to find that which is more real. To put the difference in another way, for the symbolist it is we who are the allegory. We are the 'frigid personifications', the heavens above us are the 'shadowy abstractions'; the world which we mistake for reality is the flat outline of that which elsewhere veritably is in all the round of its unimaginable dimensions.[1]

Lewis makes his division deep indeed. We may note that the separation as he intends it is more than merely logical. He is not just saying to us: 'Here is a conceptual distinction which will be useful in approaching older authors.' He means to describe two public categories of literature, which are mutually exclusive. The scholar who shows that a poem must be an allegory proves by the same token that it cannot be 'symbolical'. A little later, he says:

On the literary side the chief monuments of the symbolical idea, in the Middle Ages, are the *Bestiaries*; and I should distrust the judgement of the critic who was unaware of their strange poetry, or who did not feel it to be wholly different in kind from that of the allegories.[2]

There are, it seems, no prominent examples of 'mixed' poems.

The practical force of Lewis's distinction can be weakened in various ways. It may have been just an unlucky chance that led him to derive allegory from its literary sources only, from Virgil

[1] *The Allegory of Love*, first published Oxford 1936, reprinted with corrections 1938, pp. 44–45. This quotation and all following are taken from the 1953 impression.
[2] *ibid.*, p. 46.

and Statius, and not from its springs in the Greek (pre-)philo-
sophical writers, Heraclitus [1] and Parmenides.[2] It is also perhaps
unfortunate for his account that his central concern throughout
the book is with allegories of the 'inner man'. Where 'the given'
is a mental action or passion, 'the given' is very far from being a
definite quantity. Indeed, the mental event is so elusive as to make
'given' sound altogether too optimistic a word. There is no purely
literal language to describe 'inner' conflicts, though there is such
a language for the ordinary world of public objects – that is 'the
given' of the symbolist. It therefore follows that the metaphorical
language which we use to describe mental events is not merely
playful, is not pure, unalloyed fiction. Where literal expression is
wanting, metaphor must be set in harness. That Lewis is aware of
this emerges very clearly later in his book:

> The origins of the allegorical method turned out to be a
> longer story. We saw that allegory was in no sense a mere
> device, or figure of rhetoric, or fashion. It was not simply a
> better or worse way of telling a story. On the contrary, it was
> originally forced into existence by a profound moral revolution
> occurring in the latter days of paganism. For reasons of which
> we know nothing at all . . . men's gaze was turned inward.
> But a gaze so turned sees, not the compact 'character' of modern
> fiction, but the contending forces which cannot be described at
> all except by allegory. Hence the development of allegory, to
> supply the subjective element in literature, to paint the inner
> world, followed inevitably.[3]

Or, again, we may glance at his discussion of the difference
between the narrative poet, Chrétien de Troyes, and the allegorical poet, Guillaume de Lorris, which follows a few pages
later:

> Many people, misled by the platitudinous allegory produced in
> ages to which allegory is a toy – the allegory of Maeterlinck or
> Addison – are disposed to think that in turning to Guillaume de
> Lorris we are retreating from the real world into a shadowy
> world of abstractions. But the whole truth about Guillaume is
> missed until we see that he is more of a realist than Chrétien. Of

[1] e.g. Πόλεμος πάντων μὲν πατήρ ἐστι, πάντων δὲ βασιλεύς . . . ('War is the father
of all things, the king of all things . . .'), Heraclitus, fr. 53 [44], in H. Diels,
Fragmente der Vorsokratiker, 6th Ed., Berlin 1951, vol. 1, p. 162.

[2] See Parmenides, fr. 1, in Diels, *op. cit.*, vol. I, pp. 228–30.

[3] *The Allegory of Love*, p. 113.

the two things that he found in Chrétien it was the fantastic that he rejected and the natural that he used. Do not let us be deceived by the allegorical form. That, as we have seen, does not mean that the author is talking about non-entities, but that he is talking about the inner world – talking, in fact, about the realities he knows best. No doubt, from a grammatical or logical point of view, the land of Gorre in *Lancelot* is 'concrete', and Danger in the *Roman*, being a personification, is 'abstract'. But no one, least of all Chrétien, has ever been to the land of Gorre, while Guillaume, or any courtly lover of the period – or, for that matter, any lover in any subsequent period – has actually met Danger. In other words, the 'concrete' places and people in Chrétien are mere romantic supposals: the 'abstract' places and people in the *Romance of the Rose* are presentations of actual life.[1]

There has been a certain shifting of ground between the first quotation from Lewis and these last two; perhaps nothing which amounts to an obvious contradiction, but nevertheless a shift. While in the first passage he described the allegorical poet as leaving the given and moving in the direction of the confessedly less real, he now prefers to describe him as closing with the real by the only possible means. The mental event, so far from being 'given' as a convenient point of departure for idle poets, is only available to us at all through the labours of those poets. As Morton Bloomfield wrote, with an aptness which I think must have been unconscious. 'If Mercy kisses Peace, what else does that mean but that peace and mercy embrace?'[2]

We can distinguish a Lewis of first thoughts and a Lewis of second thoughts, a proto- and a deutero-Lewis. Deutero-Lewis dismisses with scorn that allegory which is played with as if it were a toy, but it is hard to be sure that proto-Lewis thought of it as anything but that. Proto-Lewis affirms that 'symbolism is a mode of thought, but allegory is a mode of expression',[3] deutero-Lewis coolly declares that all lovers of all ages have met Danger. It is hard to feel confident about proto-Lewis's antithesis here,

[1] *ibid.*, pp. 114–15.

[2] 'Symbolism in Mediaeval Literature', *Modern Philology*, LVI, November 1958, pp. 78–79. Bloomfield argues that much medieval literature uses not 'symbols' but 'personification', and personification is 'making what is abstract concrete'. It seems a doubtful piece of critical economy to make these categories mutually exclusive.

[3] *The Allegory of Love*, p. 48.

even within his system. The fact that the fiction obtains any credence at all in the plane of expression derives from the fact that it carried originally an appeal to the mind. Where proto-Lewis would hold that the allegorical garden in the Roman was the merest fiction, deutero-Lewis finds himself forced to distinguish it from the idle make-believe of the land of Gorre, and to found that distinction upon its closer approximation to reality.

It would be unwise to make too much of this change of approach. We may point out that in the first chapter Lewis's attention was fixed on the formation of the figure, the personification, the metaphor, and that this remains a metaphor and not a name. In the later passages he is concentrating on the *use* made of such metaphors, upon the object. We cannot, after all, deny that *some* invention goes into allegory. No one has been to the land of Gorre, and no one has heard Danger speak either, or seen the colour of his gown. So at any rate his speeches and the details of his dress are invented.

But we can no longer affirm that Danger's individuality is as much a piece of fiction as the details of his dress and behaviour. The area of *sheer* invention has been drastically reduced. The fact that Danger is highly metaphorical will not save the distinction between allegory and symbolism. After all, there are various signs that Plato himself in his efforts to define the relation between ideas and particulars was aware that terms like μέθεξις ('sharing'), μετάσχεσις ('participation') and μίμησις ('imitation') could not be taken literally,[1] yet he did not feel that this turned his metaphysics into mere fiction. The researcher into the primary constituents of matter uses language appropriate to particles, not because he is confident that the object of his research is just another particle like a grain of sand, but because he does not know how else to talk. Yet we do not wish to say that while nineteenth-century physics was a mode of thought, twentieth-century physics is a mode of expression. To bring the argument nearer home, Sigmund Freud himself affirmed[2] that the elements he distinguished in the psyche could not be given a literal status, yet he never thought of them as gay, arbitrary excursions from the real world into the world of fiction.

In tying allegory so closely to the task of representing the inner

---

[1] See W. D. Ross, *Plato's Theory of Ideas*, Oxford 1951, p. 231.
[2] See his *Introductory Lectures on Psycho-analysis,* trans. J. Rivière, London 1922, pp. 117–18.

life, Lewis was, perhaps, bringing it closer to sacramentalism than
he knew. E. Husserl once observed that by a 'change in the shad-
ing' we could transform 'a pure psychology of the inner life into a
self-styled transcendental phenomenology.'[1] There are times when
the 'Aphrodite breathed in me' of Homeric psychology[2] and the
'My Libido overcame me' of popular Freudianism seem almost to
have a common logical status. Aphrodite comes down from above
and Libido comes up from below – a spatial metaphor with all the
marks of spuriousness is all that divides them.

The effect of this reasoning is greatly to weaken Lewis's strong
opposition between sacramentalism and allegory as practised. We
can no longer think of them as marching in contrary directions,
sacramentalism towards and allegory away from 'reality'. The
distinction between allegory and vaguely transcendentalist psychology no longer rests squarely on the sheer fact of the metaphorical form, for this is common to both. Again and again men
have described the universe, viewed as being *objectively* allegorical –
as being ontologically 'stratified'– by a *method* which is itself
allegorical. Philosophers found that a many-layered universe defied
literal description, and were accordingly forced to pile metaphor
on metaphor, as the Giants piled Pelion on Ossa. Transcendentalist
metaphysics has commonly availed itself of an allegorical *medium*.
And, of course, a dualist philosophy of mind – a philosophy of
mind maintaining that there is an essential difference between the
inner and the outer universe – must find itself in like case. It is
simply impossible to unfold the workings of the ulterior world
(whether that world is a Platonic Heaven or a human mind) without raiding the public world for images and metaphors.

There is, of course, another objection to my thesis. It is, in a
way, almost the opposite of the one I have just been labouring to
refute. I have been trying to show that the language we apply to
God, Heaven, Hell and the human mind is necessarily figurative.
My objector might reply: 'Certainly it is figurative, but only
because *all* discourse is figurative. Those who take the greatest
pride in restricting themselves to literal expression are really the
abject victims of the ancient metaphors which make up the history,
and hence the structure of all language. Such people would assess
this paragraph, for example, as a very literal and "scientific" piece

---

[1] *Ideas: General Introduction to Pure Phenomenology*, trans. W. R. Boyce Gibson,
London 1931, author's preface to the English Edition, p. 16.

[2] See the earlier chapters of Bruno Snell's *The Discovery of Mind*, Oxford 1953.

of English. But they would be quite wrong. "Figurative" is itself a metaphor from shaping with finger and thumb; "discourse" is a metaphor from running; "restricting" is a metaphor from binding; "literal" is a metaphor from letters; "expression" is a metaphor from twisting, as "metaphor" is a metaphor from carrying.'

The scope of this objection can be reduced in various ways. First, as C. S. Lewis has pointed out in an admirable essay,[1] derivation is not the same thing as meaning. If *lord* means 'loaf-carver' and *dominus* 'means' 'householder', how is it that the English word translates the Latin? 'Style' may once have meant 'pen', but that is not what it means now.

More radically, the claim that all discourse is metaphorical, if granted, does not destroy my thesis only. It also destroys itself. To say that all discourse is metaphorical is to empty the word 'metaphorical' of all content. The concept 'metaphorical', in fact, presupposes the concept 'literal'. We say that a word is metaphorical when we perceive that it has been transferred from its proper, literal, application. If we claim that there is no such thing as a 'proper, literal, application', we shall find it hard to explain how people ever arrived at the conception of a 'transferred term'. The concept 'exile' has no meaning for the man who has no conception of 'home'. The concept 'borrow' has no meaning for the man who lacks the concept of property. We may assert, if we wish, that 'style' is a metaphor drawn from a physical object, a pen, but we make the modern term metaphorical only by allowing a literal sense to its etymological ancestor. If 'pen' was never the literal meaning of 'style', then the modern use can scarcely be described as a metaphor drawn from the world of physical objects. If 'pen' is no more the literal meaning of 'style' than is 'manner of writing', then it is impossible to say that one is a metaphor from the other. We are left with a mere series of meanings, which is not at all the same thing as a series of metaphors. *Litteram expellas furca, tamen usque recurrit.*

The sweeping claim of my 'objector' has now been qualified in two ways. First, to demonstrate semantic change in the history of a word is not *ipso facto* to prove that its present use is metaphorical; the fact (if it is a fact) that *tragedy* once meant 'goat-song' does not prevent us from using the same word today with a sense which is both entirely literal and entirely different from the original

[1] 'Bluspels and Flalansferes', *Rehabilitations and Other Essays*, 1939; reprinted in *The Importance of Language*, ed. Max Black (Spectrum Books), 1962.

meaning. Secondly, if we are to use the term 'metaphorical' at all, we must acknowledge the existence of a class of usages which are literal; the man who says 'Pass the sugar' is guiltless of metaphor. Thus modified, the claim becomes both more modest and more interesting. For we are left with the suggestion that a great many words retain a metaphorical force which is at the same time unsuspected and operative. To be told that *lord* once meant 'loaf-carver' is merely to receive an item of extraneous information. The discovery is accompanied by no shock of recognition[1]. But to be told that *attend* once meant 'stretch' is to discover a means of formulating something which still inheres in our present-day use of the term. The truth is that (as C. S. Lewis saw long before I did) the metaphor embedded in the history of many words becomes dispensable only when the new meaning is readily and intrinsically intelligible. Thus our idea of what a lord is is so clear as to make all allusions to the domestic economy of the early Saxons entirely otiose. But our idea of attention lacks this sort of immediate and intrinsic intelligibility, this self-sufficiency. There appear to be certain areas of discourse where we can never afford to give up the metaphors we have inherited. Perhaps the principal examples of this sort of area are, first, theology, and, second, language about the mind. But then this is what I was saying to begin with. Your metaphysician is a great metaphorist.

In blurring the distinction between allegory and 'more serious disciplines', we are not necessarily running counter to the spirit of the Middle Ages. Assertions like 'I veil eternal truths under poetical figures' are commonplace. There are, indeed, signs that men naïvely supposed that by judicious invocation of allegory a respectable 'truth-value' might be restored to all truly excellent poetry. This may well be a motive behind Dante's description of the *Thebaid* as *literaliter bellum Thebanum, allegorice homo*[1] ('literally the Theban War, allegorically man'), and Fulgentius's bizarre exegesis of the *Aeneid*[2] as an allegory of the life of man.

The characters which make works like the *Roman de la Rose* allegorical poetry, and metaphysical psychology something else, are at once more familiar and more difficult to define. The greater playfulness and exuberance in detail which we find in the poet is a symptom only. Nor, as we have seen, can the claim to be called

---

[1] Quoted in *The Allegory of Love*, p. 56.

[2] See *ibid.*, pp. 84–85, and also D. Comparetti, *Vergil in the Middle Ages*, trans. E. F. M. Benecke, London 1895, pp. 101–2, 107 ff.

poetry reside simply in the use of figures. The poetical character of a work like the *Roman* lies quite as much in its attitude to the 'given' as in its personifications. The fact that the love-affair described in the poem may be historical is not strictly relevant to the issue. It is a matter of historical fact that the Greeks fought the Persians, but this does not turn the *Persae* of Aeschylus into a history. It is unfortunate that proto-Lewis should quote with approval[1] the passage from Dante's *Vita Nuova*, XXV,[2] where he says: 'It would be a great disgrace to a man, if he should rime matters under figure and rhetorical colouring, and then, when he was asked, could not strip off that vesture and show the true sense'; for it is just this impossibility of demythologizing the allegory of the soul that deutero-Lewis brought to light.

Dante is in any case a doubtful prop to lean on. Whether we take our information from the probably spurious letter to Cangrande or from the authentic *Il Convivio*, Dante remains of all poets the one whose theory is hardest to square with his practice. In the Cangrande epistle four possible 'senses' are expounded, (i) literal, (ii) allegorical, (iii) moral, (iv) anagogical. The Biblical account of the departure of the Israelites out of Egypt is then considered as a material case. Here the literal sense (we are told) is the actual, historical journey out of Egypt; the allegorical sense is our Redemption as wrought by Christ; the moral sense is the conversion of the soul from the misery of sin to a state of grace; the anagogical sense is the passage of the soul from terrestrial corruption to heavenly glory. In *Il Convivio*, Dante sharply distinguishes poets' allegory from the allegory used in scriptural exegesis. In Trattato II, cap. i, he lists four senses for the interpretation of Scripture, but takes as his example of the second sense, the allegorical, Ovid's *poetical* account of Orpheus charming the trees and rocks, which represents (he says) the wise man softening cruel hearts by the power of his voice. But his example for the moral sense is scriptural enough – the Evangelist's account of the Transfiguration, which signifies morally that in the most secret matters we should take few companions. For the anagogical sense he uses *Exodus*, giving an account in substantial agreement with the Cangrande epistle. Dorothy L. Sayers struggled hard enough[3] to interpret the *Divine*

---

[1] *The Allegory of Love*, p. 48.

[2] Dante's *Vita Nuova*, trans. R. W. Emerson, Chapel Hill, Carolina 1960, p. 31.

[3] See 'The Fourfold Interpretation of the *Comedy*', pp. 101–26, in her *Introductory Papers on Dante*, London 1954.

Comedy in terms of the polysemantic allegory which Dante describes, but Colin Hardie had no difficulty in demolishing her case.[1] One of her principal difficulties[2] was that of finding a reasonable 'anagogical significance' in a work whose subject-matter was already radically eschatological. The easiest short cut through this sort of difficulty – though it leaves too many loose ends to be completely plausible – is to take Dante as describing in terms appropriate to the art of rhetoric the ontological structure of the universe – in other words, to allow that, poet though he is, he may retain a metaphysical preoccupation with the nature of reality.

Erich Auerbach makes a similar adjustment in his essay 'Figura'.[3] He distinguishes two medieval concepts, *allegoria* and *figura*, and derives them from the differing practices of various scriptural exegetes. He explains that in a figural relation both terms, the figure and the figured, are to be thought of as concrete realities, though the figured is likely to be felt as more 'real'. This corollary may sound a little like 'Some are more equal than others', but we must bear with him. It is a concept of reality we shall be seeing a good deal of. Moses prefigures Christ, but Christ is more real than Moses, and the Kingdom of Heaven is more real than the Promised Land (though both Moses and the Promised Land are real enough for most everyday purposes). Thus *figura* is tied very closely to the specific events of history:

> The difference between Tertullian's more historical and realistic interpretation and Origen's ethical, allegorical approach reflects a current conflict, known to us from other early Christian sources: one party strove to transform the events of the New and still more of the Old Testament into purely spiritual happenings, to 'spirit away' their historical character – the other wished to preserve the full historicity of the scriptures along with a deeper meaning.[4]

Where on this scale must we place Dante? Auerbach leaves us in no doubt. Dante is the great poet of *figura*.

[1] See his review of Miss Sayers's *Further Papers on Dante* in *Italian Studies*, XIII (1958), pp. 114 ff.

[2] See G. C. Hardie, 'The Epistle to Cangrande Again', *Deutsches Dante-Jahrbuch*, XXXVIII, Weimar 1960, pp. 57–58.

[3] In *Scenes from the Drama of European Literature*, New York 1959. The essay 'Figura' is translated by Ralph Manheim from the German text which first appeared in *Neue Dantestudien*, Istanbul 1944, pp. 11–71.

[4] *Scenes from the Drama of European Literature*, p. 36.

It must be acknowledged that Auerbach's fictive *allegoria* looks awfully like Lewis's 'allegory', while his *figura*, with its 'levels of reality' closely resembles Lewis's 'sacramentalism'. The temptation to consign all the poets to the party of Origen is strong. We may feel for a moment that the two public categories, the Fictitious and the Metaphysical, remain – but for a single exception – as firm as ever. For Lewis has lost Dante to the metaphysicians; the great Italian must be disjoined from the company of allegorical poets and placed with the makers of Bestiaries and the framers of Hermetical philosophies. The *Divine Comedy* is not allegory, but sacramentalism.

We should have to grant that Auerbach's analysis of the exegetical tradition vividly corroborates Lewis's analysis of the allegory in general, were it not for one thing: Auerbach's own account, like Lewis's; can be turned against its author. We shall find that it is possible to blur the strong antithesis of *allegoria* and *figura* while retaining a sacramentalist picture of Dante.

We must allow at once that Origen sacrificed historicity of the event. This is indeed scarcely surprising in view of the fact that a strong impulse was given to Origen in his complex task of interpretation by his conviction that the literal sense was infected by discrepancies. The claim of Scripture to be true history had therefore, he felt, been destroyed. R. M. Grant observes[1] that in his *Commentary on John* (x. 1–5, 20–34) Origen devotes some space to the differences of the Evangelists concerning the order of events at the beginning of Jesus's ministry, and also as to the time and circumstances of the Cleansing of the Temple. It is true that the *Commentary on John* was probably written after the treatise *On First Principles*, in which he gives a general argument for the allegorical status of the Scriptures from the nature of the universe and God's relation to it, but his correlative contempt for historicity must have been confirmed by his discovery of factual discrepancies.

The historicity or otherwise of the event described, of the *figura*, though of momentous theological importance in itself, is perhaps more loosely related to the logic of allegorical exegesis than Auerbach suggests. In either case the spiritual term of the relation will be of the more engrossing importance. It might be objected that Origen's method allows a virtual *carte blanche* to the wildest interpretations, yet the figural method is hardly less wild. Affinities between historical events of different ages, or between historical events and things eschatological, can be multiplied

[1] In *The Letter and the Spirit*, London 1957.

indefinitely. Similar *logical* relations will obtain in either case.

Auerbach asserts that Origen tends more to abstract significations, while figural relations remain concrete in both their terms. But the more one examines this antithesis, the more blurred it becomes. For example, he quotes[1] as an instance of figural exegesis Augustine's observation that whereas the Old Testament contains promises of temporal things, the New Testament contains in figures promises of transtemporal things, of the Kingdom of Heaven and Eternal Life. Where the figural relation is between two historical events, Auerbach is, of course, on safe ground. Such figural practice is similar to the 'innocent' historical allegorizings of Campbell, Montégut, Graves and Winstanley in the literary sphere,[2] with the important difference that the medieval figural relation is felt to be, somehow, *in rebus*; it implies an ontological, as well as a logical, relation between the terms. But can we say that these things transtemporal are more concrete than, say, the spiritual significance Origen attributes (in his *Commentary on Lamentations*) to Jerusalem?[3] There we are told that Jerusalem signifies the Soul. In asking whether such things are abstract or concrete one feels a certain conceptual discomfort. One feels that one is talking the wrong language. But if we substitute the much more comfortable antithesis Spiritual/Unspiritual, Material/Immaterial, the contrast between the figural Augustine and the allegorical Origen is somewhat diminished. Indeed, in a sacramentalist or a vaguely Platonic context, this contrast will always be diminished.

Auerbach is, I think, too rigid in his definition of the practical scope of *figura*. He is repeatedly forced to observe that the abstract *allegoria* and the concrete *figura* are mingled in the Middle Ages. For example, he says on p. 44, 'We find a good many strange and farfetched figural interpretations, often mixed with purely abstract, ethical allegory.' Again, he has to point out (pp. 44ff.) that the objective figural relation was from an early date confounded with the relation of the rhetorical image and the real – a confusion which brings it nearer to the language of sacramentalism – and on p. 57 he observes that the boundary between *figura* and *allegoria* as used was commonly fluid; *allegoria, figura, ambages, effigies, exemplum, imago, similitudo, species* and *umbra,* all interchange their functions.

[1] *Scenes from the Drama of European Literature*, p. 41.
[2] See above, Chap. I, pp. 5–6.
[3] See R. M. Grant, *op. cit.*, p. 91.

It may be noted that both *allegoria* and *figura* are used with strong ontological intentions, but that, if a choice must be made between the two, *figura* is, in eschatological contexts at any rate, the more radically sacramentalist.

When he comes to consider the poetry of Dante, Auerbach decides that it is not *allegoria* but *figura*. Thus Dante's Cato of Utica and Virgil are the fulfilment and eschatological realization of those *figurae* and *umbrae futurorum* who enjoyed historical existence in the days of ancient Rome. Beatrice is the Beatrice Dante loved on earth, but made more *real*, more herself than ever she was on earth. Dante, and by implication many other writers with him, is firmly placed in a sacramentalist context. The romantic critics of our first chapter are not the only ones to bring allegorical language to bear on metaphysical speculation.

The word *allegoria*, we must allow, answers roughly to Lewis's initial definition of *allegory*. But its range of reference is sadly contracted. It no longer covers what the world first thinks of as the greatest allegories. *The Divine Comedy, Piers Plowman, The Pilgrim's Progress*, all are equally strong in asserting the actuality of the mysterious events and places they describe.

The situation with regard to Dante is indeed tricky. As we have seen, in his prose writings we find him sternly dividing poets' allegory (roughly, Auerbach's *allegoria*) from scriptural allegory (roughly, Auerbach's *figura*) in a manner calculated to gratify proto-Lewis. Yet in his poems we find him deeply involved in transcendentalist metaphysics. Charles S. Singleton, in his *Commedia, Elements of Structure*,[1] was disposed to accept the authenticity of the Cangrande epistle, and was therefore able to argue from the use in that work of scriptural examples to explain a *poetic* intention that Dante was using scriptural allegory in *The Divine Comedy*. Certainly, once the spectre of the *figura/allegoria* distinction has been raised, it is hard to avoid the conclusion that Dante's greatest poem falls most naturally into the category of *figura*.

Of all the celebrated four senses, the easiest to extract from the *comedy* (after the literal) is the moral. Yet a 'moral signification' may without difficulty be found in almost any work of fiction, inside or outside the limits of what is usually called allegory. It is easy to explain how the fate of Paolo and Francesca reflects a moral situation common enough in this world. But it seems only a little less forceful to generalize the fate of the pretty secretary in last

---

[1] Cambridge, Mass., 1954.

week's *Woman's Own* in the same manner. True, not all the moral significations in the *Comedy* are so bathetically perspicuous: Virgil's words to Dante in the last canto of the *Inferno*, '. . . by such stairs must we go forth from so much evil', may imply allegorically that it is only by facing the worst that evil can do that we can obtain that rational knowledge which leads to sanctity. The relation here between the given situation in Hell and the implied lesson is, I suppose, sufficiently intricate to deserve the name of allegory. There are other, similar, passages. But most of the *Comedy* is easily, too easily moralized. The portentous term *sensus moralis* turns out to mean little more than 'moral tenor'.

Again, we certainly cannot claim that the poem is allegorical in virtue of the figural structures discerned in it by Auerbach. Dante is not so modest in *his* imagery as the world is in *its* imagery, for he clearly dissociates the Beatrice of the poem from the earthly Beatrice and places her in a heavenly setting. Words like 'Heaven' may have to be 'unpacked' in figurative terms, but they can hardly be said to be figurative in themselves. The Beatrice whom Dante depicts in Heaven is not, after all, the *figura*, but the 'sur-real' fulfilment of it. Where the poem ambitiously abandons the *figura* for a direct portrayal of its realization, it can hardly be called figural *in structure*. Blurring of the distinction between *figura* and *allegoria* has no effect upon this fact. For, if we substitute the terminology of *allegoria* we shall be forced, in a precisely parallel manner, to acknowledge that the Beatrice of the *Comedy* is not at all allegorical, but is nearer to being a Signification brought into the foreground. In ordinary modern terminology, Beatrice in the poem is obviously to be understood *literally*, and the suggestion that if the earthly Beatrice were substituted she would signify the heavenly Beatrice is of little interest, since the heavenly Beatrice is already available.

The case of Virgil is more complex, for he is doubly figurative. In the first place he is the sur-real fulfilment of the earthly Virgil and as such is precisely like Beatrice, already analysed. But Virgil also signifies ('morally'?) Reason, and in this respect he provides us with a case in which a *figura* is woven into the very fabric of the poem. Notice that since both terms are asserted as 'real' (both Virgil *and* Reason) the relation properly counts as figural. Yet in this case Dante refrains from running ahead to attempt a direct description of the figured, of Reason itself. He avails himself of the existing figure. Now here a man who was unaware (as the majority has always been unaware) of any distinction between *allegoria* and *figura* could naturally describe Dante as writing *allegorically*.

A close examination of the status of Virgil reveals the further fact that, though Virgil is *figural*, poet's *figura* even when it appears to be exactly like scriptural *figura* has not, in fact, the same necessary, fundamental truth-value. For where the *figura* in Scripture *is* historically true, in poetry it is necessary only that the figura be *deemed* to be historically true. We learn that Virgil is figural and not just allegorical in the weak sense when we find him saying and doing things, not *qua* Reason, but (simply) *qua* Virgil. This implies the basic feature of *figura*, viz. that the reality of Virgil is being asserted just as strongly as the reality of Reason. Yet Virgil in the *Comedy* is not, in the most brutal sense of the word, the *real* Virgil. Dante has made him out of the historical Virgil, though, of course, the creation overlaps to some extent with the fact. In the end we must acknowledge that even when Virgil acts and speaks *qua* Virgil (and not *qua* Reason), the account of these actions and words is not historically true. It is only deemed to be true. For Virgil in the *Comedy*, unlike Moses in the Bible, is *fictitious*-figural. C. S. Singleton sums up the situation in an admirable epigram: 'The fiction of the *Divine Comedy* is that it is not fiction.'[1] Perhaps I may use italics to express my point: in that Beatrice and Virgil are deemed *to be factual*, they must be classed as figural; in that they are (ultimately) only *deemed* to be factual, they must be classed as poetically rather than scripturally figural.

It begins to look as if the *Divine Comedy* embarrasses my argument, not so much because it is an airy allegory straying wantonly from the truth as because it is often so precipitately transcendentalist as not to be figurative at all. Perhaps the proper conclusion *is* that Mr. Lewis should quietly drop Dante from his company of allegorical poets and classify him with the makers of bestiaries and hermetical philosophies. We have suggested that any account of an ulterior world is bound to be allegorical for the simple reason that it is bound to borrow its terms from this world. Yet one occasionally feels doubtful whether Dante is thinking of his eschatological account as *metaphorical* at all. The dualistic structure of the universe has penetrated so far into his consciousness, and the language of the transcendent, though necessarily figurative at bottom, has found so constant and coherent a pattern of usage,

---

[1] *op. cit.*, p. 62. Yet even Singleton appears occasionally to confuse the historical and figural status of Dante's personages – see *op. cit.*, pp. 90, 91.

that the metaphor has died on his hands. Thus one suspects that Dante is often speaking *literally* of Heaven and Hell. In fact, however, I think there is enough non-literal matter in the poem to justify the description 'allegorical', used as a plain man would use it, without distinction of poet and transcendentalist.

In the first place, there runs through the poem a sense that all the multiplication of detailed incident does not in the end constitute the exhaustive truth about hell, but is rather the essentially provisional vehicle of a mystery. Our awareness of this is necessarily impressionistic, and I doubt whether it can be conclusively demonstrated. The point is obvious to some, inaccessible to others. I take comfort in the fact that this century has produced two great intuitive critics of Dante, and they have both perceived it. Charles Williams wrote, in *The Figure of Beatrice* (1943):

> I am not sure how far it may be argued that the recollection, which the poem imposes but does not stress, that all that is here seen is spirit increases the sense of symbolism; something is happening which is like this, which can only be expressed *as* this, which may (when the body is here) *be* this, but is at present only a more remote, though even more intense, fact. In that case the whole of hell is hidden though exposed: we see through a glass darkly. It may be said that Dante thought of a physical hell, and no doubt that is so, but he also thought of a spiritual. The corporal vitality of the diagram, on his own showing, is not yet here, and the spiritual reality is a fixed truth, yet infinitely recessive to the understanding.[1]

And T. S. Eliot, in his essay on Dante:

> . . . Hell is not a place but a *state* . . . Hell, though a state, is a state which can only be thought of, and perhaps only experienced, by the projection of sensory images . . .[2]

In the second place, though the Virgil of the poem is not the prefiguring sublunary Virgil but his fulfilment, yet the Virgil of the poem himself figures Reason. The Beatrice of the poem is not the prefiguring Beatrice but her fulfilment, yet the Beatrice of the poem (let us confess it) figures God. And the Journey, the whole underlying concept of the poem, is given an allegorical status in the opening line.

[1] London 1943, p. 128.
[2] In *Selected Essays*, 3rd ed., London 1951, p. 250.

But we cannot, it would seem, attack Dorothy L. Sayers for seeking an anagogical sense in the *Divine Comedy* and at the same time claim that the poem is an allegory. We wish to say that the allegorical status of the poem is saved by such things as the description of the Journey, *del cammin di nostra vita*, and the dark wood where the straight way is lost, and more of this nature. If these are images in harness, it must be allowed that the harness looks extremely anagogical.

I think we must say that Miss Sayers's main error lay in *delving* for an anagogical sense, as though the *Divine Comedy* were a Biblical text. The great contrast between the *Divine Comedy* and Scripture when it comes to anagogical signification is that in Biblical exegesis the spiritual sense commonly needs a good deal of excavation, whereas in Dante the spiritual sense is so obtrusive as almost to annihilate the metaphorical status of the work altogether. When Dante comes[1] to the dreary sunless valley, where the stones and shale slide under his feet and the abrupt chasm turns his thoughts toward chaos, and he learns that he is drawing near the place of punishment for those who were violent against their neighbours in life – we may wonder for a moment whether Dante supposes that he is giving a literal description of Hell. Yet I do not think we could sustain the doubt for long. Dante did believe that there was a place of torment, just as Guillaume de Lorris believed that different forces really did contend in his lady's mind. But neither of these things could be described unless by way of an allegory. There is no great difference, after all, in the logic of their expression. With Dante, as with Bunyan, it is the landscape that keeps the allegory vigorous. If an example of a non-allegorical eschatological poem is desired, we can hardly do better than *Paradise Lost*. In that poem there does seem to be a real danger that Milton is unaware that the language he is using should be anything but literal. We miss in him that modest reluctance to apply earthly categories to things transtemporal which appears in Dante's strange reservation at *Purgatorio*, XIII, 22 – *'Quanto di qua per un migliaio si conta.'*[2] The difference in atmosphere between Dante, Langland and Bunyan on the one hand, and Milton on the

---

[1] *Inferno*, Canto XII. In J. O. Sinclair's ed., London 1958, pp. 54 ff.

[2] 'As far as what on earth we should reckon as a mile.' The words of God the Father in Book VI of *Paradise Lost* ('Two dayes, as we compute the dayes of Heav'n', 685) may appear to reproduce the Dantean sentiment, but are, in fact, no true parallel. Where the medieval poet gives us an intuition of mystery, Milton propounds a problem in astronomy.

other, is immediately apparent. The haunting quality has fled
with the allegory.

The great critical error in dealing with these matters is to
suppose that because the degree and elaboration of personification,
etc., is so obviously fictional, the personification itself must be
fictional also. We need not think that Bunyan believed that Apollyon existed exactly as he described him. But we must not forget
that Bunyan did believe that something bearing a recognizable
resemblance to Apollyon did exist, and he probably trembled at
the thought that it lay in wait for him. The Heavenly City is a
parallel case. Bunyan's description of it is not flatly accurate and
literal. After all, he had never been there. But he hoped to. So it
is not mere fiction either. In some of its aspects the logic of such
religious language is not dissimilar to the logic of talk about the
soul. Bunyan uses his figures and personifications not because he
believes in them *tout court*, but because he does not know how else
to say what he wants to say. He would agree that it is not possible
to demythologize all his language, but he would not agree that
this admission reduced all his assertions to vanity. If he were asked
whether he really believed there was a wicket-gate at the far end
of the 'very wide field'[1] of life, he would probably say no. But if
you asked whether there really was a Journey, and Unimaginable
Bliss at the end of it, he would undoubtedly say yes.

Perhaps Lewis did not look closely enough at the rather curious
relation of similarity which holds between the figure and the
figured in allegorical contexts. Where allegory is exciting it is
exciting because of a peculiar impression of validity in the images
it uses. And one has only to bring these claims of validity into
objective prominence and one is on the very brink of sacramentalism. Even with a simple image like that of the River of Youthful
Life, at the beginning of the *Roman de la Rose*, our apprehensions
are quickened, if they are quickened at all, by a feeling akin to
recognition. 'Why, of course, the river is youthful life – that's just
right!' is the appropriate reaction. And the strange equivalence of
outer and inner is at once set in motion.

'There is nothing "mystical" or mysterious about medieval
allegory',[2] says Lewis. Yet the quality of such equivalences is
haunting, mysterious, or it is nothing. If a man thinks that life is

---

[1] *The Pilgrim's Progress*, ed. J. B. Wharey, 2nd ed., rev. by R. Sharrock, Oxford
1960, p. 10.
[2] *The Allegory of Love*, p. 48.

like a river, that man's thinking is already quasi-metaphysical. If one is proof against the aesthetic impact of metaphysical propositions, one is likely to find allegorical poetry pretty boring. Lewis, clearly, is not such a person. His initial hard-headedness is outward show only. When he comes to describe the poem in detail he is soon writing like an Elizabethan Neoplatonist. For example, here is what he says about the moment of falling in love in the *Roman*:

> . . . Guillaume, with his crystals and his well, seems to me to give us some of the real magic of eyes (and of mirrors) as that magic actually exists, not indeed outside the human mind, but outside any school of poetry.[1]

Lewis's initial view of allegory is not peculiar to him, of course. It had some force in the eighteenth century and showed its effects in the 'frigid' allegorizings of the time,[2] and then reappeared when the nineteenth-century spate of uncritically metaphysical enthusiasm had begun to dry up. It is perhaps slightly surprising to note that it was given a strong impulse by Benedetto Croce:

> . . . it is affirmed that we should make *the species shine in the individual*. If by individual be here understood the typical, here, too, we have a merely verbal variation. To typify would signify, in this case, to characterize; that is to determine and represent – the individual. Don Quixote is a type; but of whom is he a type, if not of all Don Quixotes? A type, that is to say, of himself. Certainly he is not a type of abstract concepts, such as the loss of the sense of reality, or of the love of glory . . . in art all is symbolical because all is ideal. But if the symbol be looked upon as separable – if on the one side can be expressed the symbol, and on the other the thing symbolized, we fall back again into the intellectualist error: that pretended symbol is the exposition of an abstract concept, it is an *allegory*, it is science, or art that apes science. But we must be just towards the allegorical also. In some cases, it is altogether harmless. Given the *Gerusalemme Liberata*, the allegory was imagined afterwards; given the *Adone* of Marino, the poet of the lascivious insinuated afterwards that it was written to show how 'immoderate

[1] *ibid.*, p. 129.
[2] e.g.. Thomas Gray's 'The Alliance of Education and Government', or William Collins's 'The Passions'. Both in *The Poetical Works of Gray and Collins*, ed. A. L. Poole, London 1917.

indulgence ends in pain'; given a statue of a beautiful woman, the sculptor can write on a card that the statue represents *Clemency* or *Goodness*. This allegory linked to a finished work *post festum* does not change the work of art. What is it then? It is an expression externally *added* to another expression.[1]

It is clear that we can have no such strong criticisms of Croce as we had of Lewis, mainly because his practical ambitions for the use of the term 'allegory' are more modest. It is true that there are some discrepancies between what Croce means by 'allegory' and the things which most people have agreed to call allegories, yet – every man his own Humpty-Dumpty – he is free to define his terms as he wishes. In a manner he can be held to reinforce the argument of this chapter, in so far as he dismisses as uninteresting all easily reducible symbols. Yet he seems to have no room for the partially or indistinctly reducible symbol. Indeed, where there is no distinction at all between the symbol and the thing symbolized, it is hard to see why we came to use the term 'symbol' at all.

If we claim that medieval allegory commonly differed from its eighteenth-century descendant in its warm and curious attachment to reality, it must be acknowledged that the monumentally frigid *Psychomachia*[2] of Prudentius (written, probably in Spain, in the fourth century A.D.) is an example highly invidious to our argument. It contains a few passages of poetry – a fine silver Latin description of Luxuria reeling home, trampling the flowers of an all-night party, hearing in the dawn the raucous bugles of war;[3] and there is, too, the odd sweet revival of the old alliterative genius of the language, long quenched by the decorum of the Augustans:

lilia luteolis interlucentia sertis . . .[4]
(Among yellow garlands lilies glimmering)

– but in the main it is sad stuff indeed. Yet the fact that the personages of this poem are labelled 'Pride', 'Faith', 'Fraud' and the like does not mean that, even in so turgid a work, they are regarded as mere additions, without any heuristic force. One cannot be confident that the poet has not asked himself, 'Now what

---

[1] *Aesthetic as Science of Expression and General Linguistic*, trans. Douglas Ainslie, London 1909, p. 56.
[2] The poem is printed in *Prudentius, with an English translation* by H. J. Thomson (the Loeb Classical Library) 1953.
[3] ll. 320 ff.
[4] l. 354.

must pride herself be like? . . .' and striven with some seriousness to depict her very soul.

For it is bad critical exegesis to claim that the personages of the *Psychomachia* are playful fictions arising out of mere logical constructions which are themselves to be broken down in terms of overt behaviour. The whole is far too closely tied to the baffling mental event for that. A reduction of the inner world to the terms of the outer would not just tidy up Prudentius's logic; it would silence him outright. I think it is difficult to find even in a poem as dull as this a mere formal juggling of fully understood and constant quantities.

Croce's views about the poeticalness of individuals and the unpoeticalness of 'concepts' are too confident, and his use of the categories 'individual' and 'concept' altogether too revisionary to allow him to read a medieval allegorical poet with much sympathy. If a man says, 'Last night I dreamed that I saw a lion in the swimming-bath', we can say that what he tells us both is and is not real. It is real *qua* dream; he did dream as he says. But the dream is not real; he did not really see a lion there at all.[1] It may be that the old allegorical poets were writing, or even living, in a sort of dream. Indeed they commonly asserted as much at the beginning of their poems, but then they thought this rather dignified than discredited what they had to say. Some may wish to legislate against the dream at once, others may be curious to follow out its progress in a more descriptive spirit.

Croce's views on individuals and concepts are perhaps a trifle coarse-grained, not just for talking about allegorical poems, but for any context. On 'intuitive' and 'intellective' knowledge, he says:

> What is knowledge by concepts? It is knowledge of relations of things and those things are intuitions. Concepts are not possible without intuitions just as intuition is itself impossible without the material of impressions. Intuitions are: this river, this lake, this brook, this rain, this glass of water; the concept is: water, not this or that appearance and particular example of water, but water in general, in whatever time or place it be realized; the material of infinite intuitions, but of one single and constant concept.[2]

[1] I owe this analogy to D. M. Emmet's *The Nature of Metaphysical Thinking*, London 1945, p. 66.

[2] *Aesthetic*, p. 36.

This is startlingly simple-minded in some ways. It seems to suggest that there is an agreed set of hard, constant individuals, universally recognized as such, and a set of universal concepts covering classes of objects, and that that is all there is to it. Questions like, 'What is the difference between the concept "colour" and the concept "red(ness)"?' or 'How am I to have a concept of an individual like my friend George?' or 'Can I not have an intuition of (just) Water?' or 'What sort of imagery usually accompanies the actual *having* of concepts, the *using* of terms?' – these do not arise. In a way, his aesthetic opinion reflects the artistic practice of his age – art having attained to the sophistication of individuating public objects.[1] Some had passed beyond to the individuation of the percept, the instant of seeing, so that in the paintings of Turner, for example, we sometimes feel that the individual object is half lost in the struggle to capture the instantaneousness of the perception. One suspects that Croce shares with Bishop Berkeley[2] the belief that the individuation of our imagery exactly corresponds to the individuation of public objects. In an artistic world of such hard, bright and public individuals it is easy to make the Crocean division. But for earlier times it seems less cogent. 'Harold Rex Anglorum' in the Bayeux Tapestry is portrayed less as the historical individual, Harold, than as the King. The office predominates over the man. Yet we do not find in this a predominance of concept over intuition, of the non-poetical over the poetical.

The feature that eludes Croce is the same feature that we found running through the romantic allegorical critics – that is, the thing which is half-concept, half-image, the universal which is itself thought of as a concrete object, *as an instance of itself.* Croce is familiar with the mind for which a beautiful horse (say) is an instance of beauty, but knows nothing of the mind for which Beauty is itself a beautiful thing, and hence an instance of beauty. Philosophical jargon will give us a short-hand description of this phenomenon: the instantially viewed universal. Lowell thought that Womanliness was something womanly. Lewis himself is at last forced to attribute real agency in the world to one of de Lorris's personages – to Venus, because, as he points out, she is a goddess

---

[1] See below, pp. 73 ff.

[2] See the Introduction to *The Principles of Human Knowledge* in vol. II of *The Works of George Berkeley, Bishop of Cloyne,* ed. A. A. Luce and T. E. Jessop, London 1949.

and a ruling planet;[1] and even if he still insists that *Amor* is, in Dante's terms, a mere personified accident, we have in this *Venus* something which is both Love itself and enormously loving. It is this feature, logically very curious, which gives the 'abstractions' of the allegorical poets a curiously experiential tang, and provides a plausible groundwork on which allegorical personalities may be elaborated – the personalities only, for the individuals are already there.

But if Mercy is merciful and Cruelty is cruel, some rather odd situations can develop, as the poet strives to map out the workings of the inner man. Logical oddity breeds aesthetic embarrassment. Prudentius's *Psychomachia* is full of such embarrassments. For example, it is something of a shock to find the sweetly modest *virgo Pudicitia* behaving like this:

> sed dextram furiae flagrantis et ignea dirae
> tela lupae saxo ferit imperterrita virgo,
> excussasque sacro taedas depellit ab ore.
> tunc exarmatae iugulum meretricis adacto
> transfigit gladio.   (46–50)

But the maiden, unterrified, strikes the hand of the blazing Fury and the fiery weapon of the dread she-wolf with a stone, and shattering the torch dashes it from her sacred face. Then, drawing her sword, she pierces the throat of the disarmed harlot.

Yet what else shall Modesty do when she encounters *Sodomita Libido*? It is inherent in the allegorical form that Modesty must *vanquish* Lust. Yet it is equally inherent in the form that Modesty should be blushing and modest. Prudentius, with a fine carelessness, puts into the mouth of Pride a description of the chief problem of the work:

> anne Pudicitae gelidum iecur utile bello est?
> an tenerum Pietatis opus sudatur in armis?   (238–9)

Has cold Modesty the guts for war? Or does the soft virtue of Piety sweat in arms?

The fact that *Patientia* defeats *Ira* by a process of exasperation – simply by standing still as the swords break over her head until *Ira*, in despair, commits suicide – does not seem a very great improvement. One begins to see why Prudentius is so eager to

---

[1] *The Allegory of Love*, p. 121.

make the vices defeat themselves. While *Ira* commits suicide, *Fraus* inadvertently trips up *Superbia*, *Discordia Civilis* plunders his own kin, *Amor Habendi* does not spare his own people, and *Famis* robs his own sons.

Pride, at least, makes practical use of the logical dilemma. In rhetorical exultation she points at Humility and cries

> . . . et prostrata in humum nec libera iudice sese
> Mens Humilis, quam degenerem trepidatio prodit!   (247–8)

And Humility, prostrate on the ground, by her own admission a servile spirit! Her trembling betrays her degeneracy.

That *iudice sese*, 'by her own admission', is horribly unfair, one feels. Of course Humility has to run herself down, she wouldn't be humble if she didn't. But there's no need to take her at her word. The fact that Humility condemns herself does not mean that the virtue of humility is contemptible. Nor does it mean that she can never be a match for the Vices. Pride knows no stronger foe. Prudentius is too good a Devil's Advocate in his own court. One wonders how well he could have answered these sophistries.

One of the most alarming logical tangles in the poem occurs where the choruses of Virtues are returning in triumph from the battle. Discord has concealed herself in the crowd and succeeds in dealing a privy wound to Concord. Concord, slightly shaken by this, breaks into a speech of mingled amazement and anger, ending with the words:

> quid iuvat indomitos bello sedasse Furores
> et sanctum Vitiis pereuntibus omne receptum,
> si Virtus sub pace cadit?   (697–9)

What good is it to have vanquished the indomitable Passions? What good is it that with the destruction of the Vices everything sacred is recovered – if in time of peace Virtue falls?

Things might have been safer if she had confined herself to saying, 'What is the good of quelling these Vices in war if they infiltrate in times of peace?' but by ill luck she has included the phrase *si Virtus cadit*, 'if Virtue falls'. Now it is clear from the context, despite the Loeb editor's capital V, that she does not mean that one of her fellow virtues has fallen to the ground. The awful possibility then raises itself – and swiftly becomes a certainty – that she is speaking allegorically. She thinks that viciousness has entered the hearts of her Virtues. The danger of a regress was with us from the start, of course. If the mind of man is conceived as a battlefield of warring *homunculi*, it is not surprising – just tedious – to discover that the *homunculi* themselves are composed of even tinier *homunculi*; and so on. One suspects the presence of the same phenomenon in these lines:

> discissa trahuntur
> serta Venustatis collique ac verticis aurum
> solvitur, et gemmas Discordia dissona turbat.   (440–3)

The shattered garlands of Ostentation are dragged down, the gold ornaments of her head and neck are loosed, and raucous Discord disorders her jewels.

Is the poet implying that Discord is chasing her along disordering her head-dress, or is he merely saying, in allegorical language, that her head-dress became disordered? It is hard to say. But, if this is doubtful, Concord, in her speech near the end of the poem, gives us a quite unmistakeable example.

> extincta est multo certamine saeva
> barbaries, sanctae quae circumsaepserat urbis
> indigenas, ferroque viros flammaque premebat.
> publica sed requies privatis rure foroque
> constat amicitiis: scissura domestica turbat
> rem populi, titubatque foris quod dissidet intus.
> ergo cavete, viri, ne sit sententia discors
> Sensibus in nostris . . .   (752–9)

Quenched is the savage barbarity which hemmed in the dwellers in the holy city, and pressed them hard with fire and sword. But the public peace, both urban and rural, depends upon private affections. Domestic schism confounds the state, and that which is inwardly disordered is outwardly tottering. Therefore, men, beware lest there should be any division of opinion among our sentiments . . .

In other words: we have driven off our enemies the Vices, so don't let any discord rise up among yourselves, you Virtues! The Loeb editor gives no capital letters to *sententia discors* (though he does to *Sensibus*), but there is a Chinese Box here for all that. It is as if the poet of the macrocosmic *Hamartigenia*, feeling the need to supply the subjective elements of experience, wrote the microcosmic *Psychomachia*, only to discover that in the process of composition it turned into something curiously like the old public epic after all; and so sought to describe, not the Inner Man now, but the Inner Virtue. The hopeless infinite regress is well and truly under way.

All this, it might be thought, is nothing but the last fatuity of allegorical poeticising, and could be found nowhere but among the vanities of sheer fiction. Yet consider this passage from Plato's *Parmenides* (the discussion concerns the relation of Forms to their particulars):

> . . . take Smallness: is one of us to have a portion of Smallness, and is Smallness to be larger than that portion, which is a part of it? On this supposition again Smallness itself will be larger, and anything to which the portion taken is added will be smaller, and not larger, than it was before.
>
> That cannot be so.
>
> Well then, Socrates, how are the other things going to partake of your Forms, if they can partake of them neither in part nor as wholes?
>
> Really, said Socrates, it seems no easy matter to determine in any way.
>
> Again, there is another question.
>
> What is that?
>
> How do you feel about this? I imagine your ground for believing in a single Form in each case is this: when it seems to you that a number of things are large, there seems, I suppose, to be a certain single character which is the same when you look at them all; hence you think that largeness is a single thing.
>
> True, he replied.
>
> But now take Largeness itself and the other things which are large. Suppose you look at all these in the same way in your mind's eye, will not yet another unity make its appearance – a Largeness by virtue of which they all appear large?
>
> So it would seem.
>
> If so, a second Form of Largeness will present itself, over and above Largeness itself and the things that share in it; and again, covering all these, yet another, which will make all of them large. So each of your Forms will no longer be one, but an indefinite number.[1]

---

[1] *Parmenides*, 131d–132b. The translation is from F. M. Cornford, *Plato and Parmenides*, London 1939, pp. 86–88.

This is the famous Argument of the Third Man. In it we can see certain Platonic presuppositions being subjected to a sort of *reductio ad absurdum*, by being made to jostle a little too close for comfort. The incompatible presuppositions involved have strong affinities to the discordant characteristics of allegory. Gregory Vlastos pointed out[1] that the two principal assumptions involved are, first, that any Form can be predicated of itself: Largeness is itself large; and second, that if any particular has a certain character, it cannot be identical with the Form in virtue of which we apprehend that character: if x is F, x cannot be identified with F-ness. Vlastos terms these two assumptions the self-predication assumption and the non-identity assumption respectively. Transposing the argument into the terms of allegory, we may say, 'If Humility is not humble, then who is?' (self-predication assumption); 'If Humility cannot overcome pride, who can?' (non-identity assumption). It is the work of a few moments, of course, to demonstrate the incompatibility of these two assumptions. As to the later version of the argument (*Parmenides*, 132d ff.), in which the copy notion is introduced whereby a particular stands to its Form as a copy to its original, Vlastos disposes of this by pointing out that a thing cannot be a copy of itself.

There is a short way to end this sort of argument. As Professor Ryle observes in his article on the *Parmenides*,[2] it is meaningless to say that beauty either is or is not beautiful. 'Beauty' is a mere logical construction. At one stroke he banishes the youthful Plato and the allegorical poet with him: 'Abstract nouns cannot assume the roles of proper names or demonstratives.' The *Parmenides* is an early essay in the theory of logical types. Even Dante, though more in his poetic theory than in his poetic practice, seems to belong to the same tribe, with his insistence[3] – a remote pre-echo of Russell's Axiom of Reducibility – that the poet who could not reduce his figures to non-figurative terms was a disgrace to his calling.

It all seems very straightforward. Only one puzzle remains. If things are as simple as this, how on earth did the question ever attain the status of a *problem*? Heresies, no less than orthodoxies, are phenomena, and deserve some consideration, if on that account

---

[1] 'The Third Man Argument in the *Parmenides*', *Philosophical Review*, LXIII (1954).
[2] 'Plato's "Parmenides",' I and II; *Mind*, XLVIII, 1939, nos. 190, 191.
[3] *Vita Nuova*, XXV, in *Dante's Vita Nuova*, trans. Ralph Waldo Emerson, Chapel Hill, Carolina 1960, p. 31.

alone. And perhaps the oddest feature of the phenomenon is the self-predication assumption.

A. E. Taylor, indeed, though he was the first person to bring the suppressed premise of self-predication into prominence, could not bring himself to believe[1] that Plato ever really entertained a notion so absurd. But there seems to be no doubt that he did. In the *Lysis*, 217d, he observes that when a man's hairs have turned white they have become such as that which is present in them, white through Whiteness. In the *Phaedo*, 100c, he asks whether anything else is beautiful except Beauty itself, and the whole speech of Diotima in the *Symposium* is instinct with the notion that Beauty, itself, as perceived in a state akin to that of the Beatific Vision, is supremely beautiful. Perhaps the star case, however, is *Protagoras*, 330cd, where Plato affirms that Justice is just and Holiness is holy, and asks what other things could be holy if Holiness itself was not holy.

The Greeks were encouraged to think in this way by the presence in their language of an idiom which allowed them to use the definite article with the neuter singular of the adjective instead of an abstract noun – τὸ ἀγαθόν, 'the good'. It is true that this particular locution was sometimes used to mean 'the word 'ἀγαθόν', for the Greeks lacked our device of inverted commas. But this was a special use, and it remains true to say that the phrase functioned in Greek roughly as the word 'goodness' functions in English. It was probably a little more prone than the English word to bear the sense 'what is good'; and of course 'What is good is good' is tautologously true. Thus an ancient Greek would tend to raise his eyebrows if you told him that the Good is not good. But the Platonic idiom, αὐτὸ τὸ ἀγαθόν, 'the good itself', hardly seems *designed* to express this function; it is too ostentatiously instantial.

Though the function of the Greek phrase is roughly coextensive with that of our own abstract noun, it is not *exactly* coextensive. If we examine the Greek idiom as a phenomenon, we can hardly fail to be struck by its strange air of spurious concreteness, its pseudo-sensory quality. It shares with concepts like 'the Oxford-ness of Oxford', and (with a little practice) the tea-cup-ness of tea-cups, the quality of impinging upon our *sensibilities*. A. E. Taylor, for all his benevolent refusal to believe Plato himself

---

[1] In his essay 'Parmenides, Zeno and Socrates' in *Philosophical Studies*, 1934, pp. 46 ff. The essay first appeared in *PAS*, XVI, 1915–16.

capable of any 'Third Man' nonsense, religiously translates τὸ ἕν as 'the One', though Ryle prefers to beg the question in favour of sanity by translating 'unity'. This is better philosophy than it is exegesis. It is easy to imagine Professor Ryle thinking about unity, but it is less easy to see him contemplating the One. But, if we have any sense, we will try to imagine Plato in both characters. It is hard to believe that the second expression is merely a metaphor for the first. As Cornford pointed out in a passage[1] I have already had occasion to allude to, when we meet with the phrase τὸ μεγά we should try to think not only of largeness but of 'that which is simply large and nothing else'. Plato found that he could, as a matter of psychological fact, contemplate (I will not say 'think about') Beauty as being what we see in all beautiful things, only purged of all irrelevancies.

The concept which is made to look so grotesque by the arguments of Plato's *Parmenides*, and is finally annihilated by Professor Ryle, has had a long and by no means ignominious history. It was no accident that in describing Diotima's speech I alluded to the Beatific Vision. We have only to glance at the history of theology to find the allegorical/Platonical concept in its most august guise. The Neoplatonist Synesius (*c.* A.D. 373–*c.* A.D. 414) called God νοῦς καὶ νοερός,[2] Intelligence and intelligent, and St. John himself identified the infinitely loving God with Love itself.[3] The whole practice is central to religious language.

Vlastos, in his article, asked as an implicit knockdown argument what we are to say about the Form of the Transient. Is it eternal (*qua* Form)? Or is it transient (*qua* Transient)? I would guess that Plato would have replied, though with severe misgivings, that it was eternally transient-and-nothing-else, '*eterne in mutabilitie*'. The idea is a recurrent theme of literature, and some of the best poetry in the world has been written on it. One can find it in the *Mutabilitie Cantos* of Spenser, in Keats's *Ode to a Grecian Urn*, and perhaps a hint of it in Wordsworth's

> The immeasurable height
> Of woods decaying, never to be decay'd,
> The stationary blasts of waterfalls[4]

[1] *Plato and Parmenides*, p. 87.
[2] Hymns, I, 177, in *Synesii Cyrenensis Hymni et Opuscula*, ed. N. Terzaghi, Rome 1939–44, vol. I, p. 12.
[3] I John IV, 16.
[4] *The Prelude* (1805 text), VI, 556 ff., in Helen Darbishire's revision of de Selincourt's edition, Oxford 1959, p. 210.

and it is strong in Eliot's

> Words move, music moves
> Only in time; but that which is only living
> Can only die. Words, after speech, reach
> Into the silence. Only by the form, the pattern,
> Can words or music reach
> The stillness, as a Chinese jar still
> Moves perpetually in its stillness[1]

where the metaphysical intention is clear. But the best is Shakespeare's

>   What you do
> Still betters what is done. When you speak, sweet,
> I'd have you do it ever: when you sing,
> I'd have you buy and sell so; so give alms;
> Pray so; and, for the ordering your affairs,
> To sing them too: when you do dance, I wish you
> A wave o' the sea, that you might ever do
> Nothing but that; move still, still so,
> And own no other function: each your doing,
> So singular in each particular,
> Crowns what you are doing in the present deed,
> That all your acts are queens.[2]

There is an interesting passage where St. Augustine argues that while transience, the passing of syllables and words, is essential to the understanding of poetry, the whole is held in the timeless imagination; and this time the general tone is more obviously (Neo)platonistic. At the end of the following passage his language seems almost to anticipate the Franciscan *vestigia Dei*.

> Sic enim et versus in suo genere pulcher est, quamvis duae syllabae simul dici nullo modo possint. Nec enim secunda enuntiatur, nisi prima transierit; atque ita per ordinem pervenitur ad finem, ut cum sola ultima sonat, non secum sonantibus superioribus, formam tamen et decus metricum cum praeteritis contexta perficiat. Nec ideo tamen ars ipsa qua versus fabricatur, sic tempori obnoxia est, ut pulchritudo ejus per mensuras morarum digeratur: sed simul habet omnia, quibus efficit

---

[1] 'Burnt Norton' (V). 137 in *Four Quartets*, Faber Paperback Edition, London 1959.
[2] *The Winter's Tale*, IV. iii. 135–46.

versum non simul habentem omnia, sed posterioribus priora tollentem; propterea tamen pulchrum, quia extrema vestigia illius pulchritudinis ostendat, quam constanter atque incommutabiliter ars ipsa custodit.[1]

So it is that a metrical line is beautiful in its own kind although two syllables of that line cannot be pronounced simultaneously. The second is pronounced only after the first has passed, and such is the order of procedure to the end of the line, so that when the last syllable sounds, alone, unaccompanied by the sound of the previous syllables, it yet, as being part of the whole metrical fabric, perfects the form and metrical beauty of the whole. But the versifier's art itself is not dependent on time in the same way; its beauty is not portioned out in temporally measurable units. It is simultaneously possessed of all those virtues which enable it to produce a line – a line which is not simultaneously possessed of all its virtues but which produces them in order. For the beautiful thing shows the last footprints of that beauty which art itself constantly and immutably watches over.

I cite these passages from various times and places, not in the hope of rehabilitating Plato's theory of forms, but of bringing into prominence a paradox of the imagination, which may help to explain a curious feature which Platonic metaphysics shares with allegorical poetry. Professor Ryle has said in his article on the *Parmenides* that it is no good treating abstract nouns as if they were proper nouns, and Aristotle, a good few years before, had said that the Third Man regress resulted from the false assumption that the common predicate 'Man' is an individual substance.[2] Plato was fully aware of these arguments, of course, for he put them into the mouth of Parmenides. But he was still reluctant to relinquish the notion of the Form as an individual. That may be because we have to do here, not with public individuals certainly, but perhaps with individuals of the imagination. I do not intend by this loose and tentative expression actual imaginative actions, individual mental events. After all, Plato's denial of the suggestion that the Forms are 'thoughts' follows swiftly, in 132b–c. If we are to consider imagery at all in connexion with this state of affairs, there is every sign that we shall have to consider the possibility and the propriety of regarding images *as objects*. This approach,

[1] *De Vera Religione*, XXII.42. The text is taken from *Bibliotheca Patrum Latina*, edited J. P. Migne, Paris 1861, vol. XXXIV.

[2] *De Sophisticis Elenchis*, 178b.36, in *The Works of Aristotle translated into English*, ed. W. D. Ross, London 1928, vol. I.

which treats a peculiar usage as a phenomenon, is a psychological one, and the next chapter will be taken up with an investigation of what it has to recommend it.

This chapter has treated of two concepts of allegory. The first, the theory of 'proto-Lewis' (with the ghostly support of Benedetto Croce) makes a rigid division, almost an opposition, between allegory and sacramentalism. The second proposes a number of intimate connexions and a certain community of purpose between them. We may call these two concepts non-metaphysical and metaphysical allegory respectively. The difference between them is very much a matter of applied rather than 'pure' theory. It is, no doubt, quite possible to write non-metaphysical allegory, though the language of allegory is so infected with metaphysics as to make it difficult. All the formal clarity, indeed, is on the side of proto-Lewis, but it proves an expensive clarity after all. Forever mapping out undiscovered countries, of mind, of ideas, of Heaven and Hell, the allegorical poets turn out to be very slippery fish indeed. It is possible, as A. J. Ayer does,[1] to trace all metaphysics back to an undue allegiance to linguistic forms, in which case the only difference between a metaphysician and an allegorical poet will be that the former will have the more hypertrophied delusions of grandeur. In this case both allegory and sacramentalism will be equally mere 'modes of expression,' but if that is so the category 'mode of expression' has become useless for distinguishing allegory from sacramentalism. Presumably it would be equally possible, from some sort of transcendentalist philosophical standpoint, to raise both to the level of metaphysics, in which case both become 'modes of thought'. But the quite obvious differences of intention between, at any rate, the poles of allegorical and metaphysical writing may make us wish to retain a more purely descriptive approach, and postpone revisionary techniques, whether of the reductionist or the inflationary kind. Seriously held metaphysical opinions commonly require figurative expression; allegorical poets have commonly addressed themselves to metaphysical aspects of experience. Lewis himself admits as much, and he has everything to lose by the admission.

It might be objected that, even if these propositions imply at any rate a quasi-metaphysical character for much allegorical poetry, they do not, and never can, bring it into line with the extreme

[1] In 'The Genesis of Metaphysics', in *Philosophy and Analysis*, ed. M. Macdonald, Oxford 1954, pp. 23–25.

sacramentalist position, viz. that this world is but a copy of the next. Perhaps not. Yet it is surprising how near we can bring them to one another. We have granted that, in some contexts, allegory and metaphor are the sole means of describing, on the one hand, God, the Kingdom of Heaven, the Spiritual Journey, etc., and, on the other hand, mind. If we try to understand *how* these metaphors work, we shall find that we must presuppose a structure bearing strong affinities to the metaphysical structure proposed by sacramentalism. For these metaphors will not break down into any of the first three of the four standard Aristotelian varieties,[1] the transference of the name (1) from genus to species, (2) from species to genus, (3) from species to species, and only to the fourth ('by analogy') by making the most licentious possible use of that very indulgent term. The way in which moral indecision can resemble a battlefield, or the spiritual development a journey, is not sufficiently definite to admit such lucid categorization. Yet these equivalences are universally intelligible. All we can say is, 'Journeys, battlefields, etc., are *like* these things.' The set-up now is that public, material objects are *like* mental and spiritual objects, and are, in some sense, 'beyond'. They may, indeed, be said to 'picture' them, where the word 'picture' is as irreducible a metaphor as 'journey'. Still, why should we worry now, for we are 'in blood Stepped in so far, that . . . Returning were as tedious as go o'er.' This is not quite the same thing as saying that the whole of this world is but a copy of a more real world beyond, but it is very near it. Lewis says[2] that the equivalence between the material and the immaterial can be used in two ways, allegorically or sacramentally, yet the assertion of that very equivalence is a piece of metaphysics, tending to sacramentalism.

It looks as if the vague word 'serious' is going to have to do more work than we suspected. Where the allegorical poet revels happily among figures and images, the serious metaphysician tends to become exasperated at the inadequacy of his terms. Similar logical tangles can, as we saw, be found in Prudentius and Plato alike, but Prudentius's mood of careless rapture contrasts strongly with Plato's brain-cudgelling.

Even where there is a formal similarity between the methods of the metaphysician and the poet (since both employ metaphor) there is no reason why one should not have his eye principally

[1] *Poetics*, 1457b.7–1458a.8.
[2] *The Allegory of Love*, p. 44. See above, pp. 15–16.

upon the figured, and the other upon the figure. We must also acknowledge a distinction between 'empty' and 'lively' convention, and consider the curious quantity of 'reality' (whatever that may be) which is felt to be present in, or absent from, discourse.

Interestingly, the hard-headed man who retains a theological world-view will tend, on being confronted by the incompatibility of the self-predication assumption with the non-identity assumption, to restrict allegory to the first and metaphysics to the second. Thus Dr. Johnson says,[1] 'Fame tells a tale and Victory hovers over a general or perches on a standard; but Fame and Victory can do no more.' But the effect of this is to stop allegory in its tracks, to 'de-metaphysicize' it and to relegate it to the sphere of static personification. Similarly, Lewis, writing about Statius, says, '. . . Mars is "discovered raging" when the curtain rises and before he has any reason to rage. Naturally; for when *War* is not raging he does not exist. It is his *esse* to rage.'[2] Yet how is the task of describing the inner world to be carried forward if we are not to see what the virtues and vices do *to one another*? The impulse which keeps an allegory *in train*, which exhibits the relations of mental actions and passions in time, is a metaphysical one.

Lewis's 'non-metaphysical allegory' is not an entirely useless concept. We might even grant that all poetical allegory has a non-metaphysical tendency built into it – an impulse to revel in the figure at the expense of the figured – but it is a tendency which, if fully indulged, transforms allegory into mere personification. 'Non-metaphysical allegory' properly invites the application of terms like 'empty convention' and the like. In Lewis's terms, the 'realism' which he attributes to Guillaume de Lorris must be supposed to have been achieved in the teeth of his allegorizing tendencies. It seems better, on the whole, to define allegory, modestly and loosely, as a described set of things in narrative sequence standing for a different set of things in temporal or para-temporal sequences; in short, a complex narrative metaphor. Having said so much, we can allow with equanimity that allegory is the instrument *par excellence* of the metaphysician, that de Lorris is no less an allegorist in his moments of mysteriously intimate realism than he is anywhere else, and that what the world has always called allegories are, after all, allegories.

[1] In the *Life* of Milton in his *Lives of the English Poets*, ed. G. Birkbeck Hill, Oxford 1905, vol. I, p. 185.
[2] *The Allegory of Love*, p. 51.

III

THE PSYCHOLOGICAL BASIS

The concept I have called 'the instantially viewed universal' is common to allegorical poetry (poetry with a built-in tendency to metaphysics) and to transcendentalist metaphysics (philosophizing with a built-in tendency to poetry). The phrase 'instantially viewed universal' is ambiguous, for there are various ways of regarding universals as if they were things. These ways we may divide into two classes, 'formal' and 'concrete'. It is with the second of these that this chapter is concerned.

One may think of a universal as a thing, without thinking of it as a concrete thing. The example of Bertrand Russell shows that it is quite possible to think of universals as 'independently existing', formal things without any suspicion of sensuous or para-material characteristics. There are indeed various formal arguments (or pseudo-arguments) for the existence of such reified universals. For example, it has often been alleged that since nouns must be the name of something, abstract nouns must be the name of some 'thing'.[1]

But when universals are regarded as instances of *themselves* – when the Good is regarded as something excellently good and the Beautiful as something supremely beautiful – then we are on the verge of what could be called *concrete* reification, whereby universals are not merely thought of as things, but as quasi-tangible *objects*.

The second, 'concrete' universal has no doubt often grown out

---

[1] See J. L. Austin, 'Are there *a priori* concepts?' in his *Philosophical Papers*, 1961. The paper was first published in *PAS*, suppl. vol. XVIII, 1939, pp. 83–105.

of the first 'abstract' reification. Certainly, this can happen un-
noticed in the context of primitive metaphysics, where it might be
uncritically *assumed* that 'thing' means 'concrete object'. It is thus
tempting to assume that the 'concrete' reification is a mere illegiti-
mate elaboration of an initial formal postulate. Certainly, any sort
of logical justification of the 'concrete' reification – of the notion
that the universal 'sheep' is just a very special sheep (or something
like that) – seems to be in desperate case. It may therefore be more
worth while to look for a psychological account of this recurrent
feature of human thought and expression. This philosophical 'slip
of the tongue' has, after all, shown great staying power.

I shall be arguing in this chapter for a connexion between the
concretely instantialized, self-predicable[1] universals and mental
imagery, not because a mental image can ever *be* a universal, but
because they are easily confused.

The concept in question is marked by a quality of spurious
sensuousness, a density as of material objects, which directs our
attention to the imagination. Aristotle observes that 'images are
like sensuous contents except in that they contain no matter'.[2]
Images possess this curious 'density' analogous to the obtrusive
density of material bodies, which enables them to assume the
status of *objects*. This state of affairs makes it easy for us to talk
about an 'external' and an 'internal' world, i.e. a world of images.
What we require for the explanation of our allegorical/meta-
physical concept is some instantial object which can naturally, if
not logically, be given a general-sounding name, such as Beauty.
For obvious reasons, there is little hope of discovering such an
object in the public world of material bodies. Anything we might
want to call Beauty will turn out to be just another beautiful object,
because that is the way the world is; and, we might add, that is the
way logic is also. But perhaps if we measure the objects of the
'inner' world against the objects of the 'outer', we might find that
certain of the former seem to 'comprehend' certain of the latter, in
a manner which could be mistaken for the logical relation between
a general term and an individual. Certainly, all images, in so far
as they can be thought of as objects, will be open to the sort of

---

[1] Any universal which is regarded as an instance of itself will count as 'self-
predicable'. Thus, if we suppose that pride is something which is itself very, very
proud, we make pride itself an instance of pride, and by the same token we predicate
pride of pride.

[2] *De Anima*, 432a.8, in *The Works of Aristotle translated into English*, ed. W. D.
Ross, London 1928, vol. III.

quasi-tautologous predication we apply to public objects. Cats are feline, and imaginary cats are (even more) feline. The predication of an image is perhaps a little further removed from tautology than is the self-predication of a public object. For example, to say that a dog is canine is very much like saying that a dog is a dog. But to say that an imaginary dog is (very) canine may be to say that the image is a particularly vivid evocation of the object. Again, the non-specific character of much imagery (for which I shall argue in a moment) makes us wish to say sometimes 'Well, my image wasn't of any particular dog, but it was certainly canine.' The logic of such predication is rather like the logic of talking about dreams already mentioned;[1] the lion you imagine is, *qua* lion, leonine; *qua* image, it is, of course, nothing of the sort. The effect of saying '*qua* image' is to transfer the attention to the public context, where the only identifiable object will be the electrical impulse picked up by the encephalograph or the behavioural features treated by the psychologist. H. H. Price writes:

> A visual image of a dog is not, of course, an instance of the concept Dog, but it is much nearer to being so than the word 'dog' is. It is in many ways what an actual instance of the concept would be. And if I cash the word 'yellow' in absence by means of a visual image, or the word 'squeak' by means of an auditory one, it might even be claimed that the image actually *is* an instance of the concept in question. An image of a yellow patch, it might be said, is actually itself yellow, as a buttercup seen in full daylight is, and an image of a squeak is actually itself squeaky. This claim, I think, is not altogether justified. The image does not seem to me to have the characteristic of intrusiveness or sensible forcefulness which the actual precept [*sic*] has. But the point now is that the claim is at any rate plausible.[2]

We may note that Price speaks of 'a yellow patch', and tells us no more. Some people will automatically assume that the patch he postulates would, in practice, have of necessity some particular, determinate, shape. Others will be ready to allow that it may have no particular shape at all, and that even the word 'patch' is somewhat too precise for what their imagination produces for them in response to the word 'yellow'. Such people, perusing Price's article, would have experienced no particular shock, if they had

[1] See above, p. 35.
[2] H. H. Price, 'Image Thinking', *PAS*, NS LII (1951–2), p. 155.

read, instead of the words 'a yellow patch', the single word 'yellow'. There is even a slight temptation to give the word a capital Y; it is, after all, an individual. If we succumb to this temptation, we find ourselves with the highly Platonic sentence 'Yellow, it might be said, is actually itself yellow'. Our image is, then, to adapt Cornford's words, 'yellow and nothing else',[1] just as Miranda, for Mrs. Jameson,[2] was beautiful, modest and tender, 'and these only'. If we may borrow a piece of jargon from Price, it is possible to suppose a man who would 'cash' the word 'dog' sometimes by various memory-images of particular dogs he knew, sometimes by an unspecified image which was no particular dog at all – just dog-ish-and-nothing-else. He might well feel that the second method was somehow more 'direct' than the first: that while the word 'dog' was obviously just a common noun covering all the dogs he could call to mind, it was also the *proper name* of the unspecified image. In this way a (private) object of experience is supplied in response to the formal demand that abstract nouns should be names of something.[3]

The whole of this argument depends, of course, on the existence of what we have called 'unspecified images'. It also depends on the psychological possibility of identifying concepts, ideas and images. Both of these conditions can be illuminated by examination of the clash between John Locke and Bishop Berkeley over the nature of general ideas.

Even before the argument began, the identification, or confusion, of concept, idea and image was already receiving every encouragement from linguistic usage which gave *idea* the sense 'image', and it continued to be so encouraged throughout the next century. There is a scene in Shakespeare's *Richard III* in which the Duke of Buckingham recounts to the wicked Duke of Gloucester his efforts to convince the citizens of Gloucester's claim to the throne. He explains how, among other arguments, he referred to Gloucester's physiognomy, so eloquent of his right to succeed. Precisely at the point at which we should say 'image', Buckingham uses the word 'idea':

> Withal I did infer your lineaments,
> Being the right idea of your father . . .[4]

[1] See above, p. 3 and p. 43.
[2] See above, p. 3.
[3] See above, p. 49.
[4] *Richard III*, III. vii. 12–13.

The sense 'mental image' is equally clear, though not without a certain tang of Platonism, in the forty-fifth sonnet of Spenser's *Amoretti,* where the poet says that 'the fayre idea' of his lady's 'celestiall hew' will remain immortally within his heart.[1] And as late as 1749 the usage is still lively, as may be seen from Tom Jones's words to Sophia – 'Though I despaired of possessing you, nay, almost of ever seeing you more, I doated still on your charming idea.'[2]

Moreover, the usage received strong backing from explicitly philosophical sources. Descartes, in his first philosophical work, the *Regulae,* makes it quite clear that he uses the Latin word *idea* to mean 'mental image'. For example, he asserts[3] that we do not construct two 'ideas' in our imagination, one of body and one of extension; and a little later he says that the *imaginatio* (in antithesis to the *intellectus*) *veram rei ideam fingere debet* ('the imagination ought to frame a true *idea* of the thing').[4] The French translators tend to render *idea* by the word 'idée', while the English, interestingly, translate 'image'. Perhaps this indicates a stronger semantic continuity for the sense 'image' on the Continent. Even in the *Meditations* he says that some of his thoughts are like images or things, and that it is to these alone that properly belongs the name of ideas.[5] Descartes at all events seems clear that not all of his thought 'consists of' idea/images. But in Voltaire the semantic ambivalence of the term seems to have grown into ripe philosophical confusion. In his *Dictionnaire philosophique,* which he began writing in 1751, he says under *idée* (section première):

> Qu'est-ce qu'une idée?
>
> C'est une image qui se peint dans mon cerveau.
>
> Toutes vos pensées sont donc des images?
>
> Assurément; car les idées les plus abstraites ne sont que les suites de tous les objets que j'ai aperçus.[6]

Between the *Meditations* and the *Philosophical Dictionary* lies the

---

[1] *The Works of Edmund Spenser,* ed. E. Greenlaw, C. G. Osgood, F. M. Padelford and R. Heffner, Baltimore 1932–58, vol. II of the *Minor Poems,* pp. 213–14.

[2] Henry Fielding, *Tom Jones,* Book XIII, ch. xi, in the Shakespeare Head Edition, Oxford 1926, vol. III, p. 250.

[3] *Regula,* XIV.439, in *Regulae ad Directionem Ingenii,* 'texte de l'édition Adam et Tannery, notice par Henri Gouhier', Paris 1946, p. 85.

[4] *ibid.,* p. 92 (*Regula,* XIV. 445).

[5] Meditatio III, in *Meditationes de Prima Philosophia,* ed. and trans. into French by the Duc de Luynes, introduction and notes by G. Lewis, Paris 1944, p. 37.

[6] In *Œuvres complètes de Voltaire,* Paris 1876, vol. VII.

Essay concerning Human Understanding. I do not know whether Locke is directly responsible for Voltaire's slightly defiant assertion that even the most abstract ideas are images, but there seems to be little doubt that Locke himself regarded them as having at any rate a quasi-instantial status. Even before he gives his account of the formation – one might almost say the epistemology – of general ideas, he makes it clear that he is following naturally the linguistic usage I have outlined, for he speaks[1] of 'particular things; whereof I alone having the ideas in my mind . . .'[2] So the word already carried the sense 'image' for Locke. In what follows there is no sign of any revolt against that signification.

But to deduce this a little more distinctly, it will not perhaps be amiss to trace out notions and names from their beginning, and observe by what degrees we proceed, and by what steps we enlarge our ideas from our first infancy. There is nothing more evident, than that the ideas of the persons children converse with (to instance in them alone) are, like the persons themselves, only particular. The ideas of the nurse and the mother are well framed in their minds; and, like pictures of them there, represent only those individuals; and the names of *nurse* and *mamma*, the child uses, determine themselves to those persons. Afterwards, when time and a larger acquaintance have made them observe that there are a great many other things in the world, that in some common agreements of shape, and several other qualities, resemble their father and mother, and these persons they have been used to, they frame an idea, which they find those many particulars do partake in; and to that they give, with others, the name *man*, for example. And thus they come to have a general name and a general idea. Wherein they make nothing new; but only leave out of the complex idea they had of Peter and James, Mary and Jane, that which is peculiar to each, and retain only what is common to them all.[3]

---

[1] *An Essay Concerning Human Understanding* (first published 1690), Bk. III, ch. iii, §3, in A. C. Fraser's edition, Oxford 1894, vol. II, p. 15.

[2] Frege seems to be making a similar point in his essay 'On Sense and Reference' (in *Translations from the Philosophical Writings of Gottlob Frege*, ed. P. Geach and M. Black, Oxford 1952) when he says (p. 59), 'one man's idea is not that of another'. In fact, he is merely exemplifying the semantic continuity of the sense 'image'. Frege's essay was first published in 1892. The same usage can be found in Herbert Spencer's *First Principles*, 2nd ed., 1867, e.g. p. 26.

[3] *Essay*, III.iii.7.

A paragraph or so later he uses the same model of retention and leaving out:

> . . . which new idea is made, not by any new addition, but only as before, by leaving out the shape, and some other properties signified by the name man, and retaining only a body, with life, sense, and spontaneous motion, comprehended under the name animal.[1]

It is clear that Locke considers the formation of general ideas as a sort of imaginative chemistry, in which elements are 'isolated' and subsequently referred to in their new-found imaginative isolation. We have grown accustomed in ordinary speech to make an antithesis between 'merely logical 'abstractions and 'vivid, sensuous images'. But in Locke it is the very term 'abstraction' which brings out most clearly the imagist tendency of this thinking. The word 'subtraction', or even 'detachment', could be substituted throughout without undue violence to his thought. If we are to suppose that different features are successively removed from an idea, it seems necessary to postulate some sort of continuing stuff, which subsists while the process is carried out. This continuous, malleable entity is obviously not to be found in the public world. Accordingly we must place it in the private world of the imagination, with its mysterious 'para-matter' and its resemblance to 'sensuous contents'. If a person forms his general ideas by a process of doing things to an object, and that object is not available to public inspection, it seems that we are left with the private objects of the imagination. Modern theorists of the evolution of the imagination would tend to contradict Locke in his assertion that children proceed from the particular to the general, and say instead with Aristotle that infants begin by calling all men Daddy and climb out of this stage by a process of particularization. But this does not imply that Locke is opposed to imagism as such. Whichever end of the process you care to start at, it is an *imaginative* continuum that is presupposed. When Locke comes to consider the terms 'general' and 'universal' themselves he makes a careful distinction. These two terms are mere 'creatures of the understanding' and do not belong 'to the real existence of things'.[2] Evidently, as mere logical constructions, they are opposed to the sort of ideas he has been considering up to this point. It is hard to

[1] *ibid.*, III.iii.8.
[2] *ibid.*, III.iii.11.

believe that this opposition owes nothing to the antithesis between logical and imaginative constructions.

For many people, one of the strongest motives against viewing the Lockean idea as an image, or even a quasi-image, will be derived from the extremity of his examples. 'No one could suppose that you arrive at an *image* or just-animal-and-nothing else by knocking bits off your image of man!' one might say. In fact, the example 'animal' is one of the more modest ones. We may turn to the passage concerning the triangle – the passage which stuck in Berkeley's throat:

> . . . does it not require some pains and skill to form the general idea of a triangle (which is yet none of the most abstract, comprehensive, and difficult), for it must be neither oblique nor rectangle, neither equilateral, equicrural, nor scalenon; but all and none of these at once. In effect, it is something imperfect, that cannot exist; an idea wherein some parts of several different and inconsistent ideas are put together.[1]

To do Locke justice, it must be acknowledged that he plainly felt some discomfort when he wrote these words. One suspects that he is forced to write so because he has become the slave of an imagist theory; but that he is at least struggling against his chains. One wonders whether he is, in fact, trying to describe a swift succession of related images which passed before his mind's eye, and is hoping to pass this off as a unity deserving of the name 'idea'. But he does seem to derive some comfort from the fact (as he sees it) that imaginative objects do not have to conform to the standards of consistency we require from public objects. They need not be things which could actually 'exist'. In the public world a house-front has to have a back to it, has to be located somewhere. In the imaginative world that is not so. A public triangle has to be either isosceles or not isosceles. Locke draws comfort from the fact that an imagined triangle does not have to be either of these things 'exactly'.

Bishop Berkeley spared no pains in dispossessing Locke of this very comfort. Even if the question of whether Locke regarded ideas simply as images remains *sub judice*, there is no doubt that Berkeley understood him so, and made him pay dearly for it. He affirmed that it was impossible to imagine without particularity,[2]

---

[1] *ibid.*, IV.vii.9.
[2] *A Treatise concerning the Principles of Human Knowledge*, Introduction, §10, in

and for Locke's triangle he had very strong language:

> If any man has the faculty of framing in his mind such an idea of a triangle as is here described, it is in vain to pretend to dispute him out of it, nor would I go about it.[1]

Berkeley's contention that images were necessarily highly specific found strong assent from others. Hume attacked Locke's model of abstraction or separation, saying, in words reminiscent of Descartes:[2]

> . . . 'tis evident at first sight, that the precise length of a line is not different or distinguishable from the line itself. . . . These ideas, therefore, admit no more of separation than they do of distinction and difference . . . . the general idea of a line, notwithstanding all our abstractions and refinements, has in its appearance in the mind a precise degree of quantity and quality; however it may be made to represent others, which have different degrees of both.[3]

He goes on to argue that all impressions are necessarily determinate, and that ideas, being faint copies of them, must share the characteristic of determinacy. Sir William Hamilton joined in the denunciation of Locke in still more forcible terms. He called the Lockean image a 'revolting absurdity',[4] and later referred to it as 'palpably absurd'.[5]

Much weight in the reaction against Locke was placed on the necessary particularity of images. Strangely enough, however, on this point it was the sceptics who were mistaken. In the 1860s Francis Galton began his celebrated investigation of the nature of imagery, and was soon confident of the highly schematic or, at any rate, non-specific character of many images. He made it very clear that, *pace* Hume, images are by no means necessarily subservient to the individuational features of public objects. Galton found an

---

[1] *ibid.*, §13.
[2] See above, p. 53.
[3] *A Treatise of Human Nature* (first published 1739), Bk. I, § vii, in the 1958 impression of L. A. Selby-Bigge's edition, first published Oxford 1888, pp. 18–19.
[4] *Lectures On Metaphysics*, Edinburgh 1859–60, vol. II, p. 300.
[5] *ibid.*, p. 301.

---

vol. II of *The Works of George Berkeley, Bishop of Cloyne,* ed. A. A. Luce and T. E. Jessop, London 1949. The work was first published in 1710, and republished, slightly revised, in 1734. My quotations from Luce and Jessop follow the text of 1734.

'eminent mineralogist' who assured him that he was 'able to imagine simultaneously all the sides of a crystal with which he is familiar'.[1] And Galton himself was capable, in his dream imagery, of viewing a globe 'centripetally' from all sides at once.[2] He spoke also of 'composite imagery' which he compared with the images produced by 'composite photography'. A typical 'composite photograph' would be obtained by superimposing representations of all the members of one family, with the result that an image is produced which somehow 'covers' all the Postlethwaites and yet retains a surprising appearance of individuality.[3] It is an image of just-the-archetypal-Postlethwaite. Galton, who was himself a pioneer in this sort of photography, produced a picture of the archetypal Violent Criminal and the archetypal British Soldier.[4]

Galton's paper 'Generic Images' first appeared on 25 April 1879, in the *Proceedings of the Royal Institute*. Two years later the point was firmly taken and applied by T. H. Huxley in his book on Hume. Like Galton, he makes the comparison with composite photography,[5] and asserts that a number of differing impressions could indeed leave behind a compound image in the mind, drawing support for his contentions from dream-imagery. He writes:

> An anatomist who occupies himself intently with the examination of several specimens of some new kind of animal, in course of time acquires so vivid a conception of its form and structure, that the idea may take visible shape and become a sort of waking dream. But the figure which thus presents itself is generic, not specific. It is no copy of any one specimen, but, more or less a mean of the series; and there seems no reason to doubt that the minds of children before they learn to speak, and of deaf mutes, are peopled with similarly generated generic ideas of sensible objects.[6]

For some years after the appearance of Huxley's book there was a lull[7] in the discussion of 'generic imagery'. Then in the 1890s

[1] F. Galton, *Inquiries into Human Faculty*, Everyman 1928, reprint of 2nd ed. of 1907, p. 68.

[2] *ibid.*, p. 68.

[3] *ibid.*, p. 132 and pp. 229 ff.

[4] *ibid.*, opposite p. 8.

[5] *Hume* (first published 1881), 1894, p. 111.

[6] *ibid.*, p. 113.

[7] It is true that Loewy cites E. Brücke's 'Die Darstellung der Bewegung durch die bilden den Künste', *Deutsche Rundschau*, vol. XXVI (1881), pp. 43 ff., as a notable early version of the theory.

and the early years of the twentieth century there was a whole crop of books dealing in one way or another with the subject – Bergson's *Matière et Mémoire* (1896), Th. Ribot's *L'Évolution des Idées Générales* (1897), Emanuel Loewy's *Die Naturweidergabe in der älteren griechischen Kunst* (1900), E. B. Titchener's *Experimental Psychology of the Thought Processes* (1909), and Richard Semon's *Die Mneme* (1911).

Bergson followed up Huxley's observation about children proceeding from the general to the particular enthusiastically. But at the same time he expressed a reservation which was long overdue – as to the appropriateness of the terms 'general' and 'particular' in such a context.

It would seem, then, that we start neither from the perception of the individual nor from the conception of the genus, but from an intermediate knowledge, from a confused sense of the *striking quality* or of resemblance.[1]

We have come a long way from Locke, with his gradually and successively simplified abstract image, but the central concept, the thing-which-can-call-human-and-nothing-else, seems to be with us still. But Bergson has asked an important question; why should we call this thing, image, idea, impression, or whatever it is, 'general' at all? It is only after a process of matching against public objects that it can be said to be general. And even then it is not general in the same sense that the word 'cow' is general, that is, in virtue of a logical function. For these things are not logical functions; nor are they, at all obviously, vehicles designed to convey logical functions. Bergson's whole difficulty lies in trying to describe a mental object which is prior to our sophisticated conventions. Naturally, the only way is via those conventions. This leads to one extremely interesting result; at one point he gives up the attempt to use substantival concepts, and speaks instead of 'a striking *quality*'. This brings the concept very close to the puzzling concept which I tried to isolate in the first two chapters. The uneasy status, somewhere between noun and adjective, of expressions like the Platonic αὐτὸ τὸ ἀγαθόν ('the good itself') is very like Bergson's non-determined, non-verifiable, non-falsifiable thing/quality. *Qua* thing, it is a thing not to be found in the public world; *qua* quality, we see it everywhere in this world, and only an

[1] H. Bergson, *Matter and Memory*, trans. N. M. Paul and W. S. Palmer, New York 1911, p. 205.

anamnesis to the preconceptual period of our infancy can remind us of the time when we knew it as a thing. Various other parallels between the epistemologically and the ontologically prior can no doubt be found.

Th. Ribot wrestles with the same problem in *L'Evolution des idées générales*:

> La seule formule convenable est celle-ci: L'esprit va de *l'indéfini au défini*. Si l'on fait indéfini synonyme de général, alors on peut soutenir que ce n'est pas le particulier qui apparaît au début, mais ce n'est pas non plus le général, au sens exact du terme; c'est le vague. En d'autres termes, dès que l'esprit dépasse le moment de la perception et de sa reproduction immédiate dans la mémoire, ce qui apparaît, c'est l'image générique, c'est à dire un état intermédiaire entre le particulier et le général, participant de la nature de l'un et de l'autre – une simplification confuse.[1]

Ribot shares with Bergson an awareness of the logical difficulties involved in discussing primitive material, but his form of expression nevertheless, for all Bertrand Russell's admiration[2] of it, is open to criticism. It is true that neither 'general' nor 'particular' is strictly applicable to the object under discussion but not because the object is in 'un état intermédiaire' between them. It does not appear on the scale of general and particular at all. It is not amenable to a system of individuation of which the basic particulars are public, material bodies. 'Indéfini' and 'vague' as terms are admittedly one degree better than 'general', in that they use the model of the picture or percept, and do not raise false hopes about logical functions. But none of these three terms can be applied at all strictly. They all carry with them the implications of the macrocosm. There is nothing to suggest that such primitive impressions *feel* in the least vague to the subject of them. A man who, while staying in the country, being ignorant of the finer points of agriculture, refrains from expressing an opinion on points of practical husbandry when they arise in conversation is not a man who is 'vague about farming'. He is rather a man who has not yet got round to learning about farming. There is no hesitation, indecision or cloudiness on the subject; there is just no subject. Similarly, a 'generic' image, whether it is that of an infant or of the kind that

---

[1] *op. cit.* (1897), pp. 39–40.
[2] See B. Russell, *The Analysis of Mind*, London 1921, p. 184.

occurs from time to time, half-subliminally, in our daily lives, hardly merits the stigma 'vague'. To describe it so is like giving a pupil a gamma in an examination he has not taken.

Nevertheless, a word is needed. Since it seems likely that, under the influence of attention, or of increasing maturity, images do tend to approximate more nearly to percepts in their detailedness, etc., we find it quite natural to speak of this as 'specification'; so we may describe images which have not undergone this process as 'non-specified images.' The naturalness of this is worth noting. At the same time, we must remember that the use of the word 'specification' is an odd one. Apologetic inverted commas are a useful signal of this oddity.

Richard Semon, in *Die Mneme*, revived the 'composite photograph' comparison, and asserted that the generic character of (some) imagery – the character which enables a person to imagine 'just James', that is, not James at some particular time and place, but simply James – makes possible the development of what he at first wished to describe as a sort of *physiological* abstraction.[1] The language of logical types continues to break into the language which describes imagery.

Experimental evidence for the non-specificity of imagery was gradually collected. Sartre quotes some typical examples from the investigations of Watt and Messer.

> 'I saw,' said subject I, 'something that looked like a wing.' Subject II saw a face without knowing whether it was that of a man or a woman. Subject I had 'an image that looked like a human face; a typical image, not individual'.[2]

Similarly, the order of procedure from the 'non-specified impressions of infancy to the 'specified' perceptions of maturity which we found in Bergson and Ribot appears, confirmed, in M. D. Vernon's *A Further Study of Visual Perception*, 1954, and in J. J. Gibson's *Perception and the Visual World*, 1950, p. 222.

Human beings differ very widely in their imagery. Certain of Francis Galton's correspondents were unable to discover in themselves anything remotely worthy of the name. McKellar observes[3]

[1] See *Die Mneme, als erhaltendes Prinzip im Wechsel des organischen Geschehens*, Leipzig 1911, p. 224. The term 'physiological' and Semon's observations upon it are entirely suppressed in the English version, *The Mneme*, trans. Louis Simon, London 1921.

[2] J.-P. Sartre, *The Psychology of Imagination* (no translator's name given), London 1950, p. 23.

[3] See his *Imagination and Thinking*, London 1957, pp. 19–22.

that a great deal of intolerance and angry derision tends to break out when people compare notes on the subject. People pass very readily from a description of their own imagery to prescription for the rest of mankind. The imageless mock the image-ridden and cast doubt on their veracity, the image-ridden grow romantically defiant, or stand upon their dignity. But it seems to be a generally accepted fact that 'non-specific' imagery does occur.

Thus we do have the thing we required: something which can, quite naturally, be called 'general', by a usage which does not imply any diminution of 'concreteness' or 'sensuousness' in the course of the passage from particular to general.

Of the serious claim for the substantial identity of images, ideas, and concepts, the philosopher makes short work. A. J. Furlong, C. A. Mace and D. J. O'Connor, in a symposium on 'Abstract Ideas and Images', had little difficulty in reaching agreement. Furlong pointed out[1] that our careless excesses of abstraction soon outstrip the possible scope of any composite photography. We may be able to manage an image of 'red-and-nothing-else', but what about 'colour'? C. A. Mace, in the second paper, granted the progress from 'non-specified' to 'specified' impressions, and the existence of 'generic images, schematic images, vague images, and images which in themselves are unrecognisable as representing the things they are supposed to represent',[2] but denied that anything of logical importance turned on these distinctions. O'Connor, in the third paper, said that images could serve as symbols for general reference, but were made rather less (not more) suitable for this purpose by their iconic or representational character.[3] An image is an image, instantial, inert, and a concept is a concept, to to be considered in terms of logical functioning. 'Image' and 'concept' are not even the same sort of word. One we try to define ostensively – or, at least, by a direct description of its appearance – and the other dispositionally. A man who has the concept of gravity is a man who is able to talk and think intelligently about why and how things fall to the ground. A man who has an image of a triangle is just a man with a triangle in his head.[4] Bishop Berkeley was unwise to place so much weight on the necessary

---

[1] Paper I in the Symposium, *PAS*, suppl. vol. XXVII (1953), pp. 121-36.
[2] *ibid.* (Paper II), p. 145.
[3] *ibid.* (Paper III), p. 157.
[4] There is, of course, a dispositional sense for the words 'has an image'. If someone says 'X has a curious image of the Oxford don', he is not likely to be referring to a particular mental event, but rather to a *capacity* for imagining in a certain way.

'specificity' of images, first because images are not necessarily specific, and secondly for the more important reason that an image, of whatever type, just is not what is required at all.

Evidence taken from the introspective accounts of E. B. Titchener might be held to cast doubt on Furlong's claim that logical easily and inevitably outstrips imaginative 'abstraction'. Titchener said, for example, that in addition to the fairly definite mental picture he normally had for the word 'triangle', he could quite easily

> get Locke's picture, the triangle that is no triangle and all triangles at one and the same time. It is a flashy thing, come and gone from moment to moment: it hints two or three red angles, with the red lines deepening into black, seen on a dark green ground. It is not there long enough for me to say whether the angles join to form the complete figure, or even whether all three of the necessary angles are given. Nevertheless it means triangle; it is Hamilton's palpable absurdity made real.[1]

In fact, Titchener's account does more to confirm Furlong's claim than to rebut it. In the first place, it is a long way from being 'just triangle'. It is 'red and black triangle,' 'flashing triangle'– and in both of these descriptions it is the word 'triangle' which is the less appropriate description of the idea as a phenomenon, for Titchener admits that he is not certain how many angles it has. He is forced to say of his 'non-specified' image what he says of his definite image – that it *means* triangle. And, as Mace pointed out[2] in his paper, *anything* can be made to *mean* triangle.

Our case for the relevance of 'generic' imagery to the logical oddity of allegorical concepts must therefore rest, as was suggested at the beginning of this chapter, not on the identity of generic images and concepts, but on the possibility of their confusion. The semantic ambiguity of the word 'idea' has been used, throughout its history, to promote this confusion. We can find it even in sophisticated and recent works of psychology. We may take as an example the following passage from Peter McKellar's *Thinking and Imagination*, p. 188:

> As Thurstone remarks: 'it requires inhibition of no mean order to retain the concept as such'. It is, for example, a feat of

[1] E. B. Titchener, *Lectures on the Experimental Psychology of the Thought Processes*, New York 1909, pp. 17–18.
[2] See the footnote on p. 146 of Mace, *op. cit.*

inhibition to remain conscious of the abstract idea of 'red' without allowing this to concretize into some specific red object.

It is plain that McKellar is quite ready to identify concept, idea idea and 'non-specified' image, and presumably Thurstone (though I have not read his book) was guilty of the same dangerous confusion.

All this psychological material is easily applied to Platonic or allegorical subjects. Emanuel Loewy makes the former connexion when he writes

> As the result of the visual impressions which we have received from numerous examples of the same object, there remains fixed in our minds a memory-picture, which is no other than the Platonic Idea of the object, namely a typical picture, clear of everything individual or accidental.[1]

T. H. Huxley expresses a similar view when he observes that 'the Platonic philosophy is probably the grandest example of the un-scientific use of the imagination extant'.[2]

It is interesting that this sudden growth of interest in the peculiarities of the imagination should follow close upon the period of enthusiastic metaphysicizing which provided the material of my first chapter. It is tempting to suppose that one motive of this psychology was a certain feeling of uneasiness about the status of such poetic-metaphysical language in general. The more radical positivist reaction was to come later.

The relevance of such imagery to the allegorical form is still more evident. There is a passage in Titchener's book where, in the sheer effort to describe his day-to-day imagery, he is almost writing like an allegorist:

> Whenever I read or hear that somebody has done something modestly, or gravely, or proudly, or humbly, or courteously, I see a visual hint of the modesty or gravity or pride or humility or courtesy. The stately heroine gives me a flash of a tall figure, the only clear part of which is a hand holding up a steely grey skirt; the humble suitor gives me a flash of a bent figure, the

---

[1] *The Rendering of Nature in Early Greek Art*, trans. J. Fothergill, London 1907, p. 10. The work first appeared under the title *Die Naturwiedergabe in der alteren griechischen Kunst*, Rome 1900.

[2] *Hume*, (1894), p. vii.

only clear part of which is the bowed back . . . I shall not multiply instances. All this description must be either self-evident or as unreal as a fairy-tale.[1]

It is true of these images, as it is true of all images however 'generalized', that the logical meaning is distinguishable from the image itself. But at the same time we cannot say that the image is one of any individual. At the mention of John's name, one commonly gets an image of John himself. At the mention of humility, Titchener commonly got an image. It is only too easy to proceed by a false analogy and call the image Humility herself.

Throughout this chapter I have spoken of images as if they were objects of some kind, because this language is natural to me. But it is important that this term should be more than a mere *façon de parler*. Talk of an 'inner world' is obviously greatly weakened if the world in question is to be considered as having no inspect-able objects.

A vigorous attack on the image as object was made by Jean-Paul Sartre in his book *The Psychology of the Imagination*. He argues that as in perception our attention fastens only upon certain aspects of an object, so in imagination, when the object is absent and perceptual information excluded, we retain only what we attend to. 'Generic' imagery is thus explained as resulting from the simple fact that when we attend to, say, chairs, we will be conscious of no features by the most typical; hence our imagery will be 'generic'; indeed, this is what it *means* to say that our imagery is 'generic'. To imagine John is simply to be conscious of, or attend to, John. There is no need to invoke any sort of third entity between the person doing the imagining and John himself. He writes on p. 23: 'It follows necessarily that the object as an image is never anything more than the consciousness one has of it.' Sartre is not observing that if one imagines a square, and then attends to the top right-hand corner of it, the first image tends to be replaced by an image of a corner. There is no distinction between the change of attention and the substitution of images; the phrase 'substitution of images' denotes nothing that is not denoted by the phrase 'change of attention'. This is Sartre's argument for, and explanation of, 'generic imagery'. Plainly it would have had very little effect on Bishop Berkeley:

[1] *Experimental Psychology of the Thought Processes*, pp. 13–14.

. . . it must be acknowledged that a man may consider a figure merely as triangular, without attending to the particular qualities of the angles, or relations of the sides. So far he may abstract: but this will never prove, that he can frame an abstract general inconsistent idea of a triangle. In like manner we may consider Peter so far forth as man, or so far forth as animal, without framing the forementioned abstract idea, either of man or of animal, in as much as all that is perceived is not considered.[1]

For Berkeley, attending to various features of triangles is quite different from imagining generic triangles. For Sartre, the image can have no sort of autonomy. Even when he falls into the language of objects (as he does frequently) and talks about 'looking at' images, he is clear about who is master. He writes, 'No matter how long I may look at an image, I shall never find anything in it but what I put there.'[2] It follows that images can never be used as sources of information.

In the context of twentieth-century psychological research, Sartre's opinion is a heresy. Francis Galton was the first to indicate how the imagination could be one step ahead of the consciousness by recounting the remarkable case of Mr. Petrie:

Mr. Flinders Petrie, a contributor of interesting experiments on kindred subjects to *Nature*, informs me that he habitually works out sums by aid of an imaginary sliding rule, which he sets in the desired way and reads off mentally. He does not usually visualize the whole of the rule, but only that part with which he is at the moment concerned . . . I think this is one of the most striking cases of accurate visualising power it is possible to imagine.[3]

After such an unlikely beginning, autonomous imagery gradually obtained general recognition. McKellar writes:

It may help our discussion . . . to distinguish between autonomous images whose occurrence and content are independent of the subject's conscious intentions, and *controlled* images which depend upon voluntary control. The interesting studies of imagery in relation to prejudice conducted by Gordon (1949,

---

[1] Introduction to *The Principles*, §16, in Luce and Jessop, *op. cit.*, p. 35.
[2] *The Psychology of Imagination*, p. 16.
[3] *Inquiries into Human Faculty*, p. 66.

1950) suggests an association between the tendency to form stereotypes and a predominance of autonomous rather than controlled imagery.[1]

Two pages later McKellar says that the typical eidetic imager is able to 'read' from the pages of an imagined book, and quotes Allport's experiments of 1924 in which a subject was able to give the number of buttons on the coat of a subsidiary figure in a picture which had previously been shown to him.

There is something counter-intuitive about the suggestion that we derive information from our imagery. One wishes to say *nihil in phantasia quod non prius in homine*. Accordingly, various attempts have been made to explain autonomous imagery in a causal way. McKellar cites[2] the opinion of Havelock Ellis, that 'the eye supplies entoptic glimmerings, and the brain, acting upon the suggestions received, superimposes mental pictures on these glimmerings'. But, despite the kaleidoscopic variety of such idio-retinal phenomena, they can offer no satisfactory account of, say, Flinders Petrie's slide-rule.

> We put our eyes into a pillowy cleft,
> And see the spangly gloom froth up and boil –

but more than this is needed before we can carry out complex arithmetical calculations.

One therefore says instead, 'Well, the information must have been *latent* in the subject, he really knows what a slide-rule is like and how to perform calculations upon it.' Or, of Allport's subject, one might say, 'Well, of course he knew how many buttons there were – the imagery wasn't a source of information to him, it was simply the form his recollection took.' This is, in a way, perfectly fair. Imagery (supernatural visitations apart) does not provide us with information we have never previously learned. But it does provide us with information we had temporarily forgotten. This is where Sartre seems to be mistaken. He does not say the image tells a man nothing which he does not know; he says the image tells a man nothing which his *consciousness* does not know, which he is not already *aware of*. But our waking images no less than our dreams are capable of surprising us. A man is unable to perform a calculation. He imagines a slide-rule. He is able to perform it. It is clear

[1] *Imagination and Thinking*, p. 24.
[2] *ibid.*, p. 83.

that the imager is at a loss until he contrives an object which he then uses by a process involving something very close to inspection. Sartre has no word for this object.[1] But everyday usage has. It is called an 'image'.

Gilbert Ryle in *The Concept of Mind* (1949) defended a position which is in some ways similar to Sartre's. He observes that when we imagine (say) a duck, we are not seeing a picture of a duck; nor are we seeing a phantom duck. This, I suppose, will be surprising to no one. He passes swiftly from this position to the importantly different assertion that there is no entity which we could figuratively describe as a 'pictured' duck. He tends, indeed, to attack the mental/physical antithesis by the dubious procedure of treating mental objects as if they were physical, and showing that this is absurd. For example, on p. 248 he writes of a child who imagines that her doll is smiling:

> . . . the pictured smile is not, then, a physical phenomenon, i.e. a real contortion of the doll's face; nor yet is it a non-physical phenomenon observed by the child taking place in a field quite detached from her perambulator and her nursery. There is not a smile at all, and there is not an effigy of a smile either. There is only a child fancying that she sees her doll smiling.

Ryle here uses 'effigy' with a calculated brutality which ensures that its primary physical connotations will be uppermost. A believer in the mental/physical dualism would hardly be surprised to learn that a mental image was something other than a physical effigy. Like Sartre, Ryle denies the existence of any instantial object denoted by the word 'image'. For him there are on the one hand people and on the other hand things, events, etc., and the relations between these two parties require descriptions which may be simple or complex. Where the description is complex, people tend to fall into the trap of supposing that there is some sort of complexity in the ontological structure of the universe corresponding to the logical complexity of the description. A man who is merely sparring is not doing more *things* than a man who is fighting, but

---

[1] It is arguable that Sartre (at some cost to consistency) ultimately re-admits the image as object. He allows himself, for example, to speak of the *content* of an imaginative act, and of this content as *representative* of the public object. It is only a short step from this to ask, 'What is it that *does* the representing?' The point is well put by Mary Warnock, in her *The Philosophy of Sartre*, New York 1965, pp. 26–28.

a description of the first man's activity will be more complex than a description of the second. A man who sees a tree is not doing fewer things than a man who fancies to himself that he sees a tree; the first acts categorically and the second hypothetically.

If there are no images, it might be asked how we come by the classification of imagery into visual, auditory, tactile, olfactory, gustatory and kinaesthetic. Ryle's answer is that an imagining is visual if we fancy that we see something, auditory if we fancy that we hear it, and so on. But I can imagine (or fancy) that I am looking at a rose, and I can also imagine the rose, quite simply. In the language which admits talk about objects, in the first I am myself a personage in my own imagined scene, in the second only one object is present, the rose.

How Ryle would convey this readily intelligible distinction without using object-language is not quite clear to me. Perhaps he would employ the word 'seems'[1] and say that in the first case it seems as if I am looking at a rose, while in the second case it seems as if there is a rose before me. This is not very satisfactory. If we use the word 'seems' in its most ordinary sense – as in 'this stone seems to be granite', then the antithesis would be reformulable in the following terms: 'In the first case I rather think, though I am not sure, that I am looking at a rose, while in the second case I rather think, though I am not sure, that there is a rose before my eyes.' As long as we use 'seem' in what may be called its public signification, it will not be effectual in the imaginative context. But if we follow the use of the word which has grown up for the description of imaginary things, it is immediately evident that a change of sense has taken place. The sense of 'seem' in 'I seem to be an American though really I'm an Eskimo' is plainly different from its sense in 'I seem to be standing on the top of a great mountain', where this means 'I imagine that I am standing on a high mountain'.

The alternative term 'fancy' does not improve matters very much. If I say 'I fancy that I am in the jungle', this must either mean 'I think I am in the jungle'– in which case 'fancy' corresponds closely to the 'public' sense of 'seem', and is open to the same sort of objection – or else it must mean 'I am enjoying a private drama in which I am in a jungle', and this revives the 'internal theatre' concept.

Nor does it seem much more helpful to describe imagining as a

[1] As he does *op. cit.*, p. 253.

series of abstentions.[1] If this means that humming a tune in one's head is just one effort after another to hold one's tongue, this is just false. If it means that 'to hum a tune in one's head' equals 'not to hum a tune', this is either trivial or absurd.

Ryle argues that when we say we 'see' an elephant, this does not mean we see an 'elephant', that is, that we see a dummy or pseudo-elephant somewhere. This is certainly true, but it does not exhaust the possibilities. The believer in objective though private imagery would instantly wish to point out, 'Certainly, I do not see anything, but I do "see" an "elephant",' that is, nothing of the public world at all is involved here, but both an activity and an object of the private world *are* involved.

Speaking strictly, both terms should be in inverted commas. In the first example *elephant* is allowed to stand without them because the public object stands in a logical relation to the private (since the image not only resembles, but can readily stand as a symbol for the public object),[2] but this liberty cannot be extended to *see*, since the relation here is not logical but one of unanalysable similarity.

It is not unlikely that Ryle would object to the irreducible metaphors involved in this analysis, but it seems to be a brute fact that we frequently do use metaphors (quite meaningfully) which we are not capable of reducing to non-figurative terms. Ryle himself, I suppose, would frequently be at a loss for expression if he were deprived of the numerous pictures, 'models' and similes which he uses throughout *The Concept of Mind*. There is no important difference between an irreducible metaphor and an indispensable simile.

If Sartre and Ryle are right, the language in which our psychological material has been presented by its subjects and its investigators stands in great need of revision. Yet if we try translating this language into non-objective terms, we shall soon grow dubious of the usefulness of what we do. Titchener, on hearing the word 'humility', did not have an image of a bowed back. He just attended to bowed backs in a fairly inattentive sort of way (Sartre), or else, it seemed to him that he was looking at a bowed back (Ryle). If the word 'seemed' is used in its ordinary public sense, this is sheer nonsense. If it is used in an 'inner' sense, then the whole 'inner/outer' antithesis is revived.

An interesting and useful by-product of Ryle's speculation on

[1] See *ibid.*, p. 269.
[2] See O'Connor, cited above, p. 62.

the subject of imagery was his assertion that the study of the imagination had been perverted by the model of sense-datum epistemology.[1] Ryle meant by this that it was unfortunate that people followed the model of sense-datum epistemology because it made them suppose that there must be some imaginative, objective *datum* to correspond to the sense-datum. I would rather say that while there is such a thing as a sensory field, and also as a mental image, talk about mental imagery has been vitiated by the same sort of defects as were to be found at one time in talk about sense-data. The mental image is, of course, accidental to our thinking lives, inconstant and fugitive, and not amenable to any of the usual tests of verification, public inspection and so on. As long as this is so, I suppose, there will always be philosophers who will conclude from the fact that we have no particular need for images that no one really possesses them. In fact, talk about the image as a sheer private phenomenon is likely to be even less interesting than talk about sensory fields. The model of the percept, though misleading, is better than the model of the sense-datum. We do not infer a chair by a process of conscious inference from a sense-datum; we just perceive a chair. Similarly, we do not infer an imaginary chair by a process of conscious inference from a patch of para-light in front of our (closed) eyes; we just imagine a chair. Almost any act of imagining can be said to comprise knowledge. Images are rarely, if ever, *merely* 'visual', as the image on the retina may be said to be merely visual.

It is also important to point out that an act of imagining does not necessarily imply an allusion to any one of the senses at all. I can indulge in a wish-fulfilment fantasy in which I become the world champion weight-lifter without relying exclusively on any one 'sense'. Such activity, which McKellar, following Bleuler, called 'autism' (as opposed to 'reality-adjusted thinking'), is plainly importantly different from the eidetic imaginings of a Titchener. But both are imaginings, just as the painter Constable and the botanist Linnaeus are both perceivers.

This chapter, as its heading indicates, was designed to supply a psychological basis for the mysterious thing-quality (the 'instantially viewed universal') which emerged from chapters I and II. I have argued that this entity can enjoy a logically spurious existence as long as confusion of concept and image prevails.

[1] *The Concept of Mind*, p. 255.

Grant me this confusion and I can provide in the 'non-specified image' something which can be thought of as general and at the same time envisaged as a mysterious individual; in Plato or in allegory, Pride itself is proud: in Price's psychology, the mental image Yellow is itself yellow. I have tried to strengthen this thesis by confronting two principal objections; first, the old contention that mental imagery is necessarily specific, and secondly the newer suggestion that there are no mental images, but only mental imaginings. But the biggest question of all remains to be asked, and answered. I can ask it here, but it will take another chapter to answer it. How (since mental imagery is one thing, and the public imagery of art another) are we to use what we have learned from the psychologists in our encounter with actual works of art?

IV

THE USE OF THE IMAGINATION
IN THE SIXTEENTH AND
SEVENTEENTH CENTURIES

We have to consider in this chapter how our psychological material can be used to better our understanding of public works of art. We have, up to this point, been using the phrase 'non-specific imagery' to describe mental phenomena. But in this chapter our specimens will be drawn from painting and literature. The phrase 'non-specific imagery' will work just as smoothly in the public as in the private context, but before we allow ourselves to slide from one to the other we should notice several facts.

A non-specific mental image of a face, so far as I can judge from experience, does not '*mean*' 'any face', while retaining a definite, though uninteresting physiognomy of its own; it *is* any face. But a 'non-specific' painting of a face, even when it is clearly intended to be typical rather than individual, has of necessity a perfectly definite shape. The Virgin in Cimabue's *Madonna and Child Enthroned with Angels and Prophets* may seem very far removed from the individuality of Giotto's Virgin in his *Madonna and Child Enthroned with Saints and Angels*,[1] painted about thirty years later, yet her face is just so many inches across and no more, her mouth just so far removed from her nose and no more. If it were true that no two people in the world had identical features, then it would follow that Cimabue's painting could be an accurate representation of only one individual. Cimabue's Virgin sits on a highly stylized

[1] Both pictures are reproduced in E. H. Gombrich's *Art and Illusion*, London 1960, p. 61.

throne, against a plain, gilded background, yet the throne is of a particular shape, and the 'sky' is of a particular hue which could probably occur only at sunset. But in the attempt to appraise Cimabue's painting of the sky the artificiality of the particularist approach becomes apparent. Only a man brought up exclusively on nineteenth-century painting could ever really take the gilt background for a sky at all, never mind ask what time of day it must be. In most English painting of the nineteenth century a one-one relationship holds between the painter's objects and the individual objects of real life. Of such painting it is perfectly proper to ask 'Is that the sea or the sky in the top right-hand corner?' or 'Is that an oak or an ash?' or even 'Why is that wall not in shadow?' In Cimabue's painting the Madonna is about three times as large as any of the prophets below her throne, but this does not mean that Cimabue thought the Virgin Mary was eighteen feet high; nor does it mean that he had made a mistake. But if a nineteenth-century artist paints a sheep as big as a cow he must be convicted either of ignorance or of technical incompetence.

Thus, although every item in an old picture will have a particular shape and colour, we cannot interrogate it as though it were a photograph. The objects in such paintings do not stand in a one-one relation to the objects of everyday life. Thus many questions which are significant in the context of nineteenth-century art become meaningless in the context of earlier art. The question 'Why does the Virgin's throne cast no shadow?' will not be answered by a statement of the form: 'Because the sun is not shining and the light is diffused', but rather by a statement of the form: 'Because it is not that sort of picture.' Part of the process of learning to look at pictures of an earlier age consists in un-learning the conventions of one's own time, and in particular the convention of the one-one relationship whereby the representations of painters are more and more closely assimilated to the visual field. Thus one ceases to marvel at the fact that Cimabue apparently thought that the prophets were a set of identical quadruplets, and begins to realize that the faces of the prophets are not faces of individuals at all; they are old-men-and-nothing-else.

It is true that a sort of individuation is carried out in medieval painting, but it is different in kind from the individuation of Victorian representative art. St. Peter is given a key so that you will know he is St. Peter, but no attempt is made to reproduce the historical individual St. Peter as he would actually have appeared in the visual field of someone living in the first century A.D. The pre-Raphaelites frequently tried to do just this, but that was just one of the many ways in which they differed from the painters who lived before Raphael. The medieval artist gives an apparatus of signs sufficient to enable the identification of any individuals who are important enough to be worth identifying. The rest is left schematic. But the nineteenth-century painter endeavoured to paint exactly what he saw. Since our sense of sight shows us objects in great detail, nineteenth-century painting shows us highly individuated objects; it simply follows from the convention of reproducing the visual field. It is true that perceptual glimpses can be quite as non-specified as images. The question[1] 'How many speckles were there on that glimpse you had of a speckled hen a moment ago?' (answer, 'More than ten and less than two thousand') is very like the question 'Just what shape was that non-specified image you had just then?' But there are no *candidates* for individuation in a Victorian painting, since the question has already been settled out of court. If the eye could distinguish an object, the painter must do likewise. There is no other law. The result is that the medieval painter is sometimes able to make more elaborate distinctions than the later painter. For example, Fra Angelico in depicting the Company of Heaven is able to give us a clear view of every face, whereas a John Martin would be compelled to treat the subject as a realistic crowd-scene in which some faces would be obscured by others.

Thus, where the medieval artist individuates, he tends to put his trust in signs, rather than in the simple appearance of the object itself. His art just has not attained to that state of sophistication in which appearances are rendered with anything like sufficient fidelity to secure individuation. For the so-called 'innocent eye' type of painting, the transposition of the visual field on to canvas belongs not to the first stages of art but to the last. Gombrich puts the transition epigrammatically when he says that the Egyptians painted what they knew and the Impressionists what they saw.[2]

But when a primitive artist fails to produce the individual appearance of an object, he may or may not be working in a consciously schematic manner. For it is quite possible that the

---

[1] See R. Chisholm, 'The Problem of the Speckled Hen', *Mind* LI (1942), pp. 368–73.

[2] *Art and Illusion*, p. ix.

whole process of representing is prior to the scheme of general and particular. The paintings of Giotto, though more lifelike than Cimabue's, seem very schematic and stylized to our eyes. Yet to Boccaccio[1] and his contemporaries they were so realistic as to produce the illusion of sense-perception. That is why when we wish to guess from the depiction of light in Cimabue's painting what hour of the day is intended, and find that it is very difficult to tell, we would be wise to drop the question altogether, since, despite the fact that every object in the picture has a definite hue, the questions of light and time of day simply have not arisen *at all*. Similarly, one feels that the difference between a stylized Byzantine head and an idealized figure from eighteenth-century sculpture lies partly in the fact that the Byzantine artist simply has not raised questions which the later artist has settled by a process of conscious normalization. The Byzantine *schema* is just 'the way to draw a face'; the eighteenth-century *schema* is 'the norm of all beautiful faces', 'the ideal physiognomy'.

Where art is 'naturally' schematic, that is, when the schematic character becomes apparent when viewed from a standpoint of increased sophistication, its condition is very close to that of the 'non-specified' imagery we discussed in the last chapter. The fact that a picture's being a public, material object necessitates its having complete particularity of hue, line, shape, etc., turns out to be utterly irrelevant to any understanding of it *as a picture* (as opposed to understanding it as a piece of coloured canvas). So the necessary particularity of the material object puts no sort of inevitable distance between the public work of art and the 'non-specified' character of a man's private imagery. Painting can share with imagery that character of being prior to the scheme of general and particular.

A similar account might be given of individuation in literary works of art. For example, an objector might point out that the dialogue given to dramatic characters consists of certain particular expressions and no others, and that therefore it is nonsense to talk of 'non-specified' characters (who are, after all, built up from their dialogue). But this approach will lead us to class Shakespeare's Ferdinand or Beaumont and Fletcher's Philaster as cliché-ridden stick-in-the-muds with no ideas of their own, whereas in fact they belong to that region of artistic creation where such questions are not raised. To talk so of such characters is like saying that all the

[1] *ibid.*, p. 61.

figures in Byzantine art are shown against curiously repetitious sunset skies.

But one difference between works of art and mental images is that works of art are open to public inspection. This makes it easier for the 'natural' *schemata* of the painter to be *used* in an iconic manner. Where a face is not any particular face but just 'Face' the schema can easily be given a general significance. Hence *schemata* evolved in a region prior to the structure of general and particular, when incorporated into that structure, will very easily assume a *general* significance. Thus if the artist cannot keep ahead of the sophistication of his public in his production of lifelike representations, the public will transform him into a maker of symbols. Yet he will always be able to say to them, 'I did not frame these symbols, I found them in my heart; these generalities were once individuals in my own soul.'

Thus where art is highly stylized, as in the religious cultures of Egypt or Byzantium – where there is one way to draw a face and the artist is expected to stick to it – a complex apparatus of symbols might be expected to result. And so it does.

The visual art of Elizabethan England was a strange mingling of the schematic and the symbolic with the realistic. Holbein had taught the English portrait-painters to set an unnervingly lifelike head on a richly stylized body. When we look at the face in his portrait of Henry VIII, we are confronted with the man himself; but from the neck down Regality prevails. This method is well exemplified by Isaac Oliver's drawing[1] of Queen Elizabeth. Nicholas Hilliard's design[2] for Queen Elizabeth's Great Seal of Ireland is still more emblematic in character, though some allusion is made to the Queen's actual physiognomy.

There was in those days a greater profusion of basic iconic symbols everywhere than there is today, for a very simple reason. The growth of literacy has led to the gradual usurpation by writing of the function of symbolic images. Thus the iconography of the sixteenth century is not exhausted by heraldry and literary emblems, but extends to the ordinary world of buying and selling, with its pied poles, mortars and pestles and inn signs.

The world of visual arts was, save at its most sophisticated levels, utterly dominated by the schematic and the symbolic. The

[1] Reproduced in John Woodward, *Tudor and Stuart Drawings*, London 1951, plate 7.
[2] *ibid.*, plate 5.

sense of the actual was little cultivated and standards were low. C. S. Lewis observes[1] that the bee on the title-page of Thomas Cutwood's *Caltha Poetarum* (1599) has only four legs and that some of the horses in the plates to Harington's Ariosto have human eyebrows. Literary equivalents are easily discovered. Spenser in his *Shepheardes Calender* speaks of daffodils blooming in summer.[2] For some things he may indeed have been 'a better teacher than Scotus or Aquinas', but he will never be as good a botanist as Tennyson. Again, at the beginning of the *Faerie Queene*,[3] Spenser describes for us a rather curious scene. A noble knight, ardent for valorous deeds, is spurring his 'angry steede', across a plain. Beside him, mounted upon a white ass, rides a lady, who leads by a line a 'milke white lambe'. To complete the group

> Behind her farre away a Dwarfe did lag,
> That lasie seemd in being euer last . . .

The difficulty about this group is, how on earth do they keep together? How is a lowly ass to keep pace with an 'angry steede' (and how much less a lamb, or a lazy, lagging dwarf)? To ask this question is rather like asking what time of day is intended in a Cimabue painting, or why the life-giving streams which issue from the breasts of *Alma Cantabrigia* in the Cambridge University Press emblem do not splash over the sides of her pedestal. Spenser's scene partakes of the emblematic just far enough to be lifted out of the account of the actual. As the Form of the Transient is eternally transient-and-nothing-else, so the dwarf is eternally lagging yet never left behind. It is possible that Spenser would have altered this passage if the absurdity had been pointed out to him. But it would be much less obtrusive to Elizabethan eyes than it is to ours. Indeed, compared with the glaring absurdities of older allegory, such as Prudentius's *Psychomachia*, Spenser seems to have made very modest use of allegorist's licence.

The gradual emergence in the seventeenth century of art which apes the percept is extremely interesting. In the paintings of Lely, Huysmans, Greenhill, Kneller and Hoskins an almost brutal real-

---

[1] *English Literature in the Sixteenth Century excluding Drama*, Oxford 1954, p. 322 n.

[2] *The Shepheardes Calender, January* 22, in *The Works of Edmund Spenser*, Variorum Edition, ed. E. Greenlaw, C. G. Osgood and F. M. Padelford, Baltimore 1932–58, vol. I of the *Minor Poems*, p. 16.

[3] *The Faerie Queene*, Book I, Canto i, Stanzas 1–6, in the Variorum Edition, Book I, pp. 5–6.

ism makes its appearance. The human face, as might be supposed, is the first to receive this treatment. Pink, scrubbed, un-ideal faces stare at us out of the magical world of enchanted darkness and gardens with all the shock of instantaneous perception. The eighteenth century seems to be looking at us out of the seventeenth.

The growth of this sort of realism is destructive not only of schematic art but also of the schematic way of looking at the phenomenal world. Sometimes the effect of the new realism would be simply the supplying of a deficiency. For example, I do not suppose that the illustrator of Harington's Ariosto thought that horses had human eyebrows. He just was not very clear what horses' eyebrows were like. At other times it might serve to inhibit the positive effects of an apparatus of schematic symbols. For there is a sort of perceptual back-formation in which the symbol reacts upon the percept. As Chapman put it in 1598,

> as you beholde
> Sometimes within the Sunne a face of golde,
> Form'd in strong thoughts, by that traditions force,
> That saies a God sits there and guides his course.[1]

there seems to be an interpretative element in all perception – the element sometimes referred to by psychologists as 'configuration' – which is subject to influences from various quarters. William Blake says a wise man and a fool see not the same tree. We might add that a subject of the first Queen Elizabeth is not at all likely to see the same tree as a subject of the second Queen Elizabeth. The former is likely to see a 'Royal Oak' where the latter will probably see an 'ordinary-looking deciduous tree, perhaps an oak'. I would guess, though I am not sure, that the mental imagery of our two men would show the same difference in a much more marked degree.

All this suggests that the distinction between 'the frigid abstraction' and the warm 'sensuous individual' was not so strong in the sixteenth and seventeenth century as one might suppose. The image glimmers into the symbol and the myth into the percept. Thus the constant appearance of the deliberate 'category mistake' in the literature of the time is scarcely surprising.

A good example of this sort of category-crossing can be found

---

[1] George Chapman's Continuation of Marlowe's *Hero and Leander*, the Sixt Sestyad, 157–60, in *The Works of Christopher Marlowe*, ed. C. F. Tucker-Brooke, Oxford 1910, p. 546.

in Bale's *King Johan*,[1] a curious play which was probably put together and revised between the years 1536 and 1561. In it we find historical characters, like King John and Cardinal Pandulf, conversing with 'abstractions', like Sedition and Dissimulation. This indeed is no very startling innovation. Even in as 'pure' an allegory as the *Roman de la Rose* the figure of the lover himself must be taken for a concrete individual moving among and encountering 'abstractions', and in the play of *Everyman* the protagonist, though a type, is not an instantialized quality, but rather just 'any man'. But in both these cases the 'internal' cast of the story is tolerably well preserved. The concrete protagonist can fairly easily be viewed as an *ego* subduing the passions and so on. After all, we do not only say 'My anger overcame my clemency', but also 'My anger overcame *me*'.

But it is very difficult to think of Bale's King Johan as an hypostatized ego. Even the 'abstractions' in the play dwell outside his soul. If the allegory is to rank as a *psychomachia* at all, the *psyche* in question must be that of the body politic rather that that of the king. The relation of the widow 'Englande' to 'syvyll order' and 'Sedysyon' is almost as puzzling as the relation of the Cardinal to 'Treason'. But, not content with crowding his stage with as heterogenous a set of entities as could well be conceived, Bale proceeds to confound confusion by doubling them off with one another. The editor is hard put to it to decide at times whether a mere theatrical doubling of parts is intended or whether a dramatic identification of an abstract character with a concrete. A clear example of the former is the doubling of the parts of England and Clergy where a real identification is out of the question. But Dissimulation, on his last appearance, is certainly identified with Simon of Swynsett, for he preserves his name Dissimulation as a speaker. It looks as if the Pope is identified with Usurped Power, and Nobility is identified with Private Wealth, who is in turn identified with Cardinal Pandulphus. In allegory, all things are possible.

Bale's extraordinary fluidity between abstract and concrete is that natural consequence of his conceptual apparatus. The very antithesis is clearly much less prominent in his consciousness than it is in ours. The same is true, in a less marked degree, of older authors. For example, in *Everyman* the character Good Fellowship could be renamed Good Fellow without violence. Spenser's St.

---

[1] The play is printed in the Malone Society Reprints series (1931), ed. J. H. P. Pafford under the supervision of W. W. Greg.

George is sometimes Holiness, but at other times – as, for example, when he undergoes purgation – he is undoubtedly the Holy Man. But the startling thing about *King Johan* is the way in which the whole machinery of allegory finds itself working in a particular place and at a particular time. Such, perhaps, was the peculiar genius of the sixteenth century: to see the ideal not as separated from the here-and-now but as interpenetrating it, where 'interpenetrate' was given full imaginative force. It has been said that whereas the Jews set their ideal world far off in time, at the Millenium, the Greeks removed theirs in space. But Edmund Spenser's Fairyland was England itself. Queen Elizabeth – Belphoebe – Gloriana, this escalation is not so much a succession of different symbolic meanings given to an individual as a sequence in which one configuration brightens into the next. The *Mutabilitie Cantos* are thronged with figures, divine, mythical and allegorical, but they all move in the 'sweet especial rural scene' of Arlo-hill in Ireland. Langland and Bunyan tell us that their poems are dreams, but Spenser was wide awake. The England of Michael Drayton's *Polyolbion*, stuffed with items of topographical interest and crammed with river nymphs and dragons, differs from Spenser's fairyland in degree rather than in kind.

In the world of Bale and Spenser the application of the word 'is' is greatly enlarged. Una is truth, Fairyland is England, Justice is Lord Grey, Elizabeth is Gloriana, 'King Johan' is King John, Pandulf is Nobility. The sense of 'is' in these assertions is a little stronger than might be supposed. The linguistic idiom which allows us to say 'He is hypocrisy itself' is given full imaginative indulgence.

Bale is never concerned to press the distinction between abstract and concrete or to make artistic use of it. In this respect he differs from Chaucer, who, in *The Pardoner's Tale*, for example, leads his reader on by allegorical language to expect a combat between the young men and the wicked thief Death, and ends his story with the actual death of the young men – so that Death defeated them after all. Chaucer jostles his allegorical with non-allegorical figures in order to produce a peculiar and powerful effect. The cast of Bale's play is, in comparison, an aimless aggregate.

The fallacy we must guard against in considering the literature of Elizabeth and Jacobean England is that of making the realm of the sensuously imaginative exactly coextensive with the realm of the actual and particular, and so concluding that the poetry of those days is a very non-sensuous body of material. The tacit assumption that only those images which are highly specific can have any sensuous vividness pervades the work which Rosemond Tuve has done on this subject.[1] But the critic who assumes that the scene at the beginning of the *Faerie Queene* owes nothing to the private imagination just because it flouts the laws of the public world is on very shaky ground. His error is not unlike the error of the critic who finds in medieval allegory a tissue of 'mere abstractions'. We need not assume that, because we in the twentieth century have grown disinclined to indulge our imaginations in any aberration from the individuational structure of the object, men were always so inhibited. We have seen in the last chapter that there is no necessary one-one correspondence between the object and the image, but that, on the contrary, the reverse is far more likely to be the case. The woodcuts in the 1579 edition of Spenser's *The Shepheardes Calender* may be botanically slovenly and technically inept, yet they are vigorous drawings and sometimes convey a real sense of weather and seasonal mood. The artist who depicts the sun with a broad anthropomorphic smile is not necessarily an enemy to the sensuously vivid apprehension of the sun itself.

The modern impulse to confine imagery within the bounds of perception is most clearly exemplified by the twentieth-century reaction to the poetry of the metaphysicals, a movement which was well begun before Shakespeare left off writing plays. It is commonly maintained that the intricate argument and ostentatious subtlety of these poets is exclusive of sensuousness, but that assertion, though dubious, is not our quarry here. What we must concentrate on is rather the second claim which often follows close upon the first, that the grotesque collocations of objects favoured by these poets are completely incompatible with any sensuously vivid imagining of those objects. The poetry of the Metaphysicals, it is maintained, is the poetry of men without sensuality. Only an utterly cerebral poet could write lines like

. . . My tongue shall bee my Penne, mine eyes shall raine Teares for my Inke . . .[2]

Of course, if we imagine what it would *really* be like to write with

[1] See especially her *Elizabethan and Metaphysical Imagery*, Chicago 1947, Chapter V, 'The Criterion of Sensuous Vividness', pp. 79–116.

[2] William Alabaster, 'Upon the Ensignes of Christes Crucifyinge', the first of a set of sonnets on the symbols of the Passion, lines 5–6, in *The Metaphysical Poets*, selected and ed. Helen Gardner 1960 (first published Harmondsworth 1957), p. 12.

our tongues, or to weep ink from our eyes, we shall recoil from the image. Similarly, if we imagine what it would *really* be like if our beloved had pearls for teeth, we shall not find the picture edifying. But, in fact, there is no need to use this disenchanting capacity of our imaginations at all. Take these lines from an early metaphysical poem, Sir Walter Raleigh's 'The Passionate Man's Pilgrimage, supposed to be written by one at the point of death':

> Blood must be my bodies balmer,
> No other balme will there be given
> Whilst my soule like a white Palmer
> Travels to the land of heaven,
> Over the silver mountaines,
> Where spring the Nectar fountaines:
> And there Ile kisse,
> The Bowle of blisse,
> And drinke my eternal fill
> On every milken hill.
> My soule will be a drie before,
> But after, it will nere thirst more.[1]

The idea of blood used as a balm for wounds is uncongenial to the actualizing imagination. Yet if we encountered these expressions in a modern theological work, we should all say at once that the sentiments were expressed in a curiously image-ridden way. The truth is that the vividness of imagery is not in exact proportion to its 'probability' at all. When Marlowe's Faustus cries out

> See see where Christs blood streams in the firmament[2]

the very unlikeliness of the image contributes to its excitement. And the excitement is quite as much imaginative as it is conceptual. One function of bizarre imagery like Crashaw's is, as it were, to stretch the imagination until it surprises itself. 'Category crossing' is frequent in such poetry, as also is violent association of the very great with the very small. A good example of the first is to be found in Donne's Satyres in the brilliant lines (curiously omitted by Pope from his 'versification' of the work):

---

[1] Lines 7–18, in Gardner, *The Metaphysical Poets*, p. 1.
[2] *Doctor Faustus*, l. 1432, in *The Works of Christopher Marlowe*, ed. C. F. Tucker-Brooke, p. 192.

> words, words which would teare
> The tender labyrinth of a soft maids eare[1]

and the second characteristic, the linking of the immense and the minute, appears wonderfully in these lines of Crashaw:

> Heavens thy fair eyes be:
> Heavens of ever-falling starres.[2]

The epithet 'ever-falling' belongs with the examples of motion contemplated in 'eternity' which we considered towards the end of our second chapter.[3] The effect of the lines is to precipitate the reader into a state of wonder. The sweet shock which they give to the imagination, so far from indicating that they are not intended for the imagination at all, is the very essence of their poetry.

I am not sure, however, that this explanation always holds good for the greatest metaphysical poets. But in entertaining this doubt I am far from conceding their sensuousness. For there are places in Donne, and in Crashaw, where I am disposed to think that the one reading which appeared to be out of court is, in fact, the right one. The actualizing imagination, which makes the reading of these poems so strangely shocking may, on occasion, be the proper faculty to use. In a fashion at once rapacious and enigmatic, Crashaw's 'Adoro Te' and Donne's 'The Extasie' seem to invite imaginative actualization. Take these lines of Crashaw:

> O soft self-wounding Pelican!
> Whose brest weepes Balm for wounded man.
> Ah this way bend thy benign floud
> To 'a bleeding Heart that gapes for blood.
> That blood, whose least drops soveraign be
> To wash my worlds of sins from me!

Now, it might be said that if we imagine what it would *really* be like for a pelican to turn a jet of blood on us, and wash whole worlds of sin out of us, we shall recoil from the image. Perhaps we shall. Yet I cannot help feeling that the recoil was foreseen, and in a way intended, by the poet. Not, of course, that he meant us to throw the poem away in disgust. He wrote for men with (so to speak) stronger spiritual stomachs than that. What is needed is

---

[1] Satyre II, ll. 57–58, in *The Poems of John Donne*, ed. H. J. C. Grierson, London 1912.

[2] *Sainte Mary Magdalene, or The Weeper*, ll. 7 ff., in Martin's 2nd ed., p. 308.

[3] See above, pp. 43–45.

a recoil which is felt only momentarily before being swallowed up in a generous acceptance of what is happening. The phenomenon can be paralleled in sexual experience. Notice, incidentally, that if we press the sexual analogy we shall find that the comparable form of sexuality is female rather than male, as often in powerful metaphysical poetry which is not overtly erotic in its subject-matter. Think, for example, of Donne's 'Batter my heart' and Marvell's 'The Garden'. Perhaps the most indigestible lines in the whole of Crashaw are to be found in his *Sainte Mary Magdalene*:

> He's follow'd by two faithfull fountaines
> Two walking baths; two weeping motions;
> Portable and compendious oceans.[1]

The phrase 'Portable and compendious oceans' is, I suppose, lost beyond recovery, partly because the words have been degraded by ill usage. But even when all that is adventitious in our distaste has been cleared away, there remains much that is hard to take. Certainly, we shall not find our way to an understanding of this sort of poetry by repressing our imagination. I used to think that the best way to approach it was by way of similar, but somehow more acceptable lines, like Marvell's

> So *Magdalen* in Tears more wise
> Dissolv'd those captivating Eyes,
> Whose liquid Chaines could flowing meet
> To fetter her Redeemers feet[2]

or Lovelace's

> When I lye tangled in her haire,
> And fettered to her eye . . .[3]

Here indeed we have poetry which is imaginatively rich and yet resists the actualizing imagination. Yet we read it without discomfort. The conventions of another age are perhaps more accessible than we think. The poetry soon draws our sensibility into the right channels. But the shock contained in Crashaw's lines survives any such education of the sensibility. The same is true of this from the opening of Donne's 'The Extasie' (ll. 7 to 8):

[1] In Martin's 2nd ed., p. 312.

[2] 'Eyes and Tears' stanza VIII, in *The Poems and Letters of Andrew Marvell,* ed. H. M. Margoliouth, Oxford 1952, vol. I, p. 15.

[3] From 'To *Althea, from Prison'* in *The Poems of Richard Lovelace,* ed. G. H. Wilkinson 1930, reprinted with corrections, Oxford 1953, p. 78.

> . . . Our eye-beames twisted, and did thred
> Our eyes, upon one double string . . .[1]

To approach Donne by way of Lovelace should not result in our reading Donne as if he were Lovelace. For, in fact, Donne is a very different matter. The thought of eyeballs threaded upon a string is one from which the actualizing imagination recoils. But here we are forced to acknowledge that the shock is *there* in the poem; that the recoil is *intended*, that the image is all pain and intensity, expressing with a new kind of sublimity the extreme – one might almost say the skinless – mutual awareness of the lovers.[2] The visual arts had to wait three hundred years for the introduction, by Picasso, of a comparable imaginative violence.

Such a reading of Donne is interestingly corroborated by the findings which Louis L. Martz published in his *The Poetry of Meditation*.[3] Martz showed that the years 1550 to 1610 saw the introduction into England of a new system of spiritual discipline, a system which involved, fascinatingly, a special *discipline of the imagination*. The later Elizabethans and the Jacobeans, unencumbered by that distaste for the unspontaneous which marks the moral life of our own age, deliberately set about the task of *inducing* in themselves a vivid awareness of, e.g., the Passion, by a careful evocation before the mind's eye of each detail of the scene at Calvary. This practice of *compositio loci* or 'composition of place, seeing the spot' is curiously illuminating in a consideration of Donne's peculiar imagination. Saint Ignatius in his *Spiritual Exercises* recommended that 'in contemplation or meditation on visible matters, such as the contemplation of Christ our Lord, Who is visible, the composition will be to see with the eyes of the imagination the corporeal place where the thing I wish to contemplate is found'.[4]

Martz also quotes an extremely interesting passage from the English Jesuit Richard Gibbons:

[We must see] the places where the things we meditate on were

---

[1] *The Poems of John Donne*, vol. I, p. 51.

[2] It will be apparent that I read 'The Extasie' as a serious love-poem. Of other poems in the same convention Lord Herbert's 'Ode upon a Question moved, whether Love should continue for ever' is nearer to it than is Wither's Sonnet 3 of *Fair Virtue*. See George Williamson, 'The Convention of *The Extasie*', first printed in his *Seventeenth Century Contexts*, Chicago 1960, reprinted in *Seventeenth Century English Poetry*, ed. W. R. Keast, New York 1962.

[3] Newhaven, Conn. 1962.

[4] Quoted in Martz, *op. cit.*, p. 27.

wrought, by imagining ourselves to be really present at those places; which we must endeavour to represent so lively, as though we saw them indeed, with our corporall eyes; which to performe well, it will help us much to behould before-hande some Image wherein that mistery is well represented, and to have read or heard what good Authors write of those places, and to have noted well the distance from one place to another and the height of the hills, and the situation of the townes and villages.[1]

How different is Gibbons from those printers of an earlier age who would use the same woodcut, indifferently, to represent Damascus or Rome. The handbooks taught that a man should train his imagination as an athlete trains his body. It is natural that such a system should produce certain champions, gymnasts of the imagination, whose powers should spill over into their poetry. I have mentioned the modern distaste for the unspontaneous. Certainly the artificiality of this forced training has left its mark on the best metaphysical poetry, at once brilliant and freakishly over-developed. Yet those same twentieth-century readers who feel the keenest moral distaste for the spiritual method are usually the most delighted by the poetic result.

Yet this professionally conditioned imaginative faculty was successfully joined to poetic composition by only a few of the metaphysicals and, by them, in few poems. The phenomenon was limited in extent and proved short-lived in time. Although almost every kind of poetry can be found somewhere in the works of Shakespeare, I can find in him no instance of this quasi-surrealist technique. The groundbass of metaphysical poetry continued well into the seventeenth century with imagery which has little to do with the actualizing intelligence, an imagery richly and potently unspecified. In 1624 Bishop Henry King's wife Anne died, after seven years of marriage. He wrote for her the magnificent *Exequy*, which abounds with imagery which it is impossible to actualize. For example:

> By the cleer Sun,
> My life and fortune first did run;
> But thou wilt never more appear
> Folded within my Hemisphear.[2]

---

[1] *ibid.*, p. 27.
[2] Henry King 'The Exequy, To his Matchlesse never to be forgotten Freind', pp. 29–32, in Gardner, *The Metaphysical Poets*, p. 81.

Here there can be no question of an intentionally harsh *seeing* of Bishop King's body in a celestial form. The reader is expected to understand the astronomy, to respond to the high mystery of the heavens joined as it is with the human intimacy of 'folded within', but there is no invitation to press further. The logical basis of the metaphor is adequate; and the images pass in a rich consecutiveness which is never forced into discordant simultaneity.

So from the critic who thinks that all sensuous vividness or imaginative 'density' is automatically excluded from any passage which turns grotesque if viewed in the cold light of the 'actualizing imagination', I must cautiously dissent. Not every age has felt obliged to correct its imagery by the standards of its percepts. In the sixteenth and seventeenth centuries the antithesis between the two was strong, and their poetry is, for the most part, emphatically of the image rather than of the percept.

It might be objected that, while I have shown that a thing can be vividly imaginative in character and at the same time quite unrealistic, I have not shown that such independent images share with more realistic images the quality of sensuousness. In fact, there seems to be little doubt that almost anything which can be imagined can be imagined sensuously, simply because of the 'parasensuous' character of the imagination. Erotic or pornographic drawing is frequently highly schematic in character, yet it is perhaps the clearest case there is of sensuous art. If we must find a probability test for the bizarre imagery of seventeenth-century poetry, let us ask, not 'What would it be like to see this happening in actual fact?' but rather 'What would it be like to *dream* this?'

I have used metaphysical poems as examples of the inward imagination because the authors of them made it their business to exploit the faculty which their predecessors had merely used as a matter of course. Thus, in the Metaphysicals, the peculiar character of inward imagining, so far from requiring any subtle discernment on the part of the reader, rather forces itself upon his attention. But if anyone should doubt whether imagery of the same basic type is to be found in earlier writers, let him try what his actualizing imagination can do with the following specimens (all from Shakespeare):

> I'll be a park, and thou shalt be my deer;
> Feed where thou wilt, on mountain or in dale:

Graze on my lips, and if those hills be dry,
Stray lower, where the pleasant fountains lie.

Venus and Adonis, 231–4

In winter with warm tears I'll melt the snow

Titus Andronicus, iii. i. 20

. . . their thundering shock
At meeting tears the cloudy cheeks of heaven.

Richard the Second, iii. iii. 56–57

Will all great Neptune's ocean wash this blood
Clean from my hand?

Macbeth, ii. ii. 61–62

. . . her eyes
Became two spouts . . .

The Winter's Tale, iii. iii. 24–25

The fringed curtains of thine eye advance . . .

The Tempest, i. ii. 405

As for 'category-crossings', it is well known that Shakespeare abounds in them.

I suggest, then, that the poets of the sixteenth and seventeenth centuries owed allegiance more to their imagery than to their percepts. The poems, drawings and paintings of that age imply a rich commerce between inward imagining and outward expression, achieved, perhaps, at the cost of a certain neglect of careful, public observation. Such a thesis might be held to be irremediably speculative, yet a sort of confirmation is available from an unsuspected source. The Ignatian spiritual exercises were not the only imaginative discipline current. There was also the much more ancient, more pervasively influential art of memory.

The student of this formal and elaborate art carries in his head images of complex buildings, temples, cathedrals or theatres, through which he passes in a sort of imaginative progress, following always the same route. This improbable apparatus of inner 'places' has, it is claimed, a very practical purpose. Let us suppose that our student is an orator, wishing to memorize a speech, anxious that he should develop his arguments and exhortations in their proper order. He will go through his speech and will form, for each section of it, a vividly evocative image. These images he will place in due order on the successive *loci* of his memory-building. Thus as he moves through his vast imaginary theatre he will encounter in the gateway an anchor with a broken chain, and this will cause him to open his speech with an allusion to naval questions; on passing through the gate he will see, on the great column by the entrance, the figure of a weeping woman, and this will cause him to turn in his speech to the case of the widowed plaintiff; and so on. The same memory-building can be used repeatedly, the 'imposed' images being erased much as recordings are erased from the tape in a tape-recorder. The account I have given is of the art of memory in its most basic form. The history of the art, from its origins among the Greek and Latin orators, through its various transformations, Medieval, Neoplatonic, Renascence, to its defeat by the printed book, has been admirably set out by Frances Yates.[1] Her work strongly suggests that when we read Elizabethan literature we are again and again faced with a close and intricate association of abstract and concrete which stems from an ancient tradition of mental training. For such a mental habit as the art of memory induces, the connexion between thought and image will be immediate. Thus even in the age of scholasticism, with its low estimate of the artistic imagination, we find irrepressibly imaginative art flourishing in Europe. Dr. Yates has in some degree accounted for this phenomenon. She tentatively suggests that the analogy which Panofsky perceived between the structure of a scholastic *summa* and the architecture of a great Gothic cathedral may be more than just an analogy – for 'if Thomas Aquinas memorized his own *Summa* through "corporeal similitudes" disposed on places following the order of its parts, the abstract *Summa* might be corporealized in memory into something like a Gothic cathedral full of images on its ordered places'.[2]

It is important to note that the art of memory is not, like the Ignatian method, an art of meticulous actualization. The images it employs are primarily iconic; that is to say they are tied not so much to the proliferating detail of the visual field as to the requirements of the conceiving mind. Yet if they are to serve their purpose at all they must be vivid. Once more we are made to feel the inappropriateness of that modern prejudice which automatically excludes 'sensuous vividness' from obviously 'conceptual'

[1] In her *The Art of Memory*, London 1966.
[2] *ibid.*, p. 79.

imagery. Indeed, one has only to turn to those works in which the art of memory is most plainly evident to perceive its irrelevance. Dr. Yates refers[1] to Andrea da Firenze's fresco showing the wisdom of Saint Thomas in the Chapter House of Santa Maria Novella, with its lucid structure of saints and doctors against an indeterminate background, and later offers,[2] as the supreme example of the translation into public form of memoranda-images, Giotto's frescoes of the virtues and vices in the Arena Capella at Padua. The contemplation of such pictures induces in me a Platonic frame of mind, which I trace to the paradoxical fact that they are so mysteriously perspicuous. The twentieth-century man, brought up among pictures which accommodate their scope to the mere flux of sense-perception, among photographs and magazine illustrations crowded with visual accidents, is surprised by a world of severely intelligible forms. Of course, modern painters frequently feel called upon to abandon this petrifying art of surface realism. But it seldom occurs to them that their reaction might take the form of a greater lucidity. The artist who has confined himself in the skull of a man facing due south at 4.29 p.m. on the sixth of January at a given latitude and longitude is obviously going to produce a work of art which is, in one sense of the word, highly subjective.

The train of thought I have just set out is, no doubt, strewn with philosophical mistakes and oversights. Nevertheless it is, psychologically, a *possible* train of thought. It is just another way in which the Platonizing mind can find itself moving insensibly from mental imagery to Ideas. It is perhaps worth noticing that the evolution of the art of memory follows, in this respect, a predictable course. The purely mnemotechnical images of the ancient orators became, in the hands of the Neoplatonists, the shadows of those real Ideas which lie beyond the fluctuating surface of the sensory world. Just as Plotinus changed the status of the artist by making him not the imitator of an imitation but the seer of first principles, so the Neoplatonists of the Renascence exalted the banausic images of their predecessors.[3]

In my last chapter I referred to the astounding case of Mr. Flinders Petrie, who performed arithmetical calculations by consulting an imaginary sliding rule. The question was whether this

[1] *ibid.*, pp. 79–81.
[2] *ibid.*, pp. 92–94.
[3] *ibid.*, p. 37.

anecdote embarrasses the Sartrean who holds that we never learn from our imagery. It appears that the Middle Ages and the Renascence could furnish hundreds of analogues to Mr. Flinders Petrie. The students of the old art of memory, though they need not have possessed the faculty of eidetic imagination, nevertheless consulted their imagery, and, in one sense, used it as a source of information. They interrogated their images as we interrogate our percepts.

There is some evidence that in the evolution of representational drawing a shift from image to percept is normal. Francis Galton found that for the primitive Bushmen of South Africa drawing was a process of copying their quasi-eidetic imagery on to a slate,[1] but that various Royal Academicians of his own day confessed themselves to be entirely deficient in the power of seeing mental pictures.[2] Presumably the painter who works from a real model becomes adept in repressing his private imagery.

But to say that our older poets followed their imagery rather than their percepts might be taken to imply that their art was of a highly subjective sort. This was not at all the case. For centuries the sort of imagery which would today be the private and neglected property of the subject had attained full publicity in art and ritual. Since the seventeenth century there has been an immense withdrawal from all the public forms which had been built up to express the 'non-economic' aspects of our lives. Today our imagery is indeed very idiosyncratic and lacking in symbolic force; our language would be the same if we refused to speak to anyone else, or refused to modify our expressions in the interests of intelligibility. I cannot, of course, hope to verify any statement I may make about the 'internal' mental imagery of any Englishman living three hundred and sixty years ago. But I would guess that mental imagery both acted upon the public apparatus of images and was acted upon by it. The vast Elizabethan apparatus of skulls and lilies, orbs and sceptres, royal oaks and funeral cypresses may seem to bear little relation to the sort of imagery elicited by psychologists from twentieth-century man, yet the literary Elizabethan may well have carried them about with him as part of his ordinary stock of mental pictures.

When we say that art has more of the character of mental imagery than of perception it is not entirely clear what we mean.

[1] *Inquiries into Human Faculty*, pp. 70–72.
[2] *ibid.*, p. 61.

Do we mean that such art necessarily *copies* mental imagery? E. H. Gombrich in *Art and Illusion* vigorously opposed any such notion. He alleged that Loewy's theory that the primitive artist worked from 'non-specified' mental imagery was circular –

> . . . since the primitive artist obviously does not copy the outside world, he is believed to copy some invisible inside world of mental images. For these mental images, in their turn, however, the typical pictures of primitives are the only evidence. None of us, I believe, carries in his head such schematic pictures of bodies, horses or lizards as Loewy's theory postulates.[1]

We saw enough in our last chapter to know that Gombrich's argument here rests on a factual error. The charge of circularity holds only if the drawings of primitive artists are the only evidence for schematic imagery. But this (as we have seen) is not the case. However, the fact that people do have schematic imagery does not prove that schematic drawings are necessarily copies of such imagery. Gombrich argues later in his book[2] that when we are making a snowman we are not matching our product with any image; we simply pile up snow until we recognize a man, until the minimum definition of man is satisfied.

It is, in fact, fairly easy to find examples of artists who transcribe their imagery. The evidence is strong in favour of Galton's Bushman being such an artist. Both Galton[3] and McKellar[4] classify Blake in this way. McKellar adds that Paul Klee asserts quite explicitly that he draws his source material from '*introspective observation*'.[5] But these are clearly exceptional cases. So far from showing that all public image-making involves copying, they rather imply that it normally does not. The truth seems to be that private imagining and public image-making are commonly not consecutive activities, but are rather analogous to one another. Just as we may hum a tune in our heads or allow ourselves to hum it aloud, so we may build up a complex mental picture of a castle in our imagination or we may draw it on a piece of paper. No doubt the castle a man draws will differ from the castle he would have imagined, and vice versa, but to notice this is only to distinguish the influence of the medium. Thus, when I suggest that

[1] *op. cit.*, p. 23.
[2] *ibid.*, pp. 98 ff.
[3] *Inquiries into Human Faculty*, p. 66.
[4] *Imagination and Thinking*, p. 135.
[5] *ibid.*, p. 135.

the Elizabethan's private imagery would show some conformity with his public imagery, I am relying on the presupposition that, setting aside the effects of the medium and economic circumstances, the sort of thing a man draws when he has a pencil will be very similar to the sort of thing he imagines when he has not. Thus Loewy was perhaps wrong when he claimed that primitive artists copied their images, but very probably right in the type of imagery he attributed to them. When I say that Elizabethan and Jacobean poetry is literature of the image rather than of the percept I am not necessarily postulating a relation of copying, but only suggesting that they did rather more imagining 'aloud' than we do. And the effect of this was the development of a public – or at any rate intersubjective – apparatus of images and symbols. Poetry was a popular art as it may never be again, because men could speak their hearts to one another in an instantly intelligible language. Further, it is more than likely that the very conventions had reacted upon their hearts, and made them more kindred to one another.

If this account is correct, there seems to be no reason to revise the linguistic convention which allows us to lump together private and public fictions under the one term 'imagery'. Thus we may say that the imaginary world of the Elizabethan and the Jacobean was peopled with a far more discrete set of entities than is the public world. Mental imagery and drawing are just two forms of the same thing. Each form presents its proper difficulties and imposes its peculiar modifications, but remains a form only. It was important to establish the fact that the logically curious features which we find in sophisticated allegories may be found also at the almost subliminal level of non-specific mental imagery. We thus provide allegory with a natural foundation. So far from being the last arbitrary construction of a tired artistic tradition, it has its roots in the most primitive levels of our mental lives. Even our perceptions (despite the stress I have laid on the antithesis between imagination and perception) are not wholly free from the interpretative formulations of the allegorizing intelligence. Allegory is quite as much the child of Imagination as she is of Fancy. An analysis of allegory in terms of a logical scheme of general and particular will be an adequate account of 'frigid' allegory only. As long as any haunting power is retained by an allegorical poem, that poem will also require analysis in the more baffling prelogical terms of 'non-specified' and 'individualized'.

Thus we find in Elizabethan authors the strangely 'dense' and imaginatively 'substantial' attitude to universals which we might have expected. Not even the followers of Petrus Ramus, that arch-enemy of the imagination, are exempt from this. Let us take the example of Sir Philip Sidney. Now, it has been observed[1] that there are, so to speak, two Sidneys, a Ramist and an anti-Ramist. The second has learned his art of memory not in the desiccated, anti-imaginative form expounded by Ramus but in the vividly Neoplatonic version of Giordano Bruno (as purveyed by Bruno's disciple Alexander Dicson). This is an attractive thesis and accounts for a certain fruitful tension in Sidney's writing. Yet the schizo-phrenia is not complete. The Elizabethan could never finally dis-miss his imagination. Sidney, even at his most Ramist, thinks imaginatively. Universals are not simply exemplified by individu-als; they are incarnated by them, shine through them. For example, in his *Defence of Poesie* (1595) he says that the poet is distinguished from the philosopher in that he

> yeeldeth to the powers of the minde an image of that whereof the *Philosopher* bestoweth but a wordish description, which doth neither strike, pearce, nor possesse the sight of the soule as that other doth.[2]

It might be supposed that if this were the case the poet must be confined to the illumination of concrete particulars, since it is not easy to understand how a universal is to 'shine'. But when Sidney gives his examples we soon see that he does not admit this difficulty:

> . . . let but *Sophocles* bring you *Ajax* on a stage, killing and whipping sheepe and oxen, thinking them the Army of Greekes, with their Chieftaines *Agamemnon* and *Menelaus*: and tell me if you have not a more familiar insight into Anger, then finding in the schoolemen his *Genus* and *Difference*. See whether wisdom and temperance in *Ulisses* and *Diomedes*, valure in *Achilles*, friendship in *Nisus* and *Eurialus*, even to an ignorant man carry not an apparant shining?[3]

It might be argued that all that Sidney is doing here is putting the

---

[1] See Frances Yates, *The Art of Memory*, pp. 282 ff.
[2] In *The Works of Sir Philip Sidney*, ed. A. Feuillerat, Cambridge 1923, vol. III, p. 14.
[3] *ibid.*, pp. 14–15.

paradigm case argument, saying that if you want to know what anger is like it is much better to study a really good instance of it than to theorize vaguely. But the shining and apparent image of the poet (as opposed to the philosopher's 'wordish description') is, it seems, not the image of an individual, but of a universal shining *through* an individual. A clue to the ontological presuppositions involved here is perhaps given in a passage from the writings of the rhetorician Abraham Fraunce:

> If you put downe one, more, or all the specials, you also put down the generall, for that the nature and essence of the generall is in every of the specials.[1]

Ramist authors seem indeed to have had a particular predilection for this ontological view. Rosemond Tuve observes that:

> When Puttenham describes the use of exempla (III, xix, p. 245), we seem to be reading about a poet exemplifying what he is saying by giving a concrete 'case' of it. But when Wotton in his version of Ramus gives us a passage from Ovid using 'examples', we are left in no doubt that the Ramist saw something more: 'Here the *Poet* proveth the generall, that Adversitie sheweth true vertue; by three specialls: Hector making known his valour, Typhis shewing his skill in storms, Phoebus his art in sickness' (i, 26).[2]

This poetic theory is confirmed by the ontologically suggestive character of much Elizabethan poetry. Peculiarly interesting from this point of view is the masque. It has, indeed, an additional claim upon our notice from the fact that in December 1609 or else early in 1610 Shakespeare's company began playing in the Blackfriars theatre.[3] It is to this period that *The Tempest* belongs. The previous occupants of the theatre had been a famous company of children, who had established there a convention of including in productions a considerable element of masque. This convention Shakespeare's company inherited.[4] The plays themselves were staged in what must have been an atmosphere of fairy-tale beauty. The actors performed by candle-light. This in itself could have led

---

[1] *The Lawiers Logike*, London 1588, I 6, p. 34. The word 'special' is, I gather, Ramist language for 'individual'.

[2] *Elizabethan and Metaphysical Imagery*, Chicago 1947, p. 347.

[3] See Irwin Smith, *Shakespeare's Blackfriars Playhouse*, London 1966, especially pp. 248 and 301.

[4] *ibid.*, p. 230.

to the wrong sort of naturalism. One could easily imagine how the poet who in *Romeo and Juliet* had relied on language to produce an inward awareness of darkness could now, to our infinite loss, take the short cut of simply darkening his stage. In fact, there is evidence that this is not what happened. Perhaps the simultaneous putting out of all the lights was technically impossible. At any rate, it seems that an illusion of darkness was created, as in the public playhouses, by verbal suggestion, costume and action.[1] The Duke would appear carrying a torch and listening. The Princess would be discovered wearing her nightgown, kneeling at her prayers. Candle-light at the Blackfriars was not so much a technical device as a means of shedding a generalized enchantment over the whole play.

Part of the excitement of masques and 'disguisings' seems to have consisted in recognizing that your very good friend X *was*, in several senses, what he was disguised as. In the famous *Triumph* of 1581,[2] Sir Philip Sidney, Fulke Greville, Arundel and Windsor took the parts of the 'four Foster Children of Desire', and, appearing before the 'fortress of Perfect Beauty' where the Queen sat, offered to defend her rights against all comers, bombarded the castle with flowers and perfumed water and at last engaged in the tournament. One feels that part of the intention of this elaborate compliment was to propose some essential connexion between the Queen and the idea of perfect beauty. The arrangements[3] for the marriage of Prince Arthur to Catherine of Aragon in 1501 included a masque in which Hope and Love approached a castle containing eight ladies to plead on behalf of eight knights; they were refused and forthwith the suitors took the castle by storm. Here the acting out of the real situation is hardly mistakable. This kind of ceremonious encomium is not unlike what is sometimes called, in the slang of twenty years ago, 'kidding on the level'. The imagery is both playful and seriously pointed at the same time.

Another curious feature of the masque is its way of breaking down the 'fourth wall' between the players and the audience. This feature derives from the very old tradition of 'disguisings', which existed in England long before Italian influence turned them into the more formal masque of the sixteenth century. Various masque-like disguisings were arranged for the entertainment of the Queen

[1] *ibid.*, pp. 301–3.
[2] See E. K. Chambers, *The Elizabethan Stage*, Oxford 1923, vol. I, p. 144.
[3] *ibid.*, vol. I, p. 151.

on her numerous progresses. In 1575 she arrived at Kenilworth to be greeted by Sibylla, a porter disguised as Hercules, and by the Lady of the Lake. Sixteen years later, at Elvetham, she was awakened in the morning by the pastoral singing of a Phyllida and a Corydon. At Theobalds the simple welcome of the rustic folk was offered by two figures named the Bailiff and the Dairymaid.[1] Romantic, pastoral and folk-lore elements are all drawn into a solemn play which is not so much a piece of mere fiction as a mythological unfolding of the real situation. In the second chapter of this book I argued that the fictions of allegory were often seen, not as excursions into the world of fancy, but as a peculiarly intimate way of closing with the real. Similarly, the modern reader approaches the masque expecting to find pure invention, and finds instead a curious tendency to 'act out' the real situation in heightened terms. The entities involved in a masque are sometimes even more heterogeneous than the personages of Bale's *King Johan*. At any rate, all the figures in Bale's play are *actors*.

In Milton's *Comus*, a work which belongs to the twilight of the masque, there is a passage which brings out very clearly the ontological unruliness which is always threatening to complicate or disrupt the form. The *Lady* says

> Was this the cottage, and the safe abode
> Thou told'st me of ? What grim aspects are these,
> These oughly-headed Monsters ? Mercy guard me!
> Hence with thy brew'd inchantments, foul deceiver,
> Hast thou betrai'd my credulous innocence
> With visor'd falsehood, and base forgery . . . ?[2]

'Visor'd' here refers to the garment known in fourteenth-century sources as *viseres*, or in the sixteenth century as *maskes*, from which both the name of the literary *genre* and the modern word 'mask' are derived. But why should the Lady *mention* the masks? One way of answering this question is to turn back to ll. 164–6, where Comus says

> When once her eye
> Hath met the vertue of this Magick dust
> I shall appear som harmles Villager . . .

Comus, it seems, disguises himself by putting on the mask of a

[1] *ibid.*, vol. I, pp. 122 ff.
[2] *Comus*, ll. 693–8, in *The Poetical Works of John Milton*, ed. Helen Darbishire, Oxford 1952, vol. II, p. 194.

villager. Later, when the Lady penetrates his disguise, he removes the villager's mask. When she speaks of 'visor'd falsehood' she is referring to the disguise *within* the story, and therefore no expressionist point is being made.

But this answer is not completely satisfactory. Comus appears not to leave the stage after announcing his intention to deceive the Lady. He remains, unseen by her, throughout her long speech (170–229) and overhears her echo-song (230–42). Hence, if he is really to assume the disguise of 'harmles Villager' (a disguise almost certainly requiring more than the mere putting on of a mask), he must put it on in full view of the audience. His reference to 'Magick dust', however, renders any actual disguise quite unnecessary. The 'harmles Villager' is all in the enchanted eye of the Lady. Nothing the Attendant Spirit says contradicts this account, though several of his observations appear to. For example, describing the deception of the Lady, he describes Comus as 'that damned wizard hid in sly disguise' (l. 571). But the next line – 'For so by certain signs I knew'– hints that the concealment of identity was no ordinary dressing-up, which the Attendant Spirit would have seen quite clearly, but something more mysterious. This is made plainer when we come to the Spirit's next reference to Comus's 'disguise'– at l. 645. Here he explains how he 'knew the foul enchanter, though disguised'. Note well the reasons for his knowledge; he knew the foul enchanter, not because he had seen him putting on a mask, but because, armed by the root haemony, he was proof against a *magical device* –'the very lime-twigs of his spells'. The words of the Attendant Spirit suggests strongly that Comus's disguise was more magical than theatrical; not a mask but a puff of magic dust, blown across the stage. The evidence of the stage-directions corroborates this reading. There is no direction to Comus to assume a disguise, nor is there any mention (even in the stage-direction at 658, where it might easily have been incorporated) of his putting it on. Yet other stage-directions do mention disguises – e.g. at 489, 'The attendant Spirit habited like a Shepherd.' The balance of probability is that Comus never puts on a villager's mask at all. He wears the same mask throughout, the mask of Comus. In conclusion it is perhaps worth adding that the sense 'an artificial manner assumed for deception . . . counterfeit semblance . . . deception' (as opposed to deceptive *dress*) is, according to the *Oxford English Dictionary*, well attested for the word *disguise* in the seventeenth century.

It seems probable, then, that the Lady's question really does break the closed circle of the story. Milton, as a sort of seventeenth-century Pirandello, wants to have his characters both *intra* and *extra poema* at the same time. There may be a further point of compliment to Alice Egerton, who played the Lady, figuring the 'Sun-clad power of Chastity'. Perhaps she wore no mask, and the poet intended to suggest, by means of the self-dissociating phrase he puts into her mouth, that she really did comprehend within herself the 'nature and essence' of Chastity, in a stronger sense than any of the other players could be said to represent *their* spiritual forces. Perhaps the audience, consisting as it did (at the 1634 performance) of Alice Egerton's friends and relations, felt a peculiar thrill on recognizing that here indeed was one of the 'specials' of Chastity.

A wonderfully intricate example of Shakespeare's youthful interest in illusion and reality occurs in *The Two Gentlemen of Verona* (iv. iv. 158–72):

SILVIA. How tall was she?

JULIA. About my stature; for, at Pentecost,
    When all our pageants of delight were play'd,
    Our youth got me to play the woman's part,
    And I was trimm'd in Madam Julia's gown,
    Which served me as fit, by all men's judgments,
    As if the garment had been made for me:
    Therefore I know she is about my height.
    And at that time I made her weep agood;
    For I did play a lamentable part.
    Madam, 'twas Ariadne passioning
    For Theseus' perjury and unjust flight;
    Which I so lively acted with my tears
    That my poor mistress, mov'd therewithal,
    Wept bitterly, and would I might be dead
    If I in thought felt not her very sorrow!

Anne Righter, in her book *Shakespeare and the Idea of the Play*, assembles a great many more passages of the same or similar type. Analysing this speech she writes:

. . . the real Julia, playing the part of Proteus' page Sebastian, describes an imaginary theatrical performance in which that page appeared as Ariadne before Julia herself. The passage sets up a series of illusions receding into depth of which the most remote, the tears wrung from Julia by the stage presentation of a lover's perfidy, in fact represents reality.[1]

In the later tragedies we sometimes come upon the same device, in a contracted yet greatly intensified form. Some of these have a force which has escaped the vigilance even of Mrs. Righter. When Cleopatra says (*Antony and Cleopatra*, v. ii. 218–20)

> . . . I shall see
> Some squeaking Cleopatra boy my greatness
> I' the posture of a whore

we may notice, with Mrs. Righter, that the stage is here seen as a degrading and humiliating medium, but the most wonderful thing is still unsaid. If we think of the play as performed on the Jacobean stage we shall see it at once. The lines in which Cleopatra looks forward to her degradation on the Roman stage are, on an English stage, delivered by just such a squeaking boy as Cleopatra describes. The sudden coincidence of what is speculation for Cleopatra within the story with what is fact for audience and players has a remarkable effect. It transforms the Queen's fears for the immediate future into a kind of unconscious prophecy, which looks down all the centuries from Caesar's time to Shakespeare's, all the theatres and stages from Ancient Rome to seventeenth-century London. In one way, the strange Pagan pride of the speech is untouched, retains its full and authentic magnificence. In another, Cleopatra is mocked by the mere practical circumstances of production.

There is a similar moment in *Hamlet*. The Prince is going through the ritual of swearing Horatio and Marcellus to secrecy on all that concerns the ghost. The way in which this is carried out comes very close to a certain comedy-routine still to be seen in pantomimes. The three go into a huddle and prepare to swear, but just as they are on the point of pronouncing the words the ghost's voice booms from under the stage – 'Swear!' At this they all jump (except perhaps Hamlet) and then move round to another part of the stage and begin again, only to be interrupted once more by the subterranean voice. The interesting thing is Hamlet's reaction to the ghost's first interruption:

[1] *op. cit.*, p. 103.

Ah, ha, boy! say'st thou so? art thou there, true-penny?
Come on,– you hear this fellow in the cellarage,–
Consent to swear.

I. V. 150–2.

'Cellarage' is the technical Elizabethan term for the area under the stage. Within the story, then, Hamlet is using a stage-metaphor about the 'platform' of Elsinore. But, as with Cleopatra's speech, in stage-performance the fancy coincides startlingly with the fact. The instance from *Hamlet* is the closer of the two to pure comedy, yet it retains a mysteriousness, so that the audience feels a kind of fear, even while it laughs.

If we dwell upon topics like these we are naturally led to consider the regress of fictions which seems to have haunted Shakespeare and his contemporaries, the preoccupation with plays within plays, and players within plays (for every Elizabethan fool is a player within a play). This is given an ontological colour by the ubiquity of the notion that

all the world's a stage.

This idea can be found in such early sources as Cicero,[1] Marcus Aurelius,[2] the epigrammatist Palladas,[3] and St. Augustine.[4] But the origin of it seems to lie, as we might have expected, in the works of Plato. He speaks in the *Philebus*[5] of the tragedy and comedy of life, and in the *Laws*[6] declares that every living being is a puppet of the gods. By the sixteenth century the idea had become so commonplace that we find a writer like Thomas Heywood trying to ginger it up by standing it on its head –

He that denyes then theaters should be
He may as well deny a world to me.[7]

It would not have been difficult to have used as material for

---

[1] *Cato Maior*, XVIII, 65, in *M. Tullii Ciceronis Opera*, ed. C. Orellius and I. G. Baiterus, 2nd ed., Zürich 1845–62, vol. IV, p. 605.

[2] *The Meditations of the Emperor Marcus Antoninus*, Book XI, §6, in A. S. L. Farqharson's edition, Oxford 1944, vol. I, p. 216.

[3] AP, X, 72, in *Anthologia Graeca*, ed. H. Beckby, Munich 1957, vol. III, p. 515.

[4] Augustine, *Enarratio ad Psalmum*, 127, in Migne's *Patrologia*, Augustini, vol. IV, pp. 1678 ff.

[5] *op. cit.*, 50b.

[6] *op. cit.*, I, 644d.

[7] 'The Author to his Booke', prefixed to his *Apology for Actors* (1612), printed in *The Dramatic Works of Thomas Heywood*, London 1874, vol. I, p. xlviii.

this chapter examples much more explicitly Platonic in character than anything I have, in fact, used. I might have built much on the popular Neoplatonic theory propounded by Plotinus:

εἰ δέ τις τὰς τέχνας ἀτιμάζει, ὅτι μιμούμεναι τὴν φύσιν ποιοῦσι, πρῶτον μὲν φάτεον καὶ τὰς φύσεις μιμεῖσθαι ἄλλα. Ἔπειτά δεῖ εἰδέναι, ὡς οὐχ ἀπλῶς τὸ ὁρώμενον μιμοῦνται, ἀλλ' ἀνατρέχουσι ἐπὶ τοὺς λόγους, ἐξ ὧν ἡ φύσις[1]

that is, if any man disparages the arts on the ground that they imitate nature, let him remember first that nature is itself imitative and second that art does not imitate nature but rather nature and art both imitate the same prior principles. The relevance of this poetic theory to the 'golden' poetry of the sixteenth century is generally accepted.[2] It both corroborates and offers a systematic account of our impression that sixteenth-century poetry is, among other things, an art if incarnating spiritual essences. Other Platonic notions, such as that of the Great Chain of Being (from the *Timias*) or the ladder of love (from the *Symposium* by way of Ficino's commentary) are also without doubt relevant to the picture I am trying to build up. Again, I might have dwelt on the seminal opinion of Dio Chrysostom that the function of art is to 'show forth the invisible by the visible'.[3] I avoided this approach because I was more interested in the naturalness of this curious ontological preoccupation – the degree to which it was rooted in the imaginations and feelings of the age – than I was in its validity in the tradition of authentic Platonism. I have accordingly concentrated upon the elements which go to form a spiritualist world view at an almost subliminal level. Spenser's *Four Hymns* are stuffed with Platonic or Neoplatonic notions; yet I have preferred to examine what no one would ever dream (quite rightly) of calling Platonic – the first stanzas of the *Faerie Queene*. I have indeed striven to avoid those *loci* which were open to the disenchanting explanation, 'Ah, but you see he's only repeating the doctrines which X derived from Y, and Y from Plato.' This restriction has led to some losses. It is quite possible for a poem to contain certain traditional ontological formulae and at the same time to be instinct with the sort of feeling and imagination proper to such a world view. A good

---

[1] *Ennead*, v. viii. 32, in *Plotini Opera*, ed. P. Henry and H.-R. Schwyzer, Paris 1951.
[2] See C. S. Lewis, *English Literature in the Sixteenth Century*, pp. 318 ff.
[3] Dio Chrysostom, Oratio XII (*De Dei Cognitione*), §59, in the Teubner edition of G. de Bude, Leipzig 1916, p. 218.

example of this is the 'Chinese Box' treatment of marriage in Chapman's continuation (1598) of Marlowe's *Hero and Leander*. Hero, wishing to be united with Leander, officiates as priestess at the marriage of two young lovers with whom she is acquainted. To the wedding comes the 'wilde nymph Teras' and tells the story of the marriage of Hymen and Eucharis (Marriage itself). This multiplication of images is extremely tedious unless enforced by a suspicion that it in some way reproduces the structure of the universe itself. It is quite evident that such regresses fascinated the Elizabethans, and it is hard to see how the fascination can be anything but ontological. So Chapman's poem is not only ontologically expository, but also (which is more to my purpose) it is ontologically suggestive.

Universals are incorporated into the Elizabethan world of gods, spirits and woodwoses. Love and Chastity mingle promiscuously with satyrs and mere human beings. All this is made possible by the instantial, 'thingy' view of universals which we found in Plato himself. Relations of similarity are convertible. If the particular imitates or resembles the form, it follows that the Form resembles the particular. The effect of such opinions on one's imaginative world-view is enormous. The fairly tidy structure of general and particular terms vanishes, and instead the world is peopled not so much with abstractions as with spirits.

The moral of all this for our argument is irresistible. It is easy to see how one individual thing can resemble another, or 'shine through' another, but it is harder to see how a *universal* can resemble or 'shine through' an individual; unless, that is, the universal is itself regarded as a mysterious sort of individual.

The situation is paralleled in the world of the visual arts. E. H. Gombrich, discussing the 'natural bent' of Indo-Germanic languages towards the hypostasis of concepts, comments

> The very question whether Fortuna is a 'symbol' of the vicissitudes of life or a capricious demon interfering in our fate, whether Death with the scythe is an abstraction or capable of knocking at the door, does not allow of a clear-cut answer. On this level it may be true to say that the naïve painter who had to represent 'Justice' began by trying to find out what Justice looked like.[1]

[1] 'Icones Symbolicae', *Journal of the Warburg and Courtauld Institutes*, XI (1948), p. 165.

Gombrich's suggestion about the naïve artist echoes my own suggestion in Chapter II (p. 35) that even a Prudentius may well have asked himself the strange question, 'What is Pride herself really like?' Gombrich supports his conjecture by referring to a treatise on painting by Lomazzo, first published in 1584. Lomazzo, it seems, in the seventh book of his *Trattato* makes no difference whatever between angels and the Virtues. The difference is evident to us; but our perception of the difference depends on our awareness of another difference – the radical difference between a universal and an individual.

Ernst Cassirer[1] has picked up the same trail in another place – this time the *De Umbris Idearum* of Giordano Bruno. The reader of Bruno comes to see that the allegorical masques of Renascence Italy 'extend their influence far into a field which, according to our habits of thought, should be reserved for abstract, conceptual, imageless thought'. In Bruno, 'the forces that move the inner man are viewed as cosmic potencies'. For such men, says Cassirer, allegory was not so much the decoration of thought as its vehicle. It is worth remembering that Bruno is a major exponent of the art of memory already discussed.

As soon as we find one of our older authors talking about the *resemblance* between an individual and a universal, we may mark him down as holding the special view of universals which is the subject of this book. But when we turn from logical analysis to literary or artistic criticism, we may notice something rather strange. The strangeness lies, paradoxically, in the fact that we *can* make comparative judgements about allegorical representations. If we are fully convinced that a universal is not an individual of any kind, then all attempts at image-ing the universal ought to seem equally irrelevant. Yet, in fact, we find ourselves capable of distinguishing between good and bad attempts. Plainly, some vestige of the older habit of thought lingers in our minds, or, at least, in our sensibilities. Gombrich, on p. 168 of the same article, quotes a very relevant passage from Pico della Mirandola's *Heptaplus*:[2]

The ancient fathers could not have represented one image by another had they not known the occult affinities and harmonies

[1] In his *The Individual and the Cosmos in Renaissance Philosophy*, Trans. Mario Domandi, New York 1963, p. 74.
[2] Ed. E. Garin, Florence 1942, p. 192.

of the universe. Otherwise there would not have been any reason whatever why they should have represented a thing by one image rather than by an opposite one.

We have throughout this chapter examined the practice of the Elizabethans and their successors through the glass of their imagery – imagery not restricted to the world of public and perceptible objects, but licensed to revel among all the logical functions and constructions of a complex linguistic usage. But to think of the Elizabethan pantheon as a mere set of heterogeneous non-specified images moving through a world of more narrowly individuated images is plainly almost as great a distortion as to banish the imagination altogether. There is a constant overflowing into the conceptual sphere, without which allegory could never come into being at all. Where an image has usurped a logical function it is no longer just an image, an inchoate and negligible psychological phenomenon. After all, a set of mental images, whether specified or not, is not a set of spirits, ontological Forms or anything of the sort. It is just a set of images.

Nevertheless, we have argued for a very important status for imagery in all this. All the spurious-seeming properties of 'density', instantiality, spatial characteristics, and so on, we have laid at the door of the imagination. When Plotinus says that any fire we have 'here' (in the world of particulars) makes a very poor showing compared with the fire they have 'there' (in the world of the eternal Forms),[1] we say that it is the usurping imagination which has transformed a logical distinction into a spatial one. When we suggest that the spectators in Ludlow Castle in 1634 seemed to see the form of Alice Egerton brightening into the Form of Chastity itself, we suggest that this curious excited configuration was made possible by the availability of a shared mental world of instantialized universals; and that this world was, once more, the work of the usurping imagination. Since the publication of *The Concept of Mind* it has been fashionable to argue that private mental imagery has no relevance to the preoccupations either of the artist or the thinker. Yet when we find both allegory and metaphysics dealing (each in its own way) with so curious a thing as an instantialized universal, it is natural to look to the imagination for an explanation – natural, because it is only in the imagination that the required entity, the 'thing both general and particular', can exist.

[1] *Ennead*, II.ix.4.

Yet I am still conscious of a certain discomfort. In so far as the 'Image' account of what C. S. Lewis called 'sacramentalism' is deemed exhaustive, so far it must be classed as a reductionist hypothesis. If true, it invalidates not only the more transcendentalist part of Plato, but also a large body of religious doctrine. Gods who are *just* primitive images scarcely deserve our worship. Platonism and Christian theology may be invalid indeed, or they may not. The question lies outside the scope of this book. But I doubt very much whether they can ever be invalidated by an imagist account such as I have adumbrated. The reason is that the imagist account is far from being an exhaustive one. It certainly is not strong enough to exclude every other approach. Nor is it the sole candidate for consideration.

In particular, the sort of ontological assertiveness we found in the passage quoted from Abraham Fraunce, and the way in which the figures of masque and romantic drama may be suggestive yet not individuated both raise questions which require more for their solution than a hypothetical account of the imagery involved. The puzzling notion of an ontological 'sense', together with the possibility that Shakespeare in the course of his career attempted to carry out a perfectly serious ontological separation of the ideas of love and value are topics requiring examination in detail. We have seen how non-specified imagery can be seen as lying 'behind' or 'beyond' the world of sense, and this feature of imagery has provided us with a plausible reduced sense of the word 'beyond' as it appears in some metaphysical contexts. We have yet to consider the function of the term 'beyond' as a figurative way of expressing logically interesting features of the extremely open word 'good'. In short, it seems that a psychological account of what happens when people think of qualities, mental characteristics and values in an instantial, self-predicable manner will not serve automatically as a logical account of the metaphysical usage of the term 'beyond', especially with regard to value concepts. The remainder of this book will be taken up, first, with the difficulty of distinguishing the proper senses of the metaphysical term 'beyond', secondly, with the interesting way in which the later poetry of Shakespeare exemplifies these difficulties, and, thirdly, with the way in which this exemplification may or may not be said to give an allegorical status to the later work of Shakespeare.

V

SHAKESPEARE AND THE IDEA OF LOVE

> The Imagination may be compared to Adam's dream – he awoke and found it Truth . . . KEATS

'Sacramentalists' distinguish in the universe two orders, one truly real and eternal, the other only half-real and fluid. The first of these orders they commonly describe as 'transcendent'. One tolerable clear effect of this very unclear term is to rule out any naturalistic account of how the 'real and eternal' order comes to find a place in our conceptual apparatus. The last chapter of this book, in so far as it can be read as an attempt to explain away Plato's system in terms of mental imagery, is just such a naturalistic account. Since the eternal order transcends us, our knowledge of it is only to be explained in terms of direct commerce with the supernatural; by the Platonic *anamnesis* or by the Christian Revelation.

The term 'transcendent' may perhaps be brought to yield an even more depressing picture. On the principle of *finitum non capax infiniti* it might be argued that even revelation is conveyed to us by the natural and human medium of language, and is for this reason subjected to an inevitable Procrustean reduction. In so far as it is translated into our terms, it is no longer transcendent; in so far as it is transcendent, it will resist translation into our terms. If the transcendent really transcends us it will elude description; and this is just as true of the analogical account as it is of the literal.[1] The necessarily metaphorical status of language describing mental

[1] This last point is argued by Peter Munz in his *Problems of Religious Knowledge*, London 1959.

events is not really relevant here. Mental phenomena evade literal description not because they are transcendent but because they are subjective and private.

The moral of this seems to be that the word 'transcendent', if seriously intended, should never be used to extend or elucidate discourse, but only to terminate it. Properly speaking, it silences not only the author of this book, but also Plato, the prince of Sacramentalists. 'Whereof one cannot speak, thereof one must be silent.'

This precept has certainly been more often commended than obeyed by sacramentally minded persons. A clamour of voices all saying 'The Beyond is wholly unutterable' is a very curious phenomenon. No less curious is a vein in this tradition which we may call 'apophatic'. The apophatic thinker is the man who seeks to define the Beyond, not in terms of what it is, but in terms of what it is *not*. But by the strong definition of transcendent we have outlined above, this procedure stands condemned just as much as any other. For if a thing transcends us utterly we have no more means of knowing what it is not than we have of knowing what it is. How do we *know* that the Beyond is not temporal?

If we are to take seriously concepts like 'the transcendent' and 'the beyond', we need an account of them which has slightly less paralysing effects than those we have so far observed. In the last chapter I outlined a theory of images which will give a satisfactory reduced sense for some uses of the word. But the apophatic tradition in particular will have nothing to do with this explanation. The whole *raison d'être* of apophaticism lies in its vigorous repudiation of images. It is therefore of no use to say to its supporters 'what you *really* mean is that this mysterious object or set of objects doesn't exist in the public world, but only in the private world of your images'. 'There least of all,' would be the immediate reply. It seems, then, that the reductive account of the last chapter stands in need of a supplement. This is especially true in the context of ethics, where the use of apophatic description is peculiarly persistent.

The term 'beyond' in its metaphysical use is a spatial metaphor. I suspect that 'transcendent' is also best described as a spatial metaphor, though an invisible one.[1] Perhaps if we recognize the metaphorical status of these terms we shall have a better chance of making sense of them. I therefore propose in this

[1] 'Attention' is a similarly invisible metaphor. See above, Chapter 2, p. 22.

chapter to investigate the use of such metaphors in ethical contexts, and to outline a possible connexion between intuitionist ethics and the concept of ontological hierarchy. This is the final stage in our pursuit of the instantial universal. It will be found to lead us back to the point from which we began – the poetry of Shakespeare.

The most obvious source for ethics in the context of ontological hierarchy is, of course, Plato. But, since Plato's conceptual apparatus is far removed from our own, it may be better to work towards it rather than from it. Pindar's advice was οἴκοθεν μάτευε – 'first search your own house'. If we have any similar doctrine in more familiar terms and a more familiar context, it may be as well to begin from there.

The concept of an instantial transcendent Good is by no means confined to ancient or primitive philosophers. There is more than a breath of it in the writings of G. E. Moore, a thinker at once more sophisticated and less intricate than Plato. It is true that the *Principia Ethica* of 1903 will serve our purpose better than the *Ethics* of 1912. But the spirit and intention of the earlier work are perfectly accessible to modern readers.

Moore's idea of good is unanalysable, non-natural and unified. The first of these descriptions means that 'good' is simply given, and cannot be resolved into constituent elements; the second that it is not derived from the natural world of the senses in which we all live; the third means that it is the name of one thing, common to all the objects we call good. Like Plato, Moore is very fond of the idiom 'good *itself*' – a locution which rhetorically implies that good is an individual, and might almost be allowed a capital G. Now, are we to say that Moore *finds*, by a process of analysis and argument, that good is like this, or does he *perceive* it to be so?

Much can be said in favour of the second alternative. W. K. Frankena, in his article 'The Naturalistic Fallacy',[1] expresses some distress at the way in which Moore continually presupposes what Frankena feels should be the conclusion of his argument. Frankena at last acknowledges, what is perhaps not very surprising in an avowed intuitionist, that it is all very much a matter of *inspection*:

> . . . it is difficult to see how the intuitionists can prove that the definists are at least vaguely aware of the requisite unique characteristics. The question must surely be left to the inspec-

[1] *Mind*, vol. XLVIII (1939), pp. 464-77.

tion or intuition of the definists themselves . . . If so, we must credit the verdict of their inspection . . . and then . . . the most they can be charged with is moral blindness.[1]

Six years earlier G. C. Field had expressed, by the rhetorical means of balancing a plain statement with a parenthetical afterthought, a curiously ambivalent character of ethical philosophy since *Principia Ethica*. He wrote that there was room 'for a new logic, or perhaps a psychologic, of ethics'.[2] Indeed, Moore's attack on naturalistic ethics rests quite as much on an appeal to his reader's moral perceptiveness as it does on exhaustive analysis. He takes a very few naturalistic concepts of good, and shows, by an empirical process of checking, that good just is not this sort of thing at all. Neither he nor (most of) his readers feel any obligation to go through all the naturalistic goods offered. On the contrary, we learn from the first few tries that any *such* attempt is misconceived, that good just is not that *sort* of thing. That the method of learning involves inspection Moore shows repeatedly. For example, in his account of the discovery of intrinsic value, he writes:

. . . whoever will attentively consider with himself what is actually before his mind when he asks the question 'Is pleasure (or whatever it may be) after all good?' can easily satisfy himself that he is not merely wondering whether pleasure is pleasant. And if he will try this experiment with each suggested definition in succession, he may become expert enough to recognise that in every case he has before his mind a unique object, with regard to the connection of which with any other object, a distinct question may be asked.[3]

We may note in Moore's specimen question a characteristic of the word 'good' which we found very relevant to the self-predication of Plato's Forms[4]– namely, the uneasy status, somewhere between adjective and substantive. Moore is not concerned to rebut the suggestion that pleasure is *the* highest good, nor, on the other hand, is he giving an ordinary adjectival sense to the word. He probably would not object to a reformulation like 'Does "pleasant" mean the same thing as "good"?' But this formulation suppresses

[1] *ibid.*, p. 476.
[2] 'The Place of Definition in Ethics', printed in *Readings in Ethical Theory*, ed. W. Sellars and J. Hospers, New York 1952, p. 96.
[3] *Principia Ethica*, Cambridge 1903, ch. I, §13, p. 16.
[4] See above, pp. 42 ff.

something which is hinted in Moore's different grammar, namely that 'good' not only has a different sense from 'pleasure', but a different *sort* of sense. 'Good' gives us a very mysterious thing called a non-natural quality to deal with, but 'pleasant' does nothing of the sort. Moore isolates a special *faculty* for apprehending this special ethical order of reality.

Here, then, is Moore the contemplative. But a picture of Moore the analytic philosopher can be built up which is equally convincing. We might argue that the burden of the *Principia* is not the evocation of a mysterious moral 'sense', a reminder of half-seen ideals, but a logical argument for the uniqueness of the term 'good', based on the freedom of the agent to evaluate for himself any object whatsoever. This universal licence to evaluate is particularly effective when applied to the various idolatrous Goods of naturalistic ethics. For, when confronted by anything which purports to *be* the good, I can always step back and ask, 'But is it really good?' This perennial and ubiquitous possibility seems to imply that no listing of particular things or events will ever exhaust the meaning of 'good'. The concept 'good' is not something we derive *from* the natural world; it is something we bring *to* the natural world. The world cannot be the source of that by which it may, at any moment, be judged. Hence 'good' is described as 'non-natural'.

It looks as if we must distinguish two elements in Moore's thought: first, as a sort of aesthetic metaphysic of Good, in which good is perceived as a sort of aura surrounding certain complexes (notably, the Bloomsbury ideals of friendship and aesthetic experience), and, second, a logical argument for the unique 'openness' of the word 'good'. 'Good', viewed in either of these ways, invites the description 'unanalysable', though it would seem that a different sort of unanalysability is involved in either case. It may even be that the all-embracing term 'unanalysable', with its unproclaimed equivocation, conceals a fundamental incompatibility between the two ethical doctrines we have distinguished. By the 'aura' theory, 'good' is unanalysable in a way very similar to the way in which phenomenally simple qualities like 'red' are unanalysable. The term is unanalysable because the phenomenon it is the name of is, *qua* phenomenon, unanalysable. But by the second doctrine 'good' is not the name of a phenomenon at all. On the contrary, so far from complying with some one phenomenon, all phenomena must comply with *it*. The unanalysability of 'good' in this second theory derives from its total independence of all phenomena and its consequent irreducibility to phenomenal particulars. The evidence such as we have it is that the Platonist in Moore was at the last dominant over the analyst. It is true that he seems to have wavered[1] under the attack of Stevenson,[2] who almost persuaded him to be a subjectivist in ethics. But in his last years he recanted all such temporizing, and affirmed that he could not imagine what in the world had induced him to cede as much as he did to Stevenson.[3]

The logical argument will stand as a piece of pure linguistic philosophy. It makes its point by exhibiting the logical implications of the ordinary, public usage of the word 'good'. If pleasure is all that good comes down to, what sense does it make to ask whether pleasure is good?

But, as we have seen, Moore did not put the question in quite this way. Instead he brought in a peculiar and logically otiose mental object to be used for a process of checking:

> . . . whoever will attentively consider with himself what is actually before his mind . . . he has before his mind a unique object . . .[4]

This talk of mental objects led us a few pages earlier to classify this paragraph as an example of intuitionism, of the view of 'good' as a directly perceived quality. And, indeed, Moore does seem to be saying, 'Whoever will recollect (by means of an introspectible 'non-specific' memory image)[5] what he was looking at when he was contemplating the goodness of something will realize the difference between this and pleasure.' So expressed, the view seems slightly less persuasive than it did in its plain linguistic form. It is as if he were trying to enforce his logical argument by an appeal to the 'aura' intuition. If so, the project is probably unwise. A logical usage is easily isolated, but vague intuitions of 'aural' qualities are more difficult to differentiate. Pleasure and the

---

[1] See 'A reply to my critics', printed in *The Philosophy of G. E. Moore*, ed. P. A. Schilpp, Evanston and Chicago 1942, esp. pp. 544–5.

[2] See his 'Moore's Arguments against certain forms of Ethical Naturalism' in *The Philosophy of G. E. Moore*, pp. 71–90.

[3] See A. C. Ewing's note 'G. E. Moore', *Mind*, LXXI (1962), p. 251.

[4] *Principia Ethica*, ch. I, §13, p. 16.

[5] Naturally, the image is not visual, just as goodness is not perceived by the sense of sight. We may wish to say that it is not an image but an 'image', just as we do not sense goodness but rather 'sense' it.

intuition of goodness may be easy to distinguish, but what of the intuition of beauty? How does one go about distinguishing beauty from goodness, *qua* intuitions? Perhaps the difference will be plain to some people, but certainly it will be unclear to others. On the other hand, the semantic independence of 'beautiful' and 'good' is easily demonstrated.

But it is not difficult to see why the bald argument from freedom in evaluation, stripped of any reference to mental objects or to non-natural perceptions, would have dissatisfied Moore. It seems doubtful whether one ought to cherish the right of idiosyncratic approval. If everyone valued everything differently, the word 'good' might well suffer a considerable loss of content. One's emotions cry out against the doctrine of a purely arbitrary good. The concept of valuing as appraisal in terms of (any) set of criteria seems more fundamental logically than any intuition, or ethical perception. But psychologically the importance of feeling and (supposed) perception is very great. Most people, if questioned, can be driven back upon a set of ethical axioms (as, for instance, that charity is good) which they will affirm less as working hypotheses than as revealed truth. Our legislative concepts of 'good' and 'bad' have their roots in the childish concepts of 'nice' and 'nasty'. The truth of this becomes manifest in certain great works of literature which reactivate primitive areas in the mind. Pope was criticized in his own time for breaking the rules of satire in *The Dunciad*. He had attacked the Grub Street hacks for poverty of genius, which was legitimate; but he had also attacked them for sheerly material poverty, which was not. What Pope's critics could not accept was that for the most polished poet of the Augustan Age Grub Street was not so much wicked as nasty.

Again, our ethical assertions are not without their aesthetic consequences. Reappraisal commonly involves a sort of imaginative refocussing. For example, if I see an ecclesiastical building and suppose it to be a cathedral, I may say to myself, 'That's a poor building.' But then the gravedigger tells me that it is only the parish church, and I see with new eyes and exclaim 'What a magnificent building!' The reassessment of the object in terms of a different set of criteria seems to affect the immediate aesthetic impact of the object itself. We may say that we have merely reassessed the object, but we shall be wrong. The object has not just been differently 'placed'. It also *looks* different now because of what we have done to it. We express this aesthetic back-formation from ethical reassessment in the terms of para-physical metaphor. The phenomenon is very marked in the records of mystical experience, but it is perfectly discernible in everyday life. George Fox writes in his *Journal* for the year 1648:

> Now was I come up in Spirit through the flaming sword, into the paradise of God. All things were new; and all the creation gave another smell to me than before, beyond what words can utter. I knew nothing but pureness, and innocency and righteousness . . .[1]

But one does not need to be a quaking mystic to say, 'I've never liked the look of that hack-saw since I learned that it was used for vivisecting babies.' We speak of 'seeing things in a new light', and often enough this is a dead metaphor used to express a reversal of ethical judgement. But the extract from Fox shows how this expression is capable of being a degree less metaphorical and a degree more vivid. Fox's enthusiastic utterance is relevant here because the prosaic expression derives its force from the fact that there is an aesthetic correlative to ethical judgement, and Fox is peculiarly strong on the aesthetic correlative.

Analysis has the effect of severing ethical discourse from the warmer language of reported intuitions. But the concept 'love', like 'nice' and 'nasty', stoutly resists such surgery. We love things before we pronounce them good. Love entails considerable aesthetic consequences. This does not mean that anything which is loved appears beautiful to the lover. This is true only of some objects and of some lovers. But it would be very paradoxical indeed to say, 'I've never liked the look of that house since I came to love it.'

In cynical or romantic times (the two approaches are closer than most people think) the spheres of love and value fall apart. 'I love you' is no longer held to imply 'I think you good'. Perhaps this state of affairs is, likewise, the effect of the analytic consciousness. But for an Elizabethan a discrepancy between love and esteem often presented itself as a sort of metaphysical contradiction.

Where the discovery that 'good' is logically independent of phenomenal particulars is accompanied by a conviction that good is a matter of intuition, something seen in certain complexes, inextricably linked with very substantial feelings, there is every risk that a concept of ontological hierarchy will be fathered; 'good'

[1] Ed. W. Armistead (7th ed. 1852), p. 66.

will be considered as a spiritual stuff, fitfully infused into our world from a higher realm. Either sense of the word 'unanalysable' can be mythically turned by the spatial metaphor of 'beyond', and the myth irons out all differences by assigning the conflicting parties to different worlds.

There are signs that at various times in history the areas of evaluation and of loving or hating were more closely assimilated to one another than they are today. In the thirteenth century, according to M. Gilson, Aquinas found no difficulty whatever in making them not only exactly coextensive but interdependent. He argued that the good is simply that which is desired, and that desire is simply our relation to the good.[1] To say 'I love this thing' is tantamount to saying 'This thing is good', and vice versa.

When Ferdinand tells Miranda all in one breath that he loves, prizes and honours her,[2] he is not affirming the simultaneous presence of three distinct attitudes as a post-romantic might well be if he used the words, but rather piling up near-synonyms in the effort to express a unified attitude. For a poet like Shelley love has been reduced to little more than a matter of sensations, and his life with its long record of romantic infidelities is the natural conse-quence of this reduction. But for the pre-romantic the phrase 'I love you' was not simply an account of the speaker's sensations, but quasi-performative in character, involving some degree of promise or commitment. In such a society it made sense to use the imperative mood of the verb 'love', so that we find in Shake-speare's *King John* the King of England requesting the Dauphin of France to love his niece, and the Dauphin acceding to his request with a speech in which beauty, ceremony and political prudence are strangely intermingled:

> I do, my lord; and in her eye I find
> A wonder, or a wondrous miracle,
> The shadow of myself form'd in her eye;
> Which, being but the shadow of your son
> Becomes a sun, and makes your son a shadow:
> I do protest I never lov'd myself
> Till now infixed I beheld myself,
> Drawn in the flattering table of her eye.[3]

---

[1] See E. Gilson, *Le Thomisme*, Paris 1927, pp. 264 ff.
[2] *The Tempest*, iii. i. 73.
[3] ii, i, 496–503.

It is true that the bastard Faulconbridge is given an opportunity to rail against the match in the lines immediately following, and describes the Dauphin as 'love's traitor',[1] but the judicious reader will not fall into the error of supposing the bastard to be an affronted romantic. Faulconbridge is incensed, not with the want of spontaneity in the Dauphin's affections, but with his subjection of them to selfish ends, to the service of 'commodity'. Faulconbridge does not object to the Dauphin's turning love on and off like a tap, but he does deplore the reasons for which he does it. But Shelley would have difficulty with the very concept of voluntary love, or of love as comprising an undertaking. 'How can I undertake to love when commanded?' he might say. 'Am I the master of my sensations?' But the Elizabethan use has something about it of ritual. Its logic is akin to the logic of the devotional *Credo*. And here, too, we find Shelley in dissent:

> . . . the mind *cannot* believe the existence of a God, it is also evident that as belief is a passion of the mind, no degree of criminality can be attached to disbelief, they only are reprehensible who willingly neglect to remove the false medium thro' which their mind views the subject.[2]

It is possible that the way we love is itself conditioned by our idea of what love is. The differences between the conceptual apparatus of a Sir Philip Sidney and a Shelley cast doubt upon the similarity of their actions. When Sidney loved, was he doing the same thing as Shelley was when *he* loved? Perhaps the romantic retreat into subjectivity subtly transformed the very practice of loving; perhaps the reduction of love to sensation was as much practical as it was theoretical, so that what began as a piece of revisionary metaphysics could soon pass as descriptive in character.

Again, it might be objected that the common Elizabethan antithesis between love and reason impugns any claim that love and evaluation were closely associated in the sixteenth century: the lover is ranked with the lunatic (and the poet) and Bottom the weaver declares that 'reason and love keep little company together now-a-days'.[3] Certainly, the Elizabethan was perfectly well aware of the difference between what Jonathan Swift called 'rational

---

[1] II. i. 507.

[2] From 'The Necessity of Atheism', *The Prose Works of Percy Bysshe Shelley*, ed. H. B. Forman, London 1880, vol. I, p. 309.

[3] *A Midsummer Night's Dream*, III. i. 141–2.

esteem' and 'that ridiculous passion called love'.[1] Yet to contrast love and reason is not to assert that loving has nothing to do with valuing, but rather to suggest that the value judgements it makes are often absurd. Indeed, the minute we separate love from evaluation the lover ceases to be lunatic, absurd or anything of the sort. The romantic sensationalist lover is in a way unassailable, since, like the poet. 'he nothing affirmeth'.[2]

Nevertheless, however much we may talk of the assimilation of practice to theory, it is certain that the Elizabethans, like twentieth-century man, sometimes fell out of love. To the romantic this process need not be excessively uncomfortable. But to those for whom love has acquired a metaphysical status by being inextricably linked with ethical judgement and commitment, falling out of love must be a very great shock.

I have argued that intuitionistic ethics derives much of its plausibility from the aesthetic phenomena which commonly precede and accompany evaluation. Since it is a psychological fact that an object 'looks' different when it has been evaluated differently, it becomes easy to talk in terms of perception, of 'seeing things in a different light'. For the Elizabethan, the subjectivist 'sensations' of the romantic are rather thought of as perceptions, and as perceptions of a quasi-ethical nature. Falling in love is essentially a kind of encounter. Hence, when one ceases to love a person or thing, one is confronted with a strangely shocking puzzle. Either one may be disillusioned with one's own perceptiveness, or else, baffled by the absence of any identifiable change in the object, may relegate the love-intuitions to a special, ideal realm. After all, if I have seen the original aura of goodness with my own (spiritual) eyes, it is of little avail to tell me that what I now see in some way invalidates that vision. How can a mere perception (particularly a cold, grey one) blot out a fellow perception (particularly a bright, golden one)? There need be no conflict between two objects – unless it is insisted on that they are the same thing after all. If this is once allowed, in a way the very fabric of induction is threatened; chaos is come again. A. N. Whitehead once wrote, 'Induction presupposes metaphysics.'[3] To the Elizabethan, the ordered regularity of the Cosmos sprang naturally from

---

[1] From 'A Letter to a Very Young Lady on her Marriage', in *The Prose Works of Jonathan Swift D.D.*, ed. Temple Scott 1907, vol. XI, p. 119 and p. 120.

[2] Sir Philip Sidney, *A Defence of Poesie*, in *The Complete Works of Sir Philip Sidney*, ed. A. Feuillerat, Cambridge 1923, vol. III, p. 29.

[3] *Science and The Modern World*, London 1927, p. 55.

the continuous intelligence of God. It is not absurd to claim that, for men of Shakespeare's time, God was the guarantor of induction. The kernel of this doctrine is expressed in Othello's cry

> If she be false, O ! then heaven mocks itself.
> I'll not believe it.[1]

The terrible fear that the ideal world may not be autonomous and separate after all but subdued to the imperfections of this muddy earth is wonderfully present in *Troilus and Cressida*, a sadder play than *Othello* if only because while Othello was tragically mistaken about his lady Troilus is miserably right about his. After he has learned about her infidelity, Ulysses asks, 'What hath she done, Prince, that can soil our mothers?'[2] Ulysses's question can elicit no simple, rational answer. It merely uncovers a wound. Yet because we are in the time of Queen Elizabeth the pain is not just a sensation, but embodies a metaphysical grievance also. Charles Williams caught the spirit of it when he wrote:

> There is a world where our mothers are unsoiled and Cressida is his; there is a world where our mothers are soiled and Cressida is given to Diomed. What connexion have those two worlds?[3]

Troilus answers Ulysses's question and Williams's at once: 'Nothing at all, unless that this were she.'[4] He draws out the idea in his next speech:

> This she? No, this is Diomed's Cressida.
> If beauty have a soul, this is not she;
> If souls guide vows, if vows are sanctimony,
> If sanctimony be the gods' delight,
> If there be rule in unity itself,
> This is not she. O madness of discourse,
> That cause sets up, with, and against itself;
> Bi-fold authority! where reason can revolt
> Without perdition, and loss assume all reason
> Without revolt: this is, and is not, Cressid.
> Within my soul there doth conduce a fight
> Of this strange nature that a thing inseparate

[1] *Othello*, iii. iii. 278.
[2] *Troilus and Cressida*, v. ii. 131.
[3] *The English Poetic Mind*, Oxford 1932, p. 60.
[4] *Troilus and Cressida*, v. ii. 132.

> Divides more wider than the sky and earth;
> And yet the spacious breadth of this division
> Admits no orifice for a point as subtle
> As Ariachne's broken woof to enter.
> Instance, O instance! strong as Pluto's gates;
> Cressid is mine, tied with the bonds of heaven:
> Instance, O instance! strong as heaven itself;
> The bonds of heaven are slipp'd, dissolv'd, and loos'd;
> And with another knot, five-finger-tied,
> The fractions of her faith, orts of her love,
> The fragments, scraps, the bits, and greasy relics
> Of her o'er-eaten faith, are bound to Diomed.[1]

Where sensation and evaluation are so interwoven in love, the defection of the beloved is at once painful to the sensibility and puzzling to the mind. Troilus cannot shrug his shoulders and say, 'Well, that's the end of *that* particular sentiment', because for him love was perception; he has *seen* something which he cannot forget.

If the betrayed visionary wishes to insist on the autonomy and independent reality of his vision, he may find himself constructing his ideal in either of two ways. He may wish to say that the ideal world comprises many particular, perceptible objects just as this world does, but the objects of the ideal world are distinguished from the object which mirror them here by the special property of 'radiance' which love perceives. Otherwise, he may wish to say that there is no sense in talking about a corresponding set of objects. The enumeration of objective characteristics will not enable us to distinguish the ideal and the everyday; the 'radiance' is the thing to concentrate on, and this, since it is not necessarily derived from any particular object, is best thought of as transmitted *through* the object.

If this analysis is correct, it explains a curious and recurrent feature in the records of metaphysical passion. We find men writing about the world as if every object in it, if one could only view it in itself, would be seen to be suffused with a special quality and excellence, sufficient to move everlasting love; and then, a page later, we find the same man telling us that we must avert our eyes from the worthless objects of nature and confine our contemplation to spiritual matters. Passages of Dionysiac biolatry give

---

[1] *op. cit.*, v. ii. 134–57. 141 *thy selfe* F, *it selfe* Q. 142 *By foule authority* F, *By-fould authority* Q.

place to tracts of the most negative asceticism. 'This also is Thou: neither is this Thou.'

In terms of pre-romantic psychology it is not only intelligible but natural that a failure in love should be felt to involve a contradiction in ethics, and that the passing away of a youthful joy in the world should affect the consciousness with a sort of metaphysical despair. The word 'metaphysical' sticks in the throat here, yet I think it must be allowed to pass. We often speak today of disillusionment, and there is a temptation to apply this word to the terrible experience which Hamlet, Troilus, Lear and Othello all, in their different ways, undergo. But if we attempt to do so, the word suddenly seems puny. If a man feels that in the faithlessness of his love heaven has mocked itself, we may call him 'disillusioned' from a distance of 400 years if we will, but we would hardly use the word to his face. The word is wrong because it is (in this sense) the offspring of a later age, in which the very practice of despair has changed. In a very similar way the word 'sulk' is an inadequate description of the behaviour of Achilles before Troy. The nursery language of the nineteenth century breaks upon the heroic code of Homeric times. If we call Hamlet disillusioned or Achilles a sulk, only the most foolish will fail to observe that we are using persuasive definition. There is no need to revive here the hypothesis that Shakespeare himself passed through a nervous crisis at this point in his writing career. The suggestion seems to me likely enough, and I set it aside only because it is irrelevant to the essentially critical task which is before us. Any reader can see for himself that between the years 1600 and 1601 the exuberant lyricism of Shakespeare's early verse has given place to poetry of a very different kind, that the poet is working with a new insight into quasi-metaphysical catastrophe; and that is enough for my purpose. This development has been well described in the terms of Wordsworth's poetic psychology by Charles Williams.[1] That the despair took a metaphysical form, however, is less frequently claimed, and therefore needs a more careful demonstration. The Sonnets provide a conveniently limited field for investigation.

Such demonstration is both easy and difficult, for a reason which will appear shortly. The Sonnets are from beginning to end concerned with the falling away of things into ruin and nothingness

[1] See *The English Poetic Mind*. Compare also J. Dover Wilson's *The Essential Shakespeare*, pp. 134–45.

and with the various means of shoring up our state against this ruin. One can, of course, be distressed that things should decay and be at the same time wholly innocent of metaphysics. Yet the successive remedies which Shakespeare proposes imply more and more strongly that his real grievance is radically metaphysical. In the early sonnets this is, indeed, not at all obvious. For the cure here is simply procreation. Youth's proud livery becomes a tattered weed, but man has the biological power to make good time's ravages, by begetting sons who are the image of himself. The tendency to metaphysics, such as it is, lies in the general nature of the comfort. Shakespeare does not say, 'It is true that old age will give you a moist eye and a dry hand, a decreasing leg and an increasing belly, yet there are comforts in sitting quietly at the fireside, and it is a relief to be free of the hot appetites of youth.' He does not even say, 'It will be a comfort to you to watch your children growing up.' His comfort is not really addressed to the ageing man at all. It is rather offered to the world at large. He is not sorry *for* an ageing friend. He is rather sorry *that* his friend, and the rest of the world with him, should slip into decay.

The second remedy is the immortality of poetry.

> Not marble, nor the gilded monuments
> Of princes, shall outlive this powerful rime.
>
> Sonnet LV

Never since Horace's *Exegi monumentum aere perennius* had the poet's vaunt attained this note of star-defying audacity. The basic notion that books survive people (and even statues) is unremarkable. But it is mixed with much more puzzling notions, as that the friend, by being translated into verse, has found a new mode of being exempt from the effects of time, that poetry lifts its subjects into another realm.

The concept of extended duration at last gives way to the frankly metaphysical concept of eternity when the two strands of the Sonnets – the intricate love story and the horror of mutability – are joined in the third remedy, love. It was not the poet's verses that should free his friend from the tyranny of time, but rather his love. Love itself (the now-familiar locution is forced upon us) is timeless and invulnerable.

There are various natural foundations already laid in the Sonnets for this supernatural structure. Important is the 'compensation theme', the idea that the best cure for all ills is not an inward-turned self-comfort, but the contemplation of the beloved object.

> . . . whilst I, whom fortune of such triumph bars
> Unlook'd for joy in that I honour most.
>> Sonnet XXV

> My glass shall not persuade me I am old,
> So long as youth and thou are of one date.
>> Sonnet XXII

> But if the while I think on thee, dear friend,
> All losses are restor'd and sorrows end.
>> Sonnet XXX

> Yet in these thoughts myself almost despising,
> Haply I think on thee,– and then my state,
> Like to the lark at break of day arising
> From sullen earth, sings hymns at heaven's gate;
>> For thy sweet love remember'd such wealth brings
>> That then I scorn to change my state with kings.
>> Sonnet XXIX

That one can forget one's sorrows by dwelling on one's beloved is normal enough. But Shakespeare goes on from here to place the beloved – or the love – the two will be found to intermingle strangely – in a transcendental sphere, where it may be contrasted with the impermanence of the sublunary world. This last leap into quasi-religious metaphysics cannot, I think, be broken down into logical steps, or even into pseudo-logical steps. Love and religion had been associated in Shakespeare's mind from the first.[1] The metaphysical connexion between love, value and religion which we found implicit in Othello's cry[2] assists the poet here in his defiance of time.

Spenser in his *Mutabilitie Cantos*, a work far more ostentatiously metaphysical than Shakespeare's Sonnets, rested content with the least metaphysical of the Shakespearean remedies for imperma-nence, the biological cycle. Against the metaphysical status of the third remedy, love, a specious argument can, however, be brought. It might be urged that all that Shakespeare is saying is that

---

[1] See the possibly authentic *A Lover's Complaint*, l, 250. Cf. also *Romeo and Juliet*, I. ii. 93–94.
[2] See above, p. 119.

thoughts of love dispel care, and that this, if put in its proper place with the sad merriment of the ancient poets, will be seen for what it is, the most sublunary of all cures, more comparable with the consolations of the drinker than with those of the contemplative; that Shakespeare is quite as Horatian in his third remedy as he was in the second. Yet this account simply does not fit the poems. J. B. Leishman has pointed out[1] that the *carpe diem* theme, so far from being central to Shakespeare's sonnet sequence, is conspicuously absent from it. For Shakespeare, love is not so much a way of blotting out one's cares as a way to transcend them. He celebrates not a lowered but a heightened consciousness. His horror at the flux of things is like the horror which Plato inherited from Heraclitus and Cratylus, in that it is universal, and only to be comforted by eternity.

If we follow the plain sense of Shakespeare's words, a metaphysical interpretation seems inevitable. So far, demonstration is easy. One difficulty, however, remains. Metaphysical language is peculiarly liable to turn into merely intensive imagery. If Dante describes Beatrice as heavenly, we are inclined to believe that he means what he says. But if a twentieth-century débutante uses the same word to describe her fiancé, we accept it as a mere intensive. Thus it is claimed that when Shakespeare associates his love with eternity he merely means that his love is very great. If this is true, problems such as the question of idolatry, or of the ontological status of love in the Sonnets, disappear. No one expects logical coherence in *mere* imagery.

The question is, then, which does Shakespeare resemble more closely, Dante or the débutante? The upholders of the intensive account are at an opposite pole to the seekers for hidden meaning. The first class of men maintains that the poet really means less than he appears to, the second that he means more. Perhaps we may steer a narrow course between them, and hold to the strange doctrine that he means what he says.

The dialectic of the Sonnets makes the intensive imagery account very improbable. The function of intensive imagery is ancillary; it is there to intensify something else. But for Shakespeare the metaphysical language expresses the fruition of his design, the answer to questions that have vexed him throughout his career as a poet, as well as the balm for more recent wounds. Modern criticism is often reluctant to allow metaphysical status

[1] *Themes and Variations in Shakespeare's Sonnets*, London 1961, pp. 95 ff.

to the contents of a poem, largely, I suppose, because of a vague fear that this indulgence will confound the categories of poetry and philosophy. The argument concerning the comparative truth value of poetic and various sorts of philosophical language is indeed intricate. Yet I do not think it need impede us here. In plain fact, poetry is usually made up of sentences, some of which are empirical in character, some philosophical, metaphysical, theological or what you will. This is all I intend. J. B. Leishman is anxious to assert 'the instinctiveness and unphilosophicalness of Shakespeare's idealism and spirituality'.[1] I have no quarrel with him. The whole argument of this book revolves round the proposition that metaphysics belongs as much to the primitive as to the sophisticated levels of our consciousness. To say that some of Shakespeare's poetry is metaphysical in content is a perfectly sensible statement. Whether the poetry is sensible metaphysics is a separate question which lies outside the scope of this book.

If we allow that Shakespeare is as serious in his metaphysical moments as he is anywhere else, we may look a little more closely at the concept of love and the beloved in the Sonnets. We can see the concept gradually dissociated and made autonomous, almost indeed deified. A few quotations will give an idea of its status.

> What's in the brain, that ink may character,
> Which hath not figur'd to thee my true spirit?
> What's new to speak, what new to register,
> That may express my love, or thy dear merit?
> Nothing, sweet boy; but yet, like prayers divine,
> I must each day say o'er the very same;
> Counting no old thing old, thou mine, I thine,
> Even as when first I hallow'd thy fair name.
> So that eternal love in love's fresh case
> Weighs not the dust and injury of age,
> Nor gives to necessary wrinkles place,
> But makes antiquity for aye his page;
>   Finding the first conceit of love there bred,
>   Where time and outward form would show it dead.
>   Sonnet CVIII

Now all is done, save what shall have no end . . .[2]
                                             Sonnet CX

[1] *ibid.*, pp. 119 ff.
[2] So Craig's Oxford text. Some editors preserve the reading 'have what shall have no end'.

Love's not Time's fool, though rosy lips and cheeks
Within his bending sickle's compass come;
Love alters not with his brief hours and weeks,
But bears it out even to the edge of doom.
   If this be error, and upon me prov'd,
   I never writ, nor no man ever lov'd.

Sonnet CXVI

. . . but all alone stands hugely politic,
That it nor grows with heat, nor drowns with showers.

Sonnet CXXIV

The second of these quotations, from Sonnet CX, perhaps requires a special defence of its own. In several respects Sonnet CX
is similar to Sonnets XXXVI, XL, LVII, LVIII and LXXI. That
is to say, it is one of the sonnets of self-abnegation, in which
Shakespeare abases himself, to a degree which some find embarras-
sing or offensive, before his beloved. Some of those who find
themselves embarrassed by the literal meaning like to argue that
these Sonnets are, in fact, ironic, that what we take for self-
humiliation is really a kind of censorious sarcasm. This is not an
easy position to maintain. In LVII the lines

But, like a sad slave, stay and think of nought
Save, where you are how happy you make those   .

have an authenticity of moral force which is incompatible with
irony. It is impossible to read them in a spirit of sarcastic hostility.
In Sonnet XXXVI the drab line 'I may not evermore acknowledge
thee' is characterized by nothing so much as a terrifying factual-
ness. It is not true, however, to say that these Sonnets are entirely
free from irony. In fact, they continually avail themselves of irony,
but it is irony of a special sort (seen at its most invidious and also
its most magnificent in Sonnet XCIV) in which the bitter heart of
the jest lies in the fact that the poet, after all, means what he says.
Furthermore, if the Sonnets are taken as, essentially, poems of
introspective analysis rather than poems of persuasion, much of
our embarrassment at Shakespeare's 'grovelling' will disappear.
The Sonnets are only formally part of a dialogue with an invisible
interlocutor. Fundamentally, they are prayer-like poems of self-
examination. The underlying thesis of the Sonnets is not so much
an optative 'Love me' as an indicative – 'I am I: this is what I am'.
In all persuasive love poetry, those passages in which the poet

talks about himself will be tainted with a certain rhetorical expediency, an eye for results, the poet's 'line' with women. If we take Shakespeare's Sonnets to be poetry of this type, we shall scarcely avoid recoiling from what will at once appear to be a self-insinuating humility. But read them as objective self-analysis, and the whole moral colouring is transformed. The conventions of private poetry admit us to a sort of truthfulness which may be more than we can bear. What was sugary and odious (or else sarcastic and censorious) now becomes wry, rueful, and inexorably honest. It is not that Shakespeare is too weak for us, and must be saved by an infusion of disbelief. Rather, he is too strong. Critics who believe that all literature presents its readers with a simple choice, the admission or the exclusion of irony, are in any case ill equipped for Jacobean poetry.

Yet Sonnet CX remains the strongest evidence of all for those who would read these poems as examples of straightforward irony – if only because of its strange

> Then give me welcome, next my heaven the best,
> Even to thy pure and most, most loving breast.[1]

That reiterated 'most' certainly seems to belong to the world of irony and sarcasm. Yet it is very difficult to extend this tone to the rest of the poem. I am myself rather inclined to see here a strange intrusion of the biographical into the aesthetic. At any rate, if we allow ourselves to act for a moment as biographical detectives, a sort of causal explanation can be framed. Throughout the Sonnets Shakespeare treats himself and the 'dark lady' with a terrible, clear-eyed lucidity. This lucidity is not, however, extended to the young man. If ever there is any humbug in the Sonnets, it will be found in those passages which relate to Mr. W. H. His image alone is blurred by a sort of extra-literary embarrassment. It is overwhelmingly probably that Shakespeare's love for Mr. W. H. was at least partially sexual. Thus Shakespeare may well have found himself in the uncomfortable position which frequently assails homosexuals or quasi-homosexuals, forced to oscillate between manly affection and ungovernable erotic passion. It may well be that Shakespeare was shamed into self-contempt by the cold yet constant affection of his friend – an affection maintained without difficulty by the heterosexual friend throughout a series of affairs

---

[1] I can see no real warrant for altering 'most most' to 'most' as Craig does in the Oxford text.

with women conducted on the side. It may well be that Shakespeare, anxious to excuse his friend's infidelity, had half convinced himself that W. H.'s behaviour was impeccable. But all the while there is a deeper level of Shakespeare's psychology which cries out that W. H. has betrayed something inexpressibly valuable and intimate in their relationship. All this no doubt is humanly forgivable, but it leads to artistic disorder. That 'most, most' doth protest too much indeed, but not with the mock-protestation of irony. Its shrillness was never allowed for in the conscious design of the poem. It is an intruder there, the raw signal of an imperfectly assimilated emotion. It is the same emotion which we see the poet struggling with in Sonnet XL:

> Lascivious grace, in whom all ill well shows,
> Kill me with spites; yet we must not be foes.

But here the emotion is better assimilated. The faults of W. H. are at any rate perceived with a momentary clarity; they find a place in the rhetoric of the lines, even if we feel there is as much of indulgence as of charity in the way they are instantly muffled in defensive praise.

In general, I can see no reason to doubt the fundamentally literal status of this poem (Sonnet CX). That the poet should write from a divided heart does not automatically produce irony in the resulting composition. The vision of eternal love survives with overwhelming force.

This starry doctrine of love is closely linked with his anti-Petrarchan realism. Petrarch believed in love for beauty's sake, love for the soul's sake. Shakespeare takes an almost brutal pleasure in enforcing his faith in love for love's sake; that and that only.

I am left doubtful as to whether the love of the Sonnets is of the kind to survive a disaster such as Troilus's, or merely of the kind to bring out the metaphysical status of that disaster. His insistence that faithless love is no love (Sonnet CXVI) and the comparison of his beloved's beauty to Eve's apple (Sonnet XCIII) incline me to the latter view. And indeed the former doctrine has a bad smell about it. A man who is untroubled by the defection of his beloved because he still has love itself is not a very admirable object. Is he not merely 'in love with love'?

Yet the assertion of love's autonomy must have some function. A strand of spirituality is irreducibly present still, and tempts us to the language of transcendentalism. We require an account of the concept 'love' which will admit both the autonomy and the eternalness and yet leave it immanent in human relationships. I am conscious now of writing in a language which I do not fully understand, yet I feel there is no other available for the purpose. Whether Shakespeare's concept of love is ultimately a mystery beyond our contemplation or just a muddle beyond my analytic competence, I do not know. So for the rest of this chapter the reader must be content with hints and suggestions.

The Sonnets do not take us to the end of Shakespeare's career. For the last years we are driven back upon the plays. These late dramas seem to imply a resolution of the problems I have been trying to explain. The plays of Shakespeare's middle period are infused with a sort of enormous disgust, first with what he calls 'ingratitude' in personal relationships, and then (perhaps I should say 'hence') with the world in general. If we allow ourselves to see the sequence of Shakespeare's tragedies as a developing, evolving thing, *Troilus and Cressida* seems to mark a point of crisis. *Troilus and Cressida* is not such a good play as *Macbeth*, but the *disgust* in *Troilus and Cressida* is stronger than the disgust in any other Shakespeare play.

The period of stress is worked out in the great tragedies, and then, about the year 1608, the strange new poetry of the late Romances makes its appearance. In them we find a new development in the direction of unaffected lyricism, of a near-fairy-tale sort of play, in which violence of character if not of action has been banished from the stage. Many readers (we saw a little of some of them in the first chapter) have found a transcendental quality in these plays. Yet they have nothing of the negative character one normally associates with transcendentalism. It is true that Lytton Strachey found in the author of the last plays a man tired of everything but poetry.[1] The picture he draws is in a way very reminiscent of the man we feared might result from the doctrine of the Sonnets – a man in love with love and oblivious of other human beings. Yet, after all, to press this doctrine is to misunderstand the Sonnets and to misread the Romances. There is no languor in the pungent poetry of *The Tempest*.

The shift from the tragic preoccupation to that of the Romances is not instantaneous or even clear-cut. There is an observable

[1] G. Lytton Strachey, *Books and Characters, French and English*, London 1922, 'Shakespeare's Final Period', esp. p. 60.

transition, perhaps most fascinating in the last act of *Antony and Cleopatra*. It is perhaps odd that for a vision of the self-authenticating property of love we should have to go, not to *King Lear* with its powerfully Christian frame of reference, but to the glittering, pagan *Antony and Cleopatra*. After all, in *King Lear* we are given some glimpses of an eternity of Charity, even if the vision is not strong enough to survive the murder of Cordelia. But there is no sight of Heaven in *Antony and Cleopatra* – only intimations of Elysium. The love of the play is not Charity but Eros, in triumph and humiliation. The words which foreshadow the Romances are put into the mouth, not of a Cordelia, but of a high-class whore, an irresponsible incarnation of female sexuality. They are, of course, words of an amazing beauty:

> CLEOPATRA: You laugh when boys or women tell their
> dreams; Is't not your trick?

> DOLABELLA. I understand not, madam.

> CLEOPATRA. I dream'd there was an Emperor Antony: O!
> such another sleep, that I might see
> But such another man.

> DOLABELLA. If it might please ye, –

> CLEOPATRA. His face was as the heavens, and therein stuck
> A sun and moon, which kept their course, and lighted
> The little O, the earth.

> DOLABELLA. Most sovereign creature, –

> CLEOPATRA. His legs bestrid the ocean; his rear'd arm
> Crested the world; his voice was propertied
> As all the tuned spheres, and that to friends;
> But when he meant to quail and shake the orb,
> He was as rattling thunder. For his bounty,
> There was no winter in 't, an autumn 'twas
> That grew the more by reaping; his delights
> Were dolphin-like, they show'd his back above
> The element they liv'd in; in his livery
> Walk'd crowns and crownets, realms and islands were
> As plates dropp'd from his pocket.

> DOLABELLA. Cleopatra, –

CLEOPATRA. Think you there was, or might be, such a
    man
  As this I dream'd of?

DOLABELLA. Gentle madam, no.

CLEOPATRA. You lie, up to the hearing of the gods.
  But, if there be, or ever were, one such,
  It's past the size of dreaming; nature wants stuff
  To vie strange forms with fancy; yet to imagine
  An Antony were nature's piece 'gainst fancy,
  Condemning shadows quite.

(v. ii. 74–99)

Notice the movement of the argument: Did I dream this love-vision? No, it was real. Yet even if it were a dream, it has a force and colour against which reality itself looks pale. Once this thing has been *seen*, it may be thrust aside, but it cannot be obliterated. The crucial thing about the speech is Cleopatra's willingness, in this special case, to argue *from* the idea *against* 'reality'.

Perhaps these plays give us a clue to the nature of the autonomy of love in the Sonnets. Perhaps Shakespeare finally opted for the vision-in-love after all, resolved that what he had seen could not be undermined or refuted by the chance frailties of human beings. In the Sonnets which express the theme of 'compensation' we can see the growth of the notion that love after all was something that no disaster could take from him. We can guess that the change of heart soon affected other areas of his consciousness, his attitude to poetry and to nature. The thought that whatever Cressida did leaves love itself untouched left him free to celebrate love once more.

It is easy to see why the late Shakespeare incurred the charge of senility. His Romances have the specious appearance of a second childhood because they are a renewal of innocence.

This story has certain strong affinities with Keats's fitful resolution of his worries about the falsifying imagination. Certain passages[1] from his letters are very relevant here. In them we can find the separation and 'deification' of an idea (beauty) and of the

---

[1] See the letter to Bailey of 22 November 1817, the letter to Woodhouse, 27 October 1818, and the letter to George and Georgiana Keats, written on various days in October 1818, in *The Letters of John Keats*, ed. H. E. Rollins, Cambridge, Mass. 1958, vol. I, pp. 183–7, pp. 386–8, p. 403, respectively.

assertion (which has affinities with the theological *Credo*) of the autonomous validity of the imagination. One passage in particular deserves quotation:

> O I wish I was as certain of the end of all your troubles as that of your momentary start about the authenticity of the Imagination. I am certain of nothing but of the holiness of the Heart's affections, and the truth of Imagination – What the imagination seizes as Beauty must be truth – whether it existed before or not – for I have the same Idea of all our Passions as of Love they are all, in their sublime, creative of essential Beauty – In a word, you may know my favourite Speculation by my first Book and the little song I sent in my last – which is a representation from the fancy of the probable mode of operating in these Matters – The Imagination may be compared to Adam's dream – he awoke and found it truth. I am the more zealous in this affair, because I have never yet been able to perceive how anything can be known for truth by consequitive reasoning – and yet it must be.[1]

(Letter to Bailey, 22 November 1817)

It is as if both Shakespeare and Keats had, each in his own way, seen through seeing through things. They might be saying to us '*Of course* people are false to one another, fail to live up to their own love, *of course* the world is not always as we imagine it; but that does not mean that love is not love, or imagination imagination. These things stand on their own feet and make their own way in the world. Light is not *refuted* by darkness. So why should we not after all celebrate the light?'

I have told the story in the easiest way, as a piece of literary psychology. We cannot leave the topic, however, without a few guesses at the logic of the assertions involved. There must, I feel, be a connexion, though I am not able to expound it, between Moore's attribution of unanalysability to 'good' and Shakespeare's 'deification' of love. We saw enough to understand how this way of viewing the logic of value could make a man feel that the word 'good' brought news from a far, inviolate country. If the meaning of 'good' is not to be exhausted by the enumeration of particular things, then it must be a divine spirit, having a unique authority, which has swum into our conceptual apparatus and

[1] In Rollins's edition, vol. I, pp. 184–5.

transmuted our relation with the world. This turning inside out of more common orders of reasoning has certain affinities, perhaps with Anselm's celebrated Ontological Proof[1] of the existence of God. If God is greater than anything we can conceive, says Anselm, it follows that he must exist; for anything I conceive can be made greater by the addition of actual existence, since that which exists actually is greater than that which exists mentally; therefore God must have actual existence. This argument has been the subject of much merry refutation from Aquinas[2] to Kant[3] and Broad.[4] But in its assertion of the autonomy of the idea and its wish to argue from the idea to reality it is not unlike the dialectic I have hesitantly attributed to Shakespeare and Keats. Certainly, Anselm's Proof seems, for certain intelligences at least, to have a strength beyond that of its obvious logical structure, but its admirers are commonly anxious to substitute something else (I am not sure what) for its ostensibly argumentative intention. Thus Simone Weil says that the Ontological Proof 'is mysterious because it doesn't address itself to the intelligence, but to love'.[5] And Karl Barth has argued[6] that the proof is 'essentially theological', that is, an attempt to draw out the implications of God's name and not at all a proof of his existence. He adds that Anselm admits into his discourse what others exclude, 'the aesthetics of religious knowledge'.[7]

When, in the year 399 B.C., Socrates chose to remain in Athens and die instead of saving his life by flight, there can be little doubt that, to the average Athenian of the time, his behaviour appeared αἰσχρόν, base, more fit for a slave than for a free man. Ordinary moral thinking was still infected with the success-ethic of the older 'shame culture'. The word ἀγαθός, which we translate 'good', failed, in fact, to distinguish the virtuous man from the popular thug. Now, when Socrates conceived a new ideal of human conduct, did he

---

[1] See *S. Anselmi . . . Opera Omnia*, ed. F. S. Schmitt, Edinburgh 1946, *Proslogion*, ch. III. An English translation is available in the *Library of Christian Classics*, London 1956, vol. X, *Anselm to Ockham*.

[2] *Summa Theologica*, I. ii. 1 obj. 2.

[3] In *Immanuel Kant's Critique of Pure Reason*, trans. Norman Kemp Smith, London 1961 (reprinted from the corrected 2nd impression of 1933), ch. III, §4, pp. 500–7.

[4] 'Arguments for the Existence of God', *Journal of Theological Studies*, XL (1939), esp. p. 22.

[5] *Notebooks*, trans. Arthur Wills, London 1956, vol. II, p. 375.

[6] *Anselm: Fides Quaerens Intellectum*, trans. I. W. Robertson (from the German 2nd edition of 1958), London 1960, esp. p. 16.

[7] *ibid.*, p. 16.

make something, or did he perceive something? It seems, somehow, that he did both. He revised the rules, but it seems a falsification to say this so long as we imply that his revision was merely arbitrary. He enjoyed a certain kind of perception, yet his perception could undoubtedly have been called 'subjective', since it was shared by so few. Yet the spectre of Socratic morality took on life, proved real. If the God of Anselm be taken as a focus of ideals (a legitimate way to demythologize 'not of this world'?) one can, beginning from here, learn to see how a man can find this unique extraterrestrial thing suddenly endowed with a strange, self-authenticating weight.

Various accounts of the *experience* of supreme value (the question-begging term is forced upon us) show similar features. The lover in the *Roman de la Rose* first sees the Rose reflected in a crystal which lies at the bottom of a clear well. Then he turns and sees the Rose itself.[1] This is the poet's allegorical unfolding of the moment of falling in love, which in everyday practice commonly involves a transition from inarticulate sensation to a coherent experience, requiring an object-language of its own; first the Arrow of Love, and then his language and ritual. This objective coherence of the experience of love may be repeatedly lost or forgotten. But it is capable of rediscovery, even after the defection or death of the beloved. John Donne (whose love poetry, like Shakespeare's, is often condemned as idolatrous) says to his lady:

> If ever any beauty I did see,
> which I desir'd, and got, t'was but a dreame of thee.[2]

Like Adam, de Lorris's Lover and John Donne awake and find it truth. Like the statue of Hermione in *The Winter's Tale*, the image proves real.

Whether there is a real connexion between the ideas of Shakespeare, Keats and Anselm, I do not know. I have an intuition that there is, but I cannot pretend to elucidate it satisfactorily. Such formal resemblances as I have been able to isolate must be my excuse for suggesting a more profound relation which eludes exact formulation.

There remain the late plays themselves, with their strangely

[1] In Chaucer's translation, ll. 1553–1705, in *The Works of Geoffrey Chaucer*, ed. F. N. Robinson, 2nd ed., Boston 1957, pp. 579–81.
[2] 'The Good Morrow', ll. 6–7, in *The Poems of John Donne*, ed. H. J. C. Grierson, reprinted in 1953 from the 1st ed. of 1912, p. 7.

paradisal note, with their earthy spirituality and intimate remoteness. We have suggested a sort of rehabilitation of the poet's powers of valuing the world. Keats in his letter to Bailey made use of the Myth of Eden. The *Tempest* has, almost from the first, reminded its readers of the same myth.

VI

THE TEMPEST

One of the reasons why *The Tempest* is hard to classify lies in its parentage. It has two sets of sources, first a body of romantic, fairy-tale literature and second a collection of travellers' reports. If its mother was a mermaid, its father was a sailor. It must be acknowledged that on the fairy side there is no story which we can point to as a direct influence on Shakespeare, but Iakob Ayrer's *Die Schöne Sidea* (published posthumously in his *Opus Theatricum*) and the story of Dardano and Nicephorus in the fourth chapter of Antonio de Eslava's *Noches de Invierno*[1] show, besides a strong similarity of plot, an occasional correspondence of detail, as in the episode of the log-carrying. The late date at which Ayrer's play was published makes it very unlikely that it was Shakespeare's source, but there is just enough similarity between the two plays to let us postulate a common origin. Some close analogues have been found in the *scenari* for Italian *commedia dell' arte*[2] but Kermode observes[3] that all extant *scenari* postdate Shakespeare's play. Other analogues are Diego Ortunez de Calahorra's *Espejo de Príncipes y Caballeros*, and *Fiamella*, a pastoral comedy by Bartolomeo Rossi. Here, at all events, are hints of a story available to Shakespeare, and very amenable to the Romantic style of composition he had learned in company with Beaumont and Fletcher.[4]

[1] A collection of Spanish romances published in 1609 or 1610.

[2] The notion appears to have originated in F. Neri's *Scenari delle Maschere in Arcadia*, 1913. See also Hardin Craig, *An Interpretation of Shakespeare*, New York 1948, p. 345, and H. D. Gray, *Studies in Philology*, XVIII (1921), p. 129.

[3] In his Arden Edition of *The Tempest*, 6th ed., 1958, p. lxvii.

[4] See A. H. Thorndike, *The Influence of Beaumont and Fletcher on Shakespeare*, Cambridge, Mass. 1901.

On the other side of the family correspondences are more striking, and we can speak of direct influences. There is no doubt that
the Bermuda pamphlets describing the wreck of the *Sea-Adventure*
on her way to Virginia were known to Shakespeare. Sylvester
Jourdain's *Discovery of the Barmudas* (1610), the Council of Virginia's
*True Declaration of the State of the Colonie in Virginia, with a confutation
of such scandalous reports as have tended to the disgrace of so worthy an
enterprise* (1610), and William Strachey's *True Reportory of the
Wrack,* first published in *Purchas his Pilgrimes,* 1625, but accessible
to Shakespeare from 1610, have all left traces in *The Tempest.*

The peculiar wedding of the marvellous and the circumstantial
which we find in *The Tempest* may thus be attributed, in some
measure, to the stuff of which it is made. But, nevertheless, we
must be careful not to make too much of the contrast between the
documentary naval reports and the fabulous tales of princes and
sorcerers. *Purchas his Pilgrimes,* though not so extravagant and
romantic as it appeared to the author of *The Ancient Mariner*
centuries later, was nevertheless not entirely innocent of the
marvellous. Geography itself was still soaked with imaginative
significance, for the Royal Society had not yet done its judicious
work of scientific desiccation. Spatial conceptions of Paradise,
unacknowledged allegories, and 'tall stories' were all a normal
part of the literature of travel. In the sixth century the monk
Cosmas had, as Raleigh noted, laid down the object of many a
later quest.

> If Paradise were really on the surface of the world, is there
> not a man among those who are so keen to learn and search out
> everything, that would not let himself be deterred from reach-
> ing it? When we see that there are men who will not be deterred
> from penetrating to the ends of the earth in search of silk, and
> all for the sake of filthy lucre, how can we believe that they
> would be deterred from going to get a sight of Paradise?[1]

Columbus (quite seriously) took the mouths of the Orinoco for
the threshold of Paradise, and in 1512 the Governor of Puerto
Rico landed in Florida while sailing in search of a miraculous
Fountain of Youth. It is hard to know whether to call George
Chapman's *De Guina Carmen Epicum* (1596) a Utopian or a Paradisal
account of that place. It is well known that Spenser places his
fairyland at once in England and in the human heart. But there is

[1] Quoted in W. Raleigh, *The English Voyages,* London 1928, p. 16.

another place, the prologue of the second book of the *Faerie Queene*, where he suggests, more than half seriously, that explorers may at any time *discover* Fairyland in some other part of the Globe. The interesting thing is that none of these three suggestions is felt to be incompatible with the other two, just as no conflict was recognized between Paradise as a lost primal state of felicity and Paradise as a place somewhere out in the unknown Atlantic seas. Marlowe seems to see no important distinction between geographical exploration and philosophical inquiry – at least, he speaks of them in one breath in *Doctor Faustus*:

> Shall I make spirits fetch me what I please,
> Resolve me of all ambiguities,
> Performe what desperate enterprise I will?
> Ile have them flye to *India* for gold,
> Ransacke the Ocean for orient pearle,
> *And search all corners of the new found world*
> *For pleasant fruites and princely delicates*:
> *Ile have then reade mee straunge philosophie,*
> An tell the secrets of all forraine kings . . .
>
> (ll. 107–15, my italics in ll. 112–14)

All the same, the distinction between frank fancy and documentary report remains, and if fabulous elements appear in naval records they merely gain a more startling appearance of factual truth thereby. And there is no doubt that *The Tempest* owes much of its power to an air of circumstantial actuality. Nothing could be more different than *The Tempest* from the Gothic ghost stories of the earlier Shakespeare, all graveyards and darkness. The spectres of the Enchanted Isle move in the daylight, and are for that reason twice as frightening. The Jacobeans were after all much more ready to credit the *actual* existence of the supernatural than are we. There are no sorcerers of repute in England now, but an historical Prospero can easily be found – Dr. John Dee[1] for example. Lytton Strachey's astonishing statement – 'to turn from Theseus and Titania and Bottom to the Enchanted Island, is to step out of a country lane into a conservatory'[2] – is almost the flat opposite of the truth.

Yet there is no doubt that *The Tempest* is a queer play. The

---

[1] See Bonamy Dobrée, 'The Tempest', *E & S*, NS V (1952), p. 18.
[2] 'Shakespeare's Final Period', in *Books and Characters*, p. 62.

strangeness of the island, the sounds in the air, the unnatural languor that intermittently envelops the characters, have the sinister quality of Phaedria's Isle in the *Faerie Queene*. Though the strange events of the play are in large measure accounted for by the arts of Prospero, certain things remain odd to the end. Playgoers are fairly well accustomed to that sane and purposive magic which saves a drowning man or refreshes him with sleep, but the music in the air, the voice crying in the wave, the 'strange, hollow and confused noise' which accompanies the vanishing of the reapers and nymphs at the end of the masque, the somnolence of Miranda – these gratuitous paranorma are more disturbing. Ariel mocking the drunkards by playing the song back to them on the tabor and pipe does not really worry us; we have seen similar things before in *A Midsummer Night's Dream*. But these causeless and capricious portents propel the sensibility into an unfamiliar region, and adandon it to uneasy speculation.

At the same time, the miracles and prodigies of the Enchanted Isle are related in a curiously intimate way to our experience. The hearing of strange sounds which are never properly identified, the swift recourse to useless weapons in the moments between sleep and waking – these things are especially alarming because especially near the bone. We have all lain in a twilight of inarticulate apprehension through the moments of waking. We have all known times in our everyday lives when our inattentive faculties have been surprised by confused noises, or the sound as of a name being called. E. R. Dodds in *The Greeks and The Irrational*[1] observes that dreams are a fertile source of inference to another world in primitive thought. In Shakespeare's hands, these half-glimpsed sights, half-heard sounds, this ἀπορία felt by men surprised by the nameless, become once more a means of alerting apprehensive speculation. And in the unpredictable island of *The Tempest*, we are denied that prosaic awakening which vividly refutes the night. It seems as if the poet is bent on drawing from us a different sort of credence from that ordinarily given to plays – perhaps a more primitive sort. At iii.iii.83 the Shapes (we are given no clearer stage-direction) carry out the banquet 'with mops and mows', and we never learn what they are or what their dance is about. At v.i.231 we are told how the sleeping sailors awoke to hear strange and horrific sounds and we are never told what made them. Yet to call these things loose ends would be foolish criticism. They are there

[1] London, 1951. See especially pp. 102–34.

to heat our imaginations. One feels that one can hardly call the
metaphysically speculative reaction inappropriate.

Shakespeare has another instrument for piercing to the more
primitive levels of our consciousness in the unpleasing shape of
Caliban. Caliban, though horribly unchildlike, belongs to a world
most of us have known as children. He lives in an intellectual half-
light of bites, pinches, nettle-stings, terrors, cupboard-love, glimpses of extraordinary and inexplicable beauty. These things play a
negligible part in the society of adults, but most of us remember
a society in which they were intensely familiar. It was Caliban who,
like a child, 'cried to dream again', was taught how to talk, and
shown the Man in the Moon. The character of Caliban shows us
objects which are too close to be seen in the ordinary way of
things. His world is near-sighted, tactile, downward-looking,
lacking in distant prospects.

But, despite the probing imagery of Caliban, the island itself
seems very remote. We are given the feeling of immense distances,
enforced by many images: 'Now would I give a thousand furlongs
of sea for an acre of barren ground; long heath, brown furze, anything', 'Canst thou remember A time before we came unto this
cell? . . . 'Tis far off; and rather like a dream than an assurance',
'What seest thou else In the dark backward and abysm of time?'
'She that dwells Ten leagues beyond man's life; she that from
Naples Can have no note, unless the sun were post – The man i'
th' moon's too slow – till new-born chins Be rough and razorable:
she that from whom We all were sea-swallowed . . .', 'A space
whose every cubit Seems to cry out . . .' 'In this most desolate
isle', together with the use of far-away place-names like Arabia,
Tunis and Angier.

The combination of a feeling of remoteness with an equally
strong feeling of nearness, of intimacy, is an ambiguity characteristic of dreams, and of things half perceived in the instant of
awaking. There are several wakings from sleep in the play, all
drawn with an emphasis on the equivocal character of perception
in such circumstances – Gonzalo and others in II.i., the sailors
in v.i., and Caliban's

> . . . and sometime voices,
> That, if I then had wak'd after long sleep,
> Will make me sleep again . . .   III. ii. 144–6

Miranda compares her dim memory image of the ladies who

attended her in her infancy to a dream (I. ii. 45). To these we may add the wonderful description in the minutest terms of an image glimmering upon the sight – 'The fringed curtains of thine eye advance' (I. ii. 405). There is another reference to eyelids at IV. i. 177.

The nature poetry of the play (much of it Caliban's) is extremely interesting. It, too, is full of minute observations and gigantic distances, with a strange salt-sweetness hardly to be found elsewhere. We may skim the play, creaming off images which illustrate its special flavour – 'the ooze of the salt deep . . . the veins of the earth when it is baked with frost', 'unwholesome fen . . . berries . . . brine-pits', 'yellow sands . . . the wild waves whist', 'sea-water . . . fresh brook mussels, withered roots and husks, wherein the acorn cradles', 'bogs, fens, flats', 'a rock by the seaside', 'show thee a jay's nest and instruct thee how To snare the nimble marmoset; I'll bring thee To clust'ring filberts, and sometimes I'll get thee Young scamels from the rock', 'Where crabs grow . . . pignuts', 'the quick freshes' – and the nature hymn at IV. i. 60 ff., bristling with grain and grasses, wet with rain and dew. It is strange that this great nature poem is not better loved. It may be that the focus is too clear for our post-romantic eyes. Perhaps most of us would prefer 'showery April' to Shakespeare's more intimate, tactile 'spongy April '. This truthful clarity in the natural imagery, like the circumstantial elements in the plot, helps to draw from us that special credence, at once lively and in a state of suspense, which is proper to the play. When the picture blurs we look for the emergence of bright, if unfamiliar, realities, not Gothic spectres. While the smoky ghosts of the old Histories seemed to repel our gaze, the supernatural in *The Tempest* seems to invite our minute attention or even to arise from it.

Once charmed into such an expectant frame of mind, we are quick to speculate, to postulate new 'planes of being' and vague spiritual hierarchies. The play begins with a desperate storm and shipwreck, and then the scene shifts abruptly to Prospero's cell. The crackling oaths of the rough-lunged castaways give place to the tranquil discourse of two angelic beings who might have stepped out of Blake's illustration to his *Songs of Innocence*. No sound of tempest now, the father and daughter talk together in an elaborately beautiful language, the sense variously drawn out from one line to another, which is very difficult to describe. They talk as no human beings ever talked and yet seem all the closer to our

humanity for it. The difference between the diction of the castaways and that of Prospero and Miranda, like the different systems
of perspective which Michelangelo gives to his *Ignudi* and his
Biblical personages in the Sistine Chapel, prompt us to assign to
them different 'orders of being'.

But we are also informed that Prospero is an Italian, an old
acquaintance of the castaways, sometime Duke of Milan. His
discontents and ambitions are extremely worldly. He is to be given
no dramatic walk-over as a type of Spiritual Virtue. Again we wish
to use the prefix 'half-', as often in discussing this play, and say
that Prospero and Miranda are half-dipped in another world. This
recurrent sense of ambiguity and suspension is extremely potent
dramatically.

In the first scene of Act II we have an excellent specimen of this
dramatic avoidance of the univocal. In it the 'honest old Counsel-
lor' Gonzalo is baited by the wicked plotters. The dialogue in
which this is carried out is not to be understood or enjoyed by a
lazy mind. Let us not deceive ourselves, Antonio and Sebastian are
truly witty; Gonzalo really does talk like an old fool. But Antonio
and Sebastian are themselves both foolish and wicked, while
Gonzalo is not really a fool at all. Had Shakespeare made Gonzalo's
discourse less ponderous and the witticisms of the rest feebler,
instead of allowing merit to prevail by its own sinews, the scene
would have had one-tenth of its present power. As it stands, it is
taut as a bowstring. As the scene proceeds the laughter of the
plotters, and our own laughter also, grows harsher in our ears.
Between interruptions, Gonzalo makes several pertinent observations: that they are better off than they had reason to expect, that
though the island seems to be uninhabited the necessities of life
are all to hand. He also remarks the disturbing state of their
garments, dry and unstained by the sea. The others laugh on, and
their laughter seems an echo of another laughter, in a Flemish
tavern, where other similarly jovial fellows gaily proposed to slay
Death – the *riotoures* of Chaucer's *Pardoner's Tale*.

In turning to this scene, we passed over the meeting of Ferdinand and Miranda, which is oddly colourless and at the same time
entirely glorious. Prospero, a little less than omniscient, directs the
course of the encounter. Miranda glimmers upon Ferdinand's sight
like something divine (as he says). The haunting image of Adam's
dream ('he awoke and found it Truth') seems strangely relevant.
Samuel Pepys (who seems to have seen *The Tempest* at least six

times) called it 'the most innocent play that ever I saw'.[1] This is perhaps the first meagre hint of the imagery of Eden which was to gather round the play in the writings of Coleridge, Lamb, Meredith and others.[2] Miranda speaks the forthright language of the late-Shakespearean heroine, without coquetry or irony, yet full of humanity. Ferdinand is, I feel, the lesser creature of the two. He has the air of youthful nobility which allows Miranda to take him for a spirit, yet at the same time he has something in common with other young pup heroes (to whom Shakespeare is strangely indulgent) such as Posthumus, or even Claudio. He is a flawed object, uncertainly idealistic, and lacks the sweet earth-bound candour of his lady.

As the play unfolds the character of Caliban is introduced, and, a little later, the comedians, Trinculo and Stephano. The marvellous animal poetry of Caliban contrasts strangely with the myopic inebriation of Stephano and the folly of the fool. We feel a slight shiver when Caliban deifies the drunken butler. Long ago Schlegel and Hazlitt[3] pointed out the vulgarity of the comedians and the utter absence of it in Caliban, who is without convention. One is reminded of E. M. Forster's distinction[4] between coarseness and vulgarity, the first revealing something and the second concealing something. Caliban belongs to one order, the comedians to another, Prospero to another and Miranda perhaps to yet another. The play begins to shimmer and the allegorist critic is 'amazed with matter'.

The beginning of Act III is in symmetrical contrast with the beginning of the previous scene. There we had the brutish Caliban bearing wood for his master. Here we have Ferdinand bearing wood for his lady. Ferdinand, like Caliban, is given a soliloquy. But this is no animal poetry. We hear nothing now of stings or hedgehogs. Instead we have a rounded little philosophical discourse, and breathe the upper air of the polite Renascence intellect.

[1] *The Diary of Samuel Pepys, M.A., F.R.S.*, ed. H. B. Wheatley, London 1896, entry for 7 November 1667.

[2] See *Coleridge's Shakespearean Criticism*, ed. T. M. Raysor, London 1930, vol. I, p. 133; Charles Lamb, *On the Tragedies of Shakespeare, considered with reference to their fitness for Stage Representation*, first published in *The Reflector*, 1811, printed in *The Complete Works of Charles Lamb*, ed. R. H. Shepherd, London 1892, p. 264; George Meredith, *The Ordeal of Richard Feverel*, first published 1859, in the Standard Edition, London 1914, p. 120. See also above, pp. 3ff.

[3] See above, p. 2.

[4] In *The Longest Journey* (first published 1907), The World's Classics Edition, London 1960, p. 241.

Yet he is not entirely satisfactory. We feel that where the play requires him to be luminous he is merely grey. It seems hard that Caliban should so engross the nature poetry of the play, for if a little were given to Ferdinand (as it is given to Florizel in *The Winter's Tale*) he might gain in radiance.

The crazy plot of Caliban and the comedians against Prospero is carried forward with great dramatic dexterity. We are never allowed to abandon ourselves to unreserved laughter, largely because of the character of Caliban. On the one hand his sheer nastiness (notice that he merits the conceptually primitive charge of 'nastiness' rather than the fully-fledged moral opprobrium of 'wickedness') as in his plans for Prospero –

> I'll yield him thee asleep,
> Where thou may'st knock a nail into his head.
>
> III. ii. 65–66

> Batter his skull, or paunch him with a stake,
> Or cut his wezand with thy knife.
>
> III. ii. 95–96

– and, on the other hand, his glimpses of inexplicable beauty leave the scene with an uneasy status. Caliban's description of his heart-tearing visions creates a perfect suspension in time, to which the illogical tense-sequence may be allowed to contribute.[1]

> Be not afeard: the isle is full of noises,
> Sounds and sweet airs, that give delight, and hurt not.
> Sometimes a thousand twangling instruments
> Will hum about mine ears; and sometime voices,
> That, if I then had wak'd after long sleep,
> Will make me sleep again: and then, in dreaming,
> The clouds methought would open and show riches
> Ready to drop upon me; that, when I wak'd
> I cried to dream again.
>
> III. ii. 141–9

The effect is increased a few lines later when Stephano suddenly sees all that they have been doing and plotting for the immediate future in the light of a tale told to him long ago –

---

[1] As Robert Graves suggests in *The White Goddess*, emended and enlarged edition, London 1948, p. 425.

That shall be by and by: I remember the story.

III. ii. 153

The bewilderment grows in the next scene, where Alonso, Sebastian and the rest find that they are lost. Gonzalo describes the island as a maze (III. iii. 2–3), an image which is to recur at v. i. 242. As they talk, the sound of music comes to their ears. As before, when each saw the island with different eyes, so now their perceptions diverge in the presence of the supernatural. Gonzalo is at first content with the mere beauty of it – 'marvellous sweet music!' (III. iii. 19). Sebastian and Antonio are flippant. Prospero watches, invisible, and approves Gonzalo. He mocks them with the banquet, snatched from them by Harpies. Ariel appears and denounces the villains. They draw, only to be mocked by Ariel, who all but says to them, in the best Oxford manner, 'You have made a category mistake.' Again the feeling of ἀπορία, of utter helplessness is conveyed to us. There is nothing remote from our experience in this, despite the elaborate apparatus of sorcery and fairies with which it is presented. There must be few people who have never awoken from a nightmare still grappling with an insubstantial enemy – attempting to bring physical slings and arrows to subdue a 'mental phenomenon'. Less closely connected but not irrelevant is the *feeling* which accompanies the making of a category mistake, or an attempt to yoke incomparables; as P. G. Wodehouse would say, the mind boggles. The villains boggle.

Ariel vanishes in thunder, the 'Shapes' carry out the table, and Alonso tells how he heard the name 'Prosper' in the withdrawing roar of the waves, and then in the wind and thunder. Again, the empirical character is strong. Experience will supply many such false configurations which have left us momentarily in doubt whether to form a natural or a supernatural interpretation. The play, with its life-size magician and veritable bombardment of miracles, determines us in favour of the supernatural. Sebastian and Antonio, still bemused by their own folly, cry out in hysterical defiance of the spirits that they will 'fight their legions o'er' (III. iii. 103).

Act IV opens with the sweet and orderly betrothal of Ferdinand and Miranda. Prospero, a heavyish father, enjoins the observance of the sacrament of marriage. Ariel is dispatched to invite the rabble to the ceremony, the crown of the play, where all are to be joined. It is the turning point of the plot, where δέσις gives place to λύσις – though with this particular story it is tempting to reverse Aristotle's metaphor, and refer to the end as the δέσις or binding up of the play. The betrothal is attended by a masque, and therefore, we may suppose, by elaborate music and décor. Juno and Ceres come, heralded by the rainbow messenger Iris – represented by players, it is true, but then the players are spirits – and the play seems to move into yet another dimension.[1] The transformation is almost worth calling a change of medium, and is comparable in its effect to the introduction of human voices in the last movement of Beethoven's Ninth Symphony. Goddesses, nymphs and sunburned reapers (in addition to the other characters) all come to the betrothal. The blessings of plenty are called down upon the future bride and bridegroom.

But the masque ends abruptly in a chaos of discords – 'a strange, hollow and confused noise'. Prospero at once attributes this to the conspiracy against his life. We find ourselves being propelled into the mental entertainment of a cosmic harmony, in which an impulse of ill will entails a *physical* dislocation elsewhere in the system. It is uncertain whether the disturbance we are watching is deemed to have taken place in objective reality or in Prospero's mind alone, of which the masquers are mere figments. Really, at this stage of the game, it seems to matter very little. Prospero sorrowfully meditates that we, too, shall pass like spirits. Here occurs the finest sleep image of a play filled with sleepers,

> We are such stuff
> As dreams are made on, and our little life
> Is rounded with a sleep.
>
> IV. i. 156–8

The ground is cut from under our feet and we are left with the intuition of a regress of fictions. The note has already been heard faintly in the play – at II. i. 253–4, where Antonio speaks as though he and his companions were characters in a play, but this has little effect on us. It has too much Fancy and not enough Imagination about it. Stephano's relegation of his own recent actions to a story heard long before (III. ii. 153) touches us more nearly. The idea is, of course, a Shakespearean commonplace, frequently appearing

---

[1] The true complexity of this is well caught by E. M. W. Tillyard, *Shakespeare's Last Plays*, London 1938, p. 80: 'On the actual stage the Masque is executed by players pretending to be spirits, pretending to be real actors, pretending to be supposed goddesses and rustics.'

at poetic high-points, anthology pieces, ranging from Jaques's
'All the world's a stage'[1] through Lear's 'When we are born, we
cry that we are come To this great stage of fools',[2] to Macbeth's
'tale Told by an idiot, full of sound and fury, signifying nothing'.[3]
The history of this metaphysical idea and its derivation from Plato
have been briefly discussed in an earlier chapter.[4] It is perhaps
worth adding that something very like this idea can be found in
the Greek poets who lived before Plato; for example, Pindar,
Pythian, VIII. 137 sq.; Aeschylus, *Prometheus Vinctus*, 547-50;
Sophocles, *Ajax*, 125-6.[5] I hope it will not be thought perverse if
I describe this poetry as metaphysical. Certainly Shakespeare is not
affirming that we last for ever, but rather the exact reverse. Yet the
nature of the denial is metaphysical in its assumption of pathos. It
only makes sense in the context of immortal longings. The man
who has never felt, however faintly, the tug of everlastingness
will find little to admire in these lines – a pleasing description of
cloudy towers, perhaps, but nothing more; the observation that
things decay shrinks into triviality; what else should they do?
Such a man will have no need, in the face of such thoughts, to
take a turn or two 'to still [his] beating mind'.

The fundamentally metaphysical status of Prospero's lines
emerges very clearly if we compare them with the epilogue to *A
Midsummer Night's Dream*, spoken by Puck. Indeed, the comparison will be found to have a certain property of reverberation,
for each passage is in a way typical of the play in which it appears.
It is necessary to give the two speeches in full:

If we shadows have offended,
Think but this, and all is mended,
That you have but slumber'd here
While these visions did appear.
And this weak and idle theme,
No more yielding but a dream,
Gentles, do not reprehend:
If you pardon, we will mend.
And, as I'm an honest Puck,

[1] *As You Like It*, II.vii.139.
[2] *King Lear*, IV.vi.183-4.
[3] *Macbeth*, V.v.26-8.
[4] See above, p. 102.
[5] All three references are to the Oxford Texts of these authors, the editions of
C. M. Bowra (1947), Gilbert Murray (1955) and A. C. Pearson (1931) respectively.

If we have unearned luck
Now to 'scape the serpent's tongue,
We will make amends ere long;
Else the Puck a liar call:
So, good night unto you all.
Give me your hands, if we be friends,
And Robin shall restore amends.

A Midsummer Night's Dream, v. ii. 54-69

And now Prospero:

Our revels now are ended. These our actors,
As I foretold you, were all spirits and
Are melted into air, into thin air:
And, like the baseless fabric of this vision,
The cloud-capp'd towers, the gorgeous palaces,
The solemn temples, the great globe itself,
Yea, all which it inherit, shall dissolve
And, like this insubstantial pageant faded,
Leave not a rack behind. We are such stuff
As dreams are made on, and our little life
Is rounded with a sleep.– Sir, I am vex'd:
Bear with my weakness; my old brain is troubled.
Be not disturb'd with my infirmity.
If you be pleas'd, retire into my cell
And there repose: a turn or two I'll walk,
To still my beating mind.

The Tempest, IV. i. 148-63

Puck's speech is ingenious, delightful and undisturbing. If anything, it is reassuring. Common sense is not unseated by this play
with reality and unreality, for the simple reason that the normal
scope of the terms has suffered no metaphysical revision. It is the
players who are 'shadows', the play which is 'a dream'. The audience is allowed to be utterly real. The speech is designed to end
with applause. Plainly, after such a preparation, the sudden clap-
ping from hundreds of hands will sound very human and solid.
The epilogue carefully leads the audience back to a consciousness
of its own ordinary humanity, before sending it home in happy
complacency. The ending is wholly appropriate to the play. *A
Midsummer Night's Dream* is, no doubt, a miracle of expressionist
grace and ingenuity, a gossamer construction of fictions within

fictions, dreams within a dream. But when we compare it with *The Tempest* it seems virtually innocent of any metaphysical impact. In it Shakespeare is almost as far removed from Plato as is Pirandello. I say 'almost' because I have no doubt that any Elizabethan regress of fictions will have *some* smell of Plato about it. But *A Midsummer Night's Dream* is singularly down to earth in its conceptual structure. There is one place only where the play seems likely, for a moment, to take on another dimension – a brief exchange between Demetrius and Hermia:

> DEMETRIUS. These things seem small and undistinguishable,
> Like far-off mountains turned into clouds.

> HERMIA. Methinks I see these things with parted eye,
> When everything seems double.

> IV. i. 189–92

Curiously, these are, of all the lines in the play, the most reminiscent of *The Tempest*. They begin to 'get at' the intimate experience[1] of the audience in a way which is untypical of the play as a whole. But the idea is not developed.

Now turn to Prospero's lines. Where Puck's speech was comfortable, Prospero's is uncomfortable. Where *A Midsummer Night's Dream*, at the last, assured us of our reality, *The Tempest* deprives us of that assurance. Observe how the thing is done: Prospero begins with what appears to be a consoling speech, addressed to Ferdinand, explaining the disruption of the masque. But the audience knows from the start that it is an odd sort of consolation, delivered not from a mood of easy benevolence, but from anger. Before he actually speaks, Ferdinand and Miranda watch him in consternation:

> FERDINAND. This is strange: your father's in some passion
> That works him strongly.

---

[1] It seems that Shakespeare's interest in the minutiae of perception was present from the first. It supplies the most brilliant image of *Venus and Adonis*:

> Upon his hurt she looks so steadfastly,
> That her sight dazzling makes the wound seem three;
> And then she reprehends her mangling eye,
> That makes more gashes where no breach should be . . .
> (ll. 1063–6)

But it is only in *The Tempest* that the idea of the whole work adequately reflects this piercing imaginative insight.

MIRANDA. Never till this day
Saw I him touch'd with anger so distemper'd.

IV. i. 143-5

It is something of a surprise to find Prospero addressing Ferdinand at all. The opening of the speech is probably best played abruptly. Further, as the speech unfolds we find that the comfort offered at the beginning is in no way realized. At the end Prospero turns his back on Ferdinand and Miranda, in order, as he says, to settle his disturbed thoughts. It is worth while reminding ourselves of the occasion of the speech as a whole. We suspect that the conspiracy of Caliban and the rest is the cause of the break-up of the masque, but this is rather suspicion than knowledge. Certainly we are quite unable to explain *how* the behaviour of the conspirators has led to this result. The whole episode is extremely odd, and the oddity is never cleared up. It belongs with all those other examples of the imperfectly explained supernatural which were discussed at the beginning of this chapter. In *A Midsummer Night's Dream* we may be cheated for a moment by the intricacy of the plot, but we know what form an explanation would take – for example 'You see, he has just used the love-philtre', or something of that sort. But in *The Tempest* we are led into a wilderness where we have lost even the proper form of explanation. Hence, even before Prospero begins his 'explanation in which nothing is explained', we are, so to speak, disorientated. As we have seen, Prospero's speech does nothing to cure this.

In Puck's speech it was quite easy to see what was supposed to be real, and what unreal; easy, because the unreal things were things which in any case everyone knows to be unreal – a simulated Duke of Athens, a personated Queen of the Amazons, the King and Queen of the Fairies – while the real things were, simply, ourselves. But in Prospero's speech the area of unreality has ceased to be constant and familiar. In a way it has got out of control. He begins by talking about the actor-spirits (themselves a regress of fictions). So far there is nothing absolutely unprecedented. Puck himself was capable of stepping outside the play in order to discuss it. But the circle of darkness, of unreality, continues to widen, passing over the audience itself, beyond the walls of the theatre, to engulf palace and church, and, at last, the whole world. From making the stage shimmer before our eyes Prospero passes on to cast the same spell of doubt on the earth itself. Words alone retain a vivid life, cutting deep at our inmost memories and perceptions.[1]

Act V opens with the entry of Prospero, attired, as the Folio stage-direction tells us, *in his Magicke robes.* Ariel reports that the King and his followers are thoroughly distracted. Prospero announces that he will break his charms, so that all 'shall be themselves' once more. We have a sensation as of passing from the inner world to the outer. In a great speech the spirits are dispelled and we feel ourselves falling back into Italy, into things civil and political (though, in a way, the play is all about politics). The sleeping sailors are awakened by Ariel. Assorted ἀναγνωρίσεις follow. In the interview between Alonso and Prospero we feel the link with the other late plays, with their theme of children lost in tempest and found to the playing of sweet music. We remember Perdita and Marina.

ALONSO. When did you lose your daughter?

PROSPERO. In this last tempest.

v. i. 152–3

As the play closes the theme of reconciliation and restoration grows stronger still, until at last all set sail for home with the 'calm seas' and 'auspicious gales' that Ariel gives them for his last service.

This play is obviously not an explicit allegory in which both the figure and its significance are clearly expressed in the text, in the manner of the *Psychomachia* of Prudentius. This can be shortly proved by pointing to the names of the personages in either work. The names Prospero, Miranda, Ariel might be held to be faint hints towards allegorical significance, but they are faint indeed compared with the strident labels which Prudentius has pasted on the brows of all his characters – *Patientia, Ira, Sodomita Libido,* and so on. *The Winter's Tale* might be thought more explicit, since scholarship has shown that *Hermione* was in the seventeenth century identified with *Harmonia.* Yet both were the names of a person, associated with the Theban Cycle long before Shakespeare appeared. So even here we hardly have a clear case of an abstraction personified.

But if *The Tempest* is not explicit, formal allegory, cannot it be

---

[1] I reached my conclusions about this speech before I read Anne Righter's *Shakespeare and the Idea of the Play.* I was delighted to find my analysis confirmed by hers.

allegorised? Of course, it can; but anything can. No one has yet
written a story which is utterly proof against the efforts of a
determined allegorical exegete. If a character exemplifies any
quality (and all characters do) he may be said to figure that quality.
This is the mere licence of ordinary linguistic usage; the 'semantic
areas' of 'exemplify' and 'figure' overlap.

It remains to ask whether *The Tempest* can be *shown* to be
allegorical; whether the basic logical structure which is explicit in
the *Psychomachia* can be shown to be implicit – that is less obviously
present but present all the same – in *The Tempest*. The various
attempts to do this, have been, almost without exception, metaphysical in character. In my second chapter I argued at some length
against the crude opposition of allegory and transcendentalism,
and suggested that allegory was, in fact, a very frequent medium
for the expression of transcendentalist metaphysics. But this habit
of viewing the whole world as an allegory, and then expressing
the fact allegorically, can lead, as one might expect, to some tricky
situations. Where allegory becomes, as it were, the natural habit
of the mind, it is often difficult for the more literal-minded person
to satisfy himself as to what exactly is being asserted at all. A good
example of the *anima naturaliter allegorica* in modern times is Professor J. R. Tolkien. He says (describing the dragon in *Beowulf*)

> There are in the poem some vivid touches of the right kind –
> as *þa se wyrm onwoc, wroht wæs geniwad; stonc æfter stane*[1] . . . in
> which this dragon is real worm, with a bestial life and thought
> of his own, but the conception, none the less, approaches
> *draconitas* rather than *draco*: a personification of malice, greed,
> destruction (the evil side of heroic life) and of the undiscrimi-
> nating cruelty of fortune that distinguishes not good or bad (the
> evil aspect of all life).[2]

It is clear that Tolkien is telling us something about the structure
of the universe, as well as about the Beowulfian dragon. The Old
Worm, merely by becoming indeterminate, is transformed into
draconitas. The metaphysical opinion that malice is something
active, operating in the world like an interpenetrating spirit, and
that 'dragonishness' is a sort of huge, diffused, dragon, infused like

---

[1] Taking *stonc* to mean 'moved rapidly', 'slid', translate: 'Then the worm arose,
the struggle was begun; it slid over the stone.' But *stonc* could, just possibly, mean
'stank' or 'sniffed'.

[2] 'Beowulf, the Monsters and the Critics', *PBA*, XXII (1936), pp. 258–9.

a gas through the universe, denied idiosyncratic shape and thoughts but still having the authentic dragon stench about him – this metaphysical opinion is not so much the concomitant of Professor Tolkien's observations as the very condition of them. And now we may ask the question. Does Professor Tolkien suggest that *Beowulf* is an allegory? It is almost impossible to answer. If we say yes, we must allow that, for such a sensibility, all undifferentiated, morally simple characters will be allegorical, since they will resemble more closely (while never expressing literally) the great archetypal Exemplars which properly enjoy the name of universals. Otherwise we may say 'No, clearly he doesn't mistake it for a Prudentian formal allegory; it's just his manner of speaking.' But this will blind us to the fact that Tolkien's poem is different in kind from the literal-minded man's poem.

To bring the argument back within the pale of Shakespearian criticism, we may take a passage from the critical writings of Professor Nevill Coghill:

> If I use the word 'allegory' in connection with Shakespeare I do not mean that the characters are abstractions representing this or that vice or virtue (as they do in some allegories, say the *Roman de la Rose* or *The Castle of Perseverance* itself). I mean that they contain and adumbrate certain principles, not in a crude or neat form, but mixed with other human qualities; but that these principles, taken as operating in human life, do in fact give shape and direction to the course, and therefore to the meaning of the play.[1]

How, then, is this special sort of allegory, in which principles are contained and adumbrated, to be distinguished from any other play, from which principles can be extracted? Apparently, in virtue of the activity of those principles. They *operate* 'in human life', and 'give shape and direction to the course . . . of the play'. I do not understand how a 'principle' is to do this unless it is turned into a spirit, that is, into an active, influential individual. I think we can conclude that Professor Coghill is not so much suggesting that Shakespeare's comedies are allegorical as proposing a metaphysical view of virtues and vices as active (a view authorized by much Christian religious language) and suggesting that this view was shared by Shakespeare and expressed in his plays. And indeed, he may be right.

[1] 'The Basis of Shakespearian Comedy', *E & S*, NS III (1950), p. 21.

For the nineteenth-century critics of our first chapter, proving *The Tempest* an allegory and proving it metaphysical were very nearly the same thing. It might be objected that if only we would revive the much-despised opposition between allegory and metaphysics we might be lifted out of this confusing state of affairs; either a poem is allegorical – that is, a fictitious reification of qualities, etc. – or else it is metaphysical, in which case the reification, since it is ontologically asserted, must be taken as literal; hence a poem must be described as either metaphysical or allegorical, certainly not both. Unfortunately, this lucid distinction proves to be of little use when applied to actual specimens of metaphysical/allegorical poetry, since, when the metaphysician wishes to make an ontological assertion, he is seldom *able* to make it literally at all. It is evident that almost all those who have wished to call *The Tempest* allegorical have done so on the ground that it represents metaphysical truths about the world allegorically.

That Shakespeare's poetry betrays a tendency towards metaphysics is, I think, impossible to deny. The suggestion that his metaphysical imagery may be solely intensive in function we have already considered and rejected.[1]

Allegoristic criticism was almost normal in the nineteenth century. In the twentieth, though still vigorous,[2] it has come to be considered eccentric. But one good result of the general retreat from enthusiastic allegorizing is that when a critic does brave disapproval, and allegorize, we can be tolerably sure that he is describing the play, and not just indulging in verbal high flights of his own.

The twentieth-century arguments for describing *The Tempest* as a metaphysical allegory may be classified under two heads; first those drawn from a comparison of the story-patterns of the late Romances with one other and with the plots and imagery of the earlier Tragedies; second, arguments drawn from the internal character of *The Tempest* itself, its characterization, treatment of morality, use of the supernatural. The first class may be represented by G. Wilson Knight and E. M. W. Tillyard and the second by Derek Traversi and Patrick Cruttwell.

The former critics point out that the late Romances, *Pericles, Cymbeline, The Winter's Tale* and *The Tempest*, are all concerned with

[1] See above, pp. 123–5.
[2] The most elaborate of all *Tempest* allegorizings was published in 1921 – Colin Still's *Shakespeare's Mystery Play, a study of 'The Tempest'*.

restoration and reconciliation of persons thought to be dead. The recurring feature of the storm is associated with their loss, and music with their reconciliation. This pattern may be compared with another pattern, discernible in the tragedies, in which the breakdown and death of a man is externally reflected in violent storm, and a hint of reconciliation beyond the grave is held out in the metaphors used by the heroes in their 'moments of fifth act transcendental speculation'.[1] It is thus argued that the Romances in their veritable reconciliation after tempests represent an acting out of those metaphors. It is therefore suggested that they are symbolic of a theological after-life in which all manner of things shall be well. The necessity of supposing that Shakespeare intends a life beyond the grave may well be questioned, particularly since the most explicit metaphysics in *The Tempest* is to be found in the speech in which Prospero stresses the transitoriness of this life which is rounded with a sleep (IV. i. 146–63). So long as eternal happiness is conceived in terms of extended duration, it will be difficult to find unequivocal Shakespearian support for it.

But the relation of the story-pattern of the Romances to that of the Tragedies could be accounted for with a more modest set of presumptions. For example, one might suggest that Shakespeare thought what a wonderful wish-fulfilment type of play could be written if one gave these tragic heroes their whole desire, in this world; if, after all, the beloved person were shown never to have died at all. The dramatic use of the delightfulness of reconciliation after all hope has been lost does not necessarily imply a theological belief in resurrection. If *The Tempest* is really to be taken as an account of survival after death, since it certainly is not literal it must undoubtedly be allegorical. However, I should be much happier with the alternative suggestion, hazier and perhaps unpalatable to Christian sensibilities, that the 'story' of life after death and the story of *The Tempest* both stand as myths of some mysterious state of affairs, closely connected with moral questions, which may elude literal description together.

This approach is extremely unmanageable and vague, and perhaps it is for that very reason that it admits more readily an alliance with the second approach, the approach by way of the nature of characterization and treatment of ethics in the last plays. There are indeed certain features in the Romances which are easily connected with the separation and 'eternizing' of love-value which we found

[1] G. W. Knight, *The Crown of Life*, London 1948, p. 208.

in the Sonnets and elsewhere.[1] D. A. Traversi says, of Florizel's comparison[2] of Perdita to a wave of the sea in *The Winter's Tale* (IV. iii. 140 ff.):

> This image, like the speech of which it forms a part, is, of course, much more than a beautiful piece of decorative poetry. It is rather the particular expression of a vital theme of the play . . . the relation between the values of human life which postulate timelessness, and the impersonal, 'devouring' action of time which wears these values ceaselessly away. The wave image conveys perfectly the necessary relation between the mutability of life and the infinite value of human experience which it conditions, but which is finally incommensurate with it.[3]

Traversi is quick, too, to point out the association in *The Tempest* of supernatural imagery with intuitions of value.[4] Yet the task is less easily performed for *The Tempest* than it is for *The Winter's Tale*. What we may call the Affirmation of Paradise has in *The Tempest* a far less confident tone. Miranda's first perception of the 'noble vessel' has a visionary quality, yet it is belied, as Traversi acknowledges, by the presence of the plotters in the ship. In *The Tempest* alone of the Romances the divine masque is broken up in confusion. The whole play, as compared with *The Winter's Tale*, is strangely perverse, like a piece of flawed glass. Bonamy Dobrée, in a brilliant essay,[5] pointed out the unique flavour of *The Tempest*, more shimmering, less full-bloodedly confident in its paradisal intuitions that its immediate predecessors; the wooing of Ferdinand, though piercingly ideal, is less warm than the wooing of Florizel; the forgiveness of Prospero has a touch of the priggish Senecan.

It is as if a second wave of scepticism has passed over the poet. It is quite different from the coprologous indignation of *Troilus and Cressida*. He no longer, for the sake of one transgression, denies the authenticity of love itself. But a reservation as to the truth-value of the assertions love provokes seems to have reappeared. Time, the old grey destroyer of the Sonnets, was not, after all, put down by love. After the enthusiastic reaffirmation of the

---

[1] See above, esp. pp. 123–8.
[2] Quoted above, p. 44.
[3] *Shakespeare: the Last Phase*, London 1954, pp. 151–2.
[4] *ibid.*, e.g. pp. 202, 207.
[5] 'The Tempest', *E & S*, NS V (1952), pp. 13–25.

later Sonnets and the first three Romances, a sadder and more complex reaction has set in, slightly ironical perhaps, but not at all cynical. The world has not been wholly redeemed by love; look at it. The subjective vision of the lover may transcend objective facts, but it does not obliterate them. The lover has one level, the hater another; perhaps there are a thousand more such levels, each as unreal as the rest.

Thus the quasi-mystical ethical intuitions are undermined by a doubt about reality, about the comparative status of different kinds of perception. My summary of the play in the first half of this chapter was, of course, selective. It may be as well to proclaim here the principle of selection involved. I was concerned to show Shakespeare's preoccupation, throughout the play, with the more nearly subliminal aspects of perception. It is as if Shakespeare himself became concerned, as I was in the third and fourth chapters of this book, to retreat into the preconceptual area of the mind. The chapters and the play have, in a sense, very similar subject-matter. Certainly, *The Tempest* is not related to that psychological theorizing in just the same way as the poetic specimens I cited were related to it. Those poems *exemplified* the indeterminate, configurative imagination. *The Tempest* is, for much of its length, *about* people configurating, imagining without actualizing, and so on. Patrick Cruttwell argues[1] that Shakespeare in his last plays began to take seriously the allegorical/transcendental images of his youthful poetry. In *The Winter's Tale*, indeed, it may be that an ontological force is given to such imagery. But in *The Tempest* the prominence given to the ambiguous lower reaches of our conceptual and perceptual apparatus infects all ontological dogmatism with uncertainty. Shakespeare repeatedly restricts his characters to the primitive stages of perception in their apprehension of the island and its denizens. In this way he builds up a sense of a shimmering multiplicity of levels, which, together with the gratuitous operations of the supernatural, produce in the audience a state of primitive apprehension similar to that in which the characters find themselves. We are given the impression that the island may, after all, belong wholly to the unassertive world of dreams and ambiguous perceptions. Such material is naturally baffling to the critic who wishes to sort out symbol and statement. The allegorical exegete feels he has been cheated of his proper prey.

But we have also to reckon with the intuitions of value which

[1] *The Shakespearean Moment*, London 1954, pp. 73–106.

are expressed in the meeting of Ferdinand and Miranda, and also (possibly) in the masque. That value is in these passages supernaturally conceived according to the logic treated in the earlier chapters of this book, I have little doubt. But it is somewhat puzzling to encounter these intuitions in a context so instinct with the atmosphere of ambiguous imagery. The proper relation of these ethical intuitions to the more elusive intuition that the island is only a dream or figment of the configurative imagination is difficult to determine. Certainly there is no sign of any attempt on Shakespeare's part to postulate a *genetic* relationship, to suggest that primitive configurations are the psychological parents of intuitions of value. After all, the two elements are presented in a totally different manner, the first involving the use of metaphor, the second dramatically. The imaginary status of the island is hinted by the behaviour of the characters, sometimes baffled, sometimes inconsistent. The value-intuitions are explicitly stated, by certain characters in theological imagery, and also (possibly) in the terms of a mythological spectacle. Yet it is easy to feel that some part of the vague scepticism created by the recurrence of half-subliminal perceptions has attached itself to the lovers and the persons of the masque. The differing visions which the castaways have of the island[1] may be held to throw a pale cast of doubt on the vision of Ferdinand when he falls in love with Miranda. We must allow that Shakespeare's motive in associating perceptual ambiguity with supernatural encounters is quite different from the motives behind chapter III of this book. He is not concerned to provide an instantial correlative for universals. But in our inquiry into perceptual imagery we discovered the peculiar indulgence of that area of the mind to the combining of things incompatible and the admission of things impossible. It is surely this character which it is Shakespeare's object to exploit. That property of the imagination which makes possible the instantial 'universal' is the same property as that which gives *The Tempest* its peculiar atmosphere of ontological suspension. This Shakespeare effects by giving the imaginative 'limbo of possibles' a dramatic impulse in the direction of reality, that is, by backing up the glimpses enjoyed by his characters with just enough magical apparatus to determine us in favour of a supernatural explanation without losing our sense of the 'internal' flavour of the experience. The truth is that these ambiguities have at least two functions. If they make the reports

[1] II. i. 46–55.

of the characters dubious, they make the playwright convincing. We cannot trust characters who contradict one another and continually stumble in their encounters with the supernatural. But we must trust the playwright who shows us both their insights and their stumblings.

Shakespeare has, in a perfectly legitimate manner, contrived to have his cake and eat it. He gives us the heart-tearing intuitions of heavenly value, but in a radically empirical and undogmatic way which disarms the cynical critic. He seems to say, 'I have seen this, and this, and this. You receive it as I found it. The interpretation I leave to you.' Certainly, the challenge has been accepted!

Is *The Tempest* allegorical? If I have done my work properly, the question should have shrunk in importance. The principal object of this book has been to show that allegorical poetry is more curiously and intimately related to life than was allowed by the petrifying formula of C. S. Lewis. One result of this is that the question 'Is this work allegorical?' ceases to have the clear significance it would have for a man to whom allegory, as the most ostentatiously fictitious of all literary forms, is directly opposed to a serious preoccupation with the real universe. Nevertheless, I am willing to give a few arbitrary rulings. The simplified characters of the play are not *ipso facto* allegorical, but it is no great sin to take them as types. The sense that beauty and goodness and harmony are ontologically prior to their subjects does not become full-bloodedly allegorical until the masque, where the spirits, nymphs, etc., may without straining be taken as a mythological acting out of the mystery of the betrothal. It is hardly worth while to call the island itself allegorical ('the mind of man' and so on). Certainly it shimmers between subjectivity and objectivity, presents itself differently to different eyes, yet it will not keep still long enough for one to affix an allegorical label. For the island, as for most of the elements of the play, I should prefer to coin a rather ugly term –'pre-allegorical'. Ariel and Caliban of all the characters in the play come nearest to being allegories of the psychic processes, but it would certainly be a mistake not to realize that they are very much more besides. If the suggestion of the unique authority of love and value were only a little more explicit, we might allow the word 'allegorical' for the play as a whole, and consider the restoration of the supposedly dead as a myth of this ethic, but, as things are, we cannot.

The minutely perceptive scepticism of *The Tempest* defeats the stony allegorist and the rigid cynic equally. The mystery is never allowed to harden into an ontological dogma to be reduced to symbols or rejected with contempt. Instead we have an extraordinarily delicate and dramatic play, which, until the Last Day makes all things clear, will never be anything but immensely suggestive.

One important claim can be made. The suggestiveness of *The Tempest* is metaphysical in tendency, and the indeterminate *concepts* adumbrated do have the logical oddity which we have followed through from the first chapter. Love *is* conceived as a supernatural force, and any number of protestations of metaphor and apologetic inverted commas cannot do away with the fact that a sort of deification, and therefore *a fortiori* reification has taken place. Whether these concepts should be allowed to be meaningful, or whether they should be permitted only a 'merely aesthetic' force (and that presumably spurious) I do not know. The unassertive candour of Shakespeare's imagination has left the question open. But the nineteenth-century allegorists were at any rate concerning themselves with the right (i.e. the peculiar) sort of concept. Their heresy is less than that of the hard-headed, poetry-has-nothing-to-do-with-ideas school. Their claims to have found *the* exclusive allegorical interpretation may be left to their foolish internecine strife, but their noses told them truly that the smell of metaphysics was in the air. If we look upon their effusions less as appraisals of the play than as reactions to it, they will be more acceptable. We may think of them as we think of the women who miscarried on seeing the Eumenides of Aeschylus: as critics they may have been injudicious, but as an audience they were magnificent – though perhaps a little too lively.

BIBLIOGRAPHY
OF BOOKS REFERRED TO IN THE TEXT

NOTE. The following list of works is divided into two sections, A and B. In section A, reference is made to books, in section B to periodicals.

SECTION A

AESCHYLUS. *Tragoediae*. Ed. Gilbert Murray (Oxford Text), 1955.

ANSELM. *S. Anselmi . . . Opera Omnia*. Ed. F. S. Schmitt. Edinburgh 1946.

— *Fides Quaerens Intellectum*. Trans. I. W. Robertson. London 1960.

Anthologia Graeca. See under *Greek Anthology*.

AQUINAS, THOMAS. *Summa Theologiae*. Ottawa 1953.

ARISTOTLE. *Aristotelis De Anima*. Ed. W. D. Ross (Oxford Text), 1956.

— *The Works of Aristotle translated into English*. Ed. W. D. Ross. London 1928.

AUERBACH, E. *Scenes from the Drama of European Literature*. New York 1959.

AUGUSTINE. See under MIGNE.

AURELIUS, M. *The Meditations of the Emperor Marcus Antoninus*. Ed. A. S. L. Farquharson. Oxford 1944.

BALE, JOHN. *King Johan*. The Malone Society Reprints. Ed. J. H. P. Pafford under the supervision of W. W. Greg. Oxford 1931.

BARTH, KARL. *Anselm: Fides Quaerens Intellectum. Anselm's Proof of the Existence of God in the Context of his Theological Scheme*. Trans. by I. W. Robertson from the German 2nd edition of 1958. London 1960.

BARTLETT, J. *Concordance to Shakespeare*. Reprint of the 1st edition of 1894. London 1956.

BEAUMONT, F., and FLETCHER, J. *The Works of Francis Beaumont and John Fletcher*. Variorum Edition. London 1904–12.

BERGSON, H. *Matter and Memory*. Trans. N. M. Paul and W. S. Palmer. New York 1911.

BERKELEY, G. *The Works of George Berkeley, Bishop of Cloyne*. Ed. A. A. Luce and T. E. Jessop. London 1949.

Bible, the Authorised Version.

BUNYAN, J. *The Pilgrim's Progress*. Ed. J. B. Wharey. 2nd ed. revised by R. Sharrock. Oxford 1960.

CAMPBELL, T. *Remarks on the Life and Writings of William Shakespeare*. London 1838.

CASSIRER, E. *The Individual and the Cosmos in Renaissance Philosophy*. Trans. Mario Domandi. New York 1963.

— *Language and Myth*. Trans. S. Langer. New York 1946.

CHAMBERS, E. K. *The Elizabethan Stage*. Oxford 1923.

— *The Mediaeval Stage*. Oxford 1903.

CHAPMAN, GEORGE. *The Poems of George Chapman*. Ed. Phyllis B. Bartlett. New York and London 1941.

CHAUCER, G. *The Works of Geoffrey Chaucer*. Ed. F. N. Robinson. 2nd ed. Boston 1957.

CHERNISS, H. *Aristotle's Criticisms of Plato and the Academy*. Baltimore 1944.

CHRYSOSTOM, DIO. In *Dio Chrysostomus*. Ed. G. de Budé. Leipzig 1916.

CICERO, M. TULLY. *Cato Maior*. Vol. IV of *M. Tullii Ciceronis Opera*. Ed. I. C. Orellius and I. G. Baiterus. 2nd ed. Zurich 1845–62.

COLERIDGE, S. T. *Biographia Literaria*. Ed. G. Watson. London 1956.

— *Coleridge's Shakespearean Criticism*. Ed. T. M. Raysor. London 1930.

COLLINS. See under GRAY.

COMPARETTI, D. *Vergil in the Middle Ages*. Trans. E. F. M. Benecke. London 1895.

CORNFORD, F. M. *Plato and Parmenides*. London 1939.

— *Plato's Cosmology*. London 1937.

COUCH, A. T. QUILLER. See under Q.

CRAIG, H. *An Interpretation of Shakespeare*. New York 1948.

CRASHAW, R. *The Poems English Latin and Greek of Richard Crashaw*. Ed. L. C. Martin. 2nd ed. London 1957.

CROCE, B. *Aesthetic as Science of Expression and General Linguistic*. Vol. I of *Philosophy of the Spirit*. Trans. Douglas Ainslie. London 1909.

CRUTTWELL, MAURICE JAMES PATRICK. *The Shakespearean Moment*. London 1954.

CURTIUS, E. R. *European Literature and the Latin Middle Ages*. First published Berlin 1948. Trans. W. R. Trask. London 1953.

DANBY, J. F. *Poets on Fortune's Hill*. London 1952.

DANTE ALIGHIERI. *Dante's Convivio*. Trans. W. W. Jackson. Oxford 1909.

— *Divine Comedy*. 1954 reprint of the edition of 1899 with translation and comment by J. D. Sinclair. London 1958.

— *A Translation of Dante's Eleven Letters* by C. S. Latham. Ed. G. R. Carpenter. Boston and New York 1892.

— *The Vision of Dante.* Trans. H. F. Cary. 3rd ed. London 1844.

— *Dante's Vita Nuova.* Trans. R. W. Emerson. Chapel Hill, Carolina 1960.

DESCARTES, R. *Meditationes de Prima Philosophia.* Ed. and trans. into French by the Duc de Luynes. Introduction and notes by G. Lewis. Paris 1944.

— *Regulae ad Directionem Ingenii.* 'Texte de l'édition Adam et Tannery, notice par Henri Gouhier.' Paris 1946.

DIELS, H. *Die Fragmente der Vorsokratiker.* 6th ed. Berlin 1951.

DODDS, E. R. *The Greeks and the Irrational.* London 1951.

DONNE, J. *The Poems of John Donne.* Ed. H. J. C. Grierson. London 1912.

DOWDEN, E. *Shakspere – his Mind and Art.* London 1875.

DRAYTON, M. *The Works of Michael Drayton.* Ed. J. W. Hebel. Tercentenary Edition. Oxford 1961.

ELIOT, T. S. *Four Quartets.* Faber Paperback Edition. London 1959.

— *Selected Essays.* 3rd ed. London 1951.

EMMET, D. M. *The Nature of Metaphysical Thinking.* London 1945.

Encyclopaedia Britannica. 7th ed. Edinburgh 1838.

Everyman. Ed. A. C. Cawley (Old and Middle English Texts). London 1961.

FIELDING, HENRY. *Tom Jones.* Shakespeare Head Edition. Oxford 1926.

FOX, GEORGE. *Journal.* Ed. W. Armistead. 7th ed. London 1852.

FORSTER, E. M. *The Longest Journey.* World's Classics Edition. London 1960.

FRAUNCE, A. *The Lawiers Logike.* London 1588.

FREGE, F. L. G. 'On Sense and Reference', In *Translations from the Philosophical Writings of Gottlob Frege*, pp. 56–78. Ed. P. Geach and M. Black. Oxford 1952. The essay was first published in 1892.

FREUD, SIGMUND. *Introductory Lectures on Psycho-analysis.* Trans. Joan Rivière. London 1922.

GALTON, FRANCIS. *Inquiries into Human Faculty.* Everyman Edition. 1928 reprint of the 2nd edition of 1907.

GARDNER, HELEN (ed.). *The Metaphysical Poets.* Harmondsworth 1960.

GIBSON, J. J. *The Perception of the Visual World.* Cambridge, Mass. 1950.

GILSON, E. *History of Christian Philosophy in the Middle Ages.* London 1955.

— *Le Thomisme, introduction au système de Saint Thomas d'Aquin.* Paris 1927.

GOMBRICH, E. H. *Art and Illusion.* London 1960.

GRANT, R. M. *The Letter and the Spirit.* London 1957.

GRANVILLE-BARKER, H. *Prefaces to Shakespeare*. The two-volume edition incorporating certain changes from the 1st edition of 1930. New York 1958.

GRAVES, ROBERT. *Poetic Unreason*. London 1925.

— *The White Goddess*. London 1948.

GRAY, T., and COLLINS, W. *The Poetical Works of Gray and Collins*. Ed. A. L. Poole. London 1917.

Greek Anthology. *Anthologia Graeca*. Ed. H. Beckby. Munich 1957.

HALL, E. *Chronicle*. Collated from the editions of 1548 and 1550 by an anonymous editor. London 1809.

HAMILTON, SIR WILLIAM. *Lectures on Metaphysics*. Edinburgh 1859–60.

HAZLITT, W. *The Complete Works of William Hazlitt*. Ed. P. P. Howe. London 1934.

HEINE, H. *Shakespeares Mädchen und Frauen*. First published 1838. Trans. Ida Benecke under the title *Heine on Shakespeare*. Westminster 1895.

HERBERT, G. *The Works of George Herbert*. Ed. F. E. Hutchinson. The slightly corrected reprint of the edition of 1941. Oxford 1953.

HEYWOOD, T. *The Dramatic Works of Thomas Heywood*. London 1874.

HUGO, FRANÇOIS-VICTOR. *Œuvres complètes de W. Shakespeare*. Paris 1859.

HUME, D. *A Treatise of Human Nature*. Ed. L. A. Selby-Bigge. Reprint of the 1st edition of 1888. Oxford 1958.

HUSSERL, E. *Ideas: General Introduction to Pure Phenomenology*. Trans. W. R. Boyce Gibson. London 1931.

HUXLEY, T. H. *Hume*. First published 1881. London 1894.

JAMES, WILLIAM. *The Principles of Psychology*. London 1890.

— *The Varieties of Religious Experience*. New York 1902.

JAMESON, MRS. A. B. *Characteristics of Women, Moral, Poetical, and Historical*. London 1832.

JOHNSON, S. *Lives of the English Poets*. Ed. G. Birkbeck Hill, Oxford 1905.

JONSON, B. *Ben Jonson*. Ed. C. H. Herford and Percy Simpson. Oxford 1925.

KANT, I. *Immanuel Kant's Critique of Pure Reason*. Trans. Norman Kemp Smith. Reprint of the corrected 2nd Impression of 1933. London 1961.

KEATS, JOHN. *The Letters of John Keats*. Ed. H. E. Rollins. Cambridge, Mass. 1958.

KIRK, G. S. *Heraclitus: the Cosmic Fragments*. Cambridge 1954.

KNIGHT, G. W. *The Crown of Life*. London 1948.

— *Myth and Miracle*. London 1929.

LAMB, C. *The Complete Works of Charles Lamb*. Ed. R. H. Shepherd. London 1892.

LANGER, S. K. *Philosophy in a New Key.* 3rd ed. Cambridge, Mass. 1957.

LEAVIS, F. R. *The Common Pursuit.* Harmondsworth 1962.

LEISHMAN, J. B. *Themes and Variations in Shakespeare's Sonnets.* London 1961.

LEWIS, C. S. *The Allegory of Love.* 1953 impression of the corrected reprint of 1938. Oxford 1953.

—— *English Literature in the Sixteenth Century, excluding Drama.* Oxford 1954.

Library of Christian Classics. Edited by J. Baillie, John T. McNeill and Henry P. Van Dusen. London 1953– .

LOCKE, J. *An Essay concerning Human Understanding.* Ed. A. C. Fraser. Oxford 1894.

LOEWY, E. *The Rendering of Nature in Early Greek Art.* Trans. J. Fothergill. London 1907.

LOVEJOY, A. O. *The Great Chain of Being.* Cambridge, Mass. 1936.

LOVELACE, R. *The Poems of Richard Lovelace.* Ed. G. H. Wilkinson. 1953 corrected reprint of the edition of 1930. Oxford 1953.

LOWELL, J. R. *Among my Books.* Everyman Edition. London 1870.

MACKAIL, H. W. *Lectures on Poetry.* London 1911.

MCKELLAR, PETER. *Imagination and Thinking.* London 1957.

MARETT, R. R. *The Threshold of Religion.* 2nd ed. London 1914.

MARLOWE, C. *The Works of Christopher Marlowe.* Ed. C. F. Tucker-Brooke. Oxford 1910.

MARTZ, L. L. *The Poetry of Meditation.* Newhaven, Conn. 1962.

MARVELL, A. *The Poems and Letters.* Ed. H. M. Margoliouth. 2nd ed. Oxford 1952.

MEREDITH, GEORGE. *The Ordeal of Richard Feverel.* Standard Edition. London 1914.

MÉZIÈRES, ALFRED. *Shakspere, ses œuvres et ses critiques.* Paris 1860.

MIGNE, J.-P. (ed.). *Bibliotheca Patrum Latina,* otherwise entitled *Patrologia Latina.* Paris 1861.

MILTON, J. *The Poetical Works of John Milton.* Ed. Helen Darbishire. Oxford 1952.

MONTAIGNE. *The Essays of Michael, Lord of Montaigne.* Trans. John Florio. Everyman Edition (n.d.) based on the 3rd edition (1632) of Florio's translation.

MOORE, G. E. *Principia Ethica.* Cambridge 1903.

MUIR, K. *Shakespeare's Sources.* London 1957.

MUNZ, PETER. *Problems of Religious Knowledge.* London 1959.

A New Oxford Dictionary. 1888.

Palatine Anthology. See under *Greek Anthology.*

Patrologia Latina. See under MIGNE.

PEPYS, S. *The Diary of Samuel Pepys, MA, FRS.* Ed. H. B. Wheatley. London 1893–99.

PETTET, E. C. *Shakespeare and the Romance Tradition*. London and New York 1949.

PHILLPOTTS, J. SURTEES (ed.). *The Tempest of Shakespeare*. The Rugby Edition. London 1876.

PINDAR. *Carmina*. Ed. C. M. Bowra (Oxford Text). 1947.

PLATO. *The Dialogues of Plato*. Trans. B. Jowett. 4th ed. re-edited by D. J. Allan and H. E. Dale. Oxford 1953.

PLOTINUS. *Plotini Opera*. Ed. Henry and Hans-Rudolf Schwyzer. Paris 1951.

PRUDENTIUS. 'Psychomachia', in *Prudentius*. Trans. H. J. Thomson. Loeb Classical Library. 1953.

PURCHAS, SAMUEL. *Purchas his Pilgrimes*. First published 1625. The Merton Library Copy. 1626.

QUILLER-COUCH, A. T., and J. D. WILSON (eds.). *The Tempest*. The Cambridge Shakespeare. 1921.

DE QUINCEY. Article on Shakespeare contributed to the 7th edition of the *Encyclopaedia Britannica*. 1838.

RALEIGH, W. *The English Voyages*. London 1928.

— *Shakespeare*. Slightly revised version of the 1907 edition. London 1909.

RIBOT, TH. *L'Évolution des idées générales*. Paris 1897.

RIGHTER, ANNE. *Shakespeare and the Idea of the Play*. London 1962.

ROSS, W. D. *Plato's Theory of Ideas*. Oxford 1951.

RUSKIN, J. *Munera Pulveris*. First published New York 1872. In *The Works of John Ruskin*. Ed. E. T. Cook and A. Wedderburn. London 1905.

RUSSELL, BERTRAND. *The Analysis of Mind*. London 1921.

RYLE, GILBERT. *The Concept of Mind*. London 1949.

SARTRE, J.-P. *The Psychology of Imagination*. (No translator's name given.) London 1950.

SAYERS, D. L. 'The Fourfold Interpretation of the *Comedy*', in her *Introductory Papers on Dante*, pp. 101–26. London 1954.

SCHILPP, P. A. (ed.). *The Philosophy of G. E. Moore*. Evanston and Chicago 1942.

SCHLEGEL. A. W. *A Course of Lectures on Dramatic Art and Literature*. Trans. J. Black, revised A. H. W. Morrison. Bohn's Standard Library. 1846.

SELLARS, W., and J. HOSPERS (eds.). *Readings in Ethical Theory*. New York 1952.

SEMON, RICHARD. *Die Mneme, als erhaltendes Prinzip im Wechsel des organischen Geschehens*. Leipzig 1911. English Version *The Mneme*. Trans. Louis Simon. London 1921.

SHAKESPEARE, WILLIAM. The three-volume Oxford Shakespeare. Ed. W. J. Craig: (i) The *Comedies*. The 1952 reprint of the 1st edition of 1911. (ii) The *Histories and Poems*. The 1958 reprint of the 1st edition of 1912. (iii) The *Tragedies*. The 1956 reprint of the 1st edition of 1912.

— *The Tempest*. Ed. H. H. Furness. The New Variorum Shakespeare. 1892.

— *The Tempest*. Ed. Frank Kermode. The Arden Shakespeare. 1958.

— *The Tempest*. Ed. A. T. Quiller-Couch and J. Dover Wilson. The Cambridge Shakespeare. 1921.

Other volumes in the Variorum, Arden and Cambridge series have also been used for purposes of reference.

The Shakespeare Allusion Book. Originally compiled by C. M. Ingleby, Miss L. Toulmin Smith and F. J. Furnivall, with the assistance of the New Shakespeare Society. Re-edited, revised and rearranged with an introduction by John Munro (1909) and now reissued with a preface by Sir Edmund Chambers, 1932.

SHELLEY, P. B. *The Prose Works of Percy Bysshe Shelley*. Ed. H. B. Foreman. London 1880.

SIDNEY, SIR PHILIP. *The Works of Sir Philip Sidney*. Ed. A. Feuillerat. Cambridge 1912–26.

SINGLETON, C. S. *Commedia, Elements of Structure*. Cambridge, Mass. 1954.

SMITH, DAVID NICHOL. *Eighteenth Century Essays on Shakespeare*. Glasgow 1903.

— *Shakespeare Criticism*. The 1944 reprint of the World's Classics Edition of 1916.

SMITH, IRWIN. *Shakespeare's Blackfriars Playhouse*. London 1966.

SNELL, BRUNO. *The Discovery of Mind*. Trans. T. G. Rosenmeyer. Oxford 1953.

SOPHOCLES. *Fabulae*. Ed. A. C. Pearson (Oxford Text). 1931.

SPALDING, K. J. *The Philosophy of Shakespeare*. Oxford 1953.

SPENCER, HERBERT. *First Principles*. 2nd ed. London 1867.

SPENSER, E. *The Works of Edmund Spenser*. Variorum Edition. Ed E.. Greenlaw, C. G. Osgood, F. M. Padelford and R. Heffner. Baltimore 1932–58.

STILL, COLIN. *Shakespeare's Mystery Play, a study of 'The Tempest'*. London 1921.

STRACHEY, G. LYTTON. *Books and Characters, French and English*. London 1922.

SWIFT, J. *The Prose Works of Jonathan Swift, D.D.* Ed. Temple Scott. Bohn's Standard Library. 1897-1908.

SYNESIUS. *Synesii Cyrenensis Hymni et Opuscula*. Ed. N. Terzaghi. Rome 1939–44.

TAYLOR, A. E. 'Parmenides, Zeno and Socrates', in *Philosophical Studies*. London 1934. The essay first appeared in *PAS* XVI (1915-16).

THOMAS AQUINAS. See under A.

THORNDIKE, A. H. *The Influence of Beaumont and Fletcher on Shakespeare.* Worcester, Mass. 1901.

TILLYARD. E. M. W. *Shakespeare's Last Plays.* London 1938.

TITCHENER, E. B. *Lectures on the Experimental Psychology of the Thought-Processes.* New York 1909.

TRAVERSI, DEREK. *Shakespeare: the Last Phase.* London 1954.

TUVE, R. *Elizabethan and Metaphysical Imagery.* Chicago 1947.

VAUGHAN, HENRY. *The Works of Henry Vaughan.* Ed. L. C. Martin. 2nd ed. Oxford 1957.

VERNON, M. D. *A Further Study of Visual Perception.* Cambridge 1952.

VOLTAIRE. *La Dictionnaire philosophique.* Vol. VII of *Œuvres complètes de Voltaire.* Paris 1876.

WARNOCK, MARY. *The Philosophy of Sartre.* New York 1965.

WEIL, SIMONE. *Notebooks.* Trans. Arthur Wills. London 1956.

WHITEHEAD, A. N. *Science and the Modern World.* Cambridge 1927.

WILLIAMS, C. W. S. *Charles Williams, Selected Writings.* Chosen by Anne Ridler. London 1961.

— *The English Poetic Mind.* Oxford 1932.

— *The Figure of Beatrice.* London 1943.

WILLIAMS, GEORGE. 'The Convention of *The Extasie.*' First printed in *Seventeenth Century Contexts.* Chicago 1960. Reprinted in *Seventeenth Century English Poetry.* Ed. W. R. Keast. New York 1962.

WILSON, DANIEL. *Caliban: the Missing Link.* London 1873.

WILSON, J. DOVER. *The Essential Shakespeare.* Cambridge 1932. For his editions see under SHAKESPEARE.

WOODWARD, JOHN. *Tudor and Stuart Drawing.* London 1951.

WORDSWORTH, W. *The Prelude, or Growth of a Poet's Mind.* Ed. E. de Selincourt. 2nd ed. revised by Helen Darbishire. Oxford 1959.

YATES, FRANCES A. *The Art of Memory.* London 1966.

SECTION B

AUSTIN, J. L. 'Are there *a priori* Concepts?' *PAS*, suppl. vol. XVIII (1939), pp. 83–105.

BROAD, C. D. 'Arguments for the Existence of God.' *Journal of Theological Studies*, XL (1939), pp. 16–30, 156–67.

BELOFF, J. R. 'Perception and Extrapolation.' *Bulletin of the British Psychological Society*, XXXII (1957), p. 44.

BLOOMFIELD, M. 'Symbolism in Mediaeval Literature.' *Modern Philology*, LVI (1958), pp. 73–81.

CHISHOLM, R. 'The Problem of the Speckled Hen.' *Mind*, LI (1942), pp. 368–73.

COGHILL, NEVILL. 'The Basis of Shakespearian Comedy.' *E & S*, New Series III (1950), pp. 1–28.

— 'Six Points of Stage Craft in *The Winter's Tale.*' *Shakespeare Survey*, XI (1958), pp. 31–41.

DOBRÉE, B. 'The Tempest.' *E & S*, New Series V (1952), pp. 13–26.

DYSON, H. V. D. 'The Emergence of Shakespeare's Tragedy.' *Proc. Brit. Acad.*, XXXVI (1950), pp. 69–93.

EWING, A. C. 'G. E. Moore.' (A note). *Mind*, LXXI (1962), p. 251.

FURLONG, A. J. 'Abstract Ideas and Images.' *PAS*, suppl. vol. XXVII (*Berkeley and Modern Problems*) (1953), pp. 121–36.

GERARD, A. 'On the Logic of Romanticism.' *Essays in Criticism*, VII (1957), pp. 262–73. The article is translated by George Watson from the original in *L'Athénée*, XLV (1956).

GIBSON, J. J. 'The Visual Field and the Visual World.' *Psychological Review*, LIX (1952), pp. 148–51.

GOMBRICH, E. H. '*Icones Symbolicae.*' *Journal of the Warburg and Courtauld Institutes*, XI (1948), pp. 163–92.

HARDIE, COLIN. 'The Epistle to Cangrande Again.' *Deutsches Dante-Jahrbuch*, XXXVIII (Weimar 1960), pp. 51–74.

— Review of D. L. Sayers's *Further Papers on Dante* in *Italian Studies*, XIII (1958), pp. 114 ff.

HOSPERS, J. 'The Concept of Artistic Expression.' *PAS*, New Series LV (1954–5), pp. 313–44.

— 'The Croce-Collingwood Theory of Art.' *Philosophy*, XXI (1956), pp. 291–308.

LEWIS, C. S. 'Bluspels and Flalansferes', in *Rehabilitations and Other Essays*, 1939; reprinted in *The Importance of Language*, ed. Max Black (Spectrum Books), 1962.

MACE, C. A. 'Abstract Ideas and Images.' *PAS*, suppl. vol. XXVII (*Berkeley and Modern Problems*) (1953), pp. 137–48.

MONTÉGUT, E. 'Une Hypothèse sur *le Tempête* de Shakespeare.' *Revue des Deux Mondes*, LVIII (1865), pp. 733 ff.

MURDOCH, IRIS. 'Nostalgia for the Particular.' *PAS*, New Series LII (1951–2), pp. 243–60.

NOSWORTHY, J. M. 'The Narrative Sources of *The Tempest.*' *RES*, XXIV (1948), pp. 281–94.

O'CONNOR, D. J. 'Abstract Ideas and Images.' *PAS*, suppl. vol. XXVII (*Berkeley and Modern Problems*) (1953), pp. 149–58.

POPPER, K. R. 'The Principle of Individuation.' *PAS*, suppl. vol. XXVII (*Berkeley and Modern Problems*) (1953), pp. 97–120.

PRICE, H. H. 'Image Thinking.' *PAS*, New Series LII (1951–2), pp. 135–67.

RUSSELL, EDWARD R. 'The Religion of Shakespeare.' *The Theological Review*, LV (1876), pp. 459 ff.

RYLE, GILBERT. 'Plato's "Parmenides".' Two papers in *Mind*, XLVIII (1939), pp. 129–51, 302–25.

TOLKIEN, J. R. R. 'Beowulf, the Monsters and the Critics.' *Proc. Brit. Acad.*, XXII (1936), pp. 245–95.

VLASTOS, G. 'The Third Man Argument in the Parmenides.' *Philosophical Review*, 1954 (1954), pp. 319–49.

WARNOCK, G. J. 'Concepts and Schematism.' *Analysis*, IX, 5 (1949), pp. 77–82.

INDEX